Ultimate Go Notebook

First Edition

Version 1.0

WILLIAM KENNEDY

with HOANH AN

For online information and ordering of this and other Ardan Labs books, please visit www.ardanlabs.com. The publisher offers discounts on this book when ordered in quantity. For more information, please contact

Special Sales Department
Ardan Labs Press
12973 SW 112 ST, Suite 153
Miami, FL 33186
Email: orders@ardanlabs.com

Administrator: Nick Caputo
Typesetter: Erick Zelaya
Cover Designer: Andrea Saavedra
Core Reviewer: Matthew Sanabria
Core Reviewer: Michael Bang

ISBN: 978-1-7373844-2-7
Patch: 39

Welcome

Back in August 2019, Hoanh An started a project in Github called the Ultimate Go Study Guide. It was a collection of notes he took after taking the Ultimate Go class. Surprisingly, it got a lot of attention and eventually had more stars and activity than the actual repo for the class. This shows the power of open sourcing material.

Then Hoanh decided to publish a book from his notes and repo. When I saw what Hoanh had written and the excitement his followers had, I reached out to him. We decided I would review and refactor his original work and we would publish a book together. This is that book and it represents the notes I would like any student to make while taking the class.

I want to thank everyone in the Go community for their support and help over the years in creating this material. When I started learning Go in March 2013, I didn't have any idea I would be able to accumulate all this knowledge and share it with all of you. Learning is a journey that takes time and effort. If this material can help jump start your learning about Go, then the time and effort was worth every minute.

Thanks,
-- Bill Kennedy

Intended Audience

This notebook has been written and designed to provide a reference to everything that I say in the Ultimate Go class. It's not necessarily a beginner's Go book since it doesn't focus on the specifics of Go's syntax. I would recommend the Go In Action book I wrote back in 2015 for that type of content. It's still accurate and relevant.

Many of the things I say in the classroom over the 20 plus hours of instruction has been incorporated. I've tried to capture all the guidelines, design philosophy, whiteboarding, and notes I share at the same moments I share them. If you have taken the class before, I believe this notebook will be invaluable for reminders on the content.

If you have never taken the class, I still believe there is value in this book. It covers more advanced topics not found in other books today. I've tried to provide a well rounded curriculum of topics from types to profiling. I have also been able to provide examples for writing generic function and types in Go, which will be available in version 1.18 of Go.

The book is written in the first person to drive home the idea that this is my book of notes from the Ultimate Go class. The first chapter provides a set of design philosophies, quotes, and extra reading to help prepare your mind for the material. Chapters 2-13 provide the core content from the class. Chapter 14 provides a reediting of important blog posts I've written in the past. These posts are presented here to enhance some of the more technical chapters like garbage collection and concurrency.

If you are struggling with this book, please provide me any feedback over email at bill@ardanlabs.com. I will always do my best to correct and teach anything that is not obvious or clear.

Thanks,
-- Bill Kennedy

Acknowledgements

WILLIAM KENNEDY

I would like to dedicate this book to my kids (Brianna, Melissa, Amanda, Jarrod, Thomas) and the love of my life, Alejandra. Thank you for the constant support and understanding you provide me on a daily basis. I don't believe this project would have been completed if I didn't have all of you in my life.

I would also like to thank my Ardan family, Ed, John, Miguel, and Erick. Without your support over the past 10 years, I wouldn't be capable of spending the time on projects like this.

HOANH AN

I want to thank my family and my partner, Dani, for always being there, supporting me, and encouraging me to keep working on the project since the very early days. You are the most beautiful, kind, and smartest person I've known and loved.

I want to thank Bill and the Ardan team for your understanding and support over the last year. Additionally, I want to thank all of the Ultimate Go Study Guide's supporters for taking the time and making the effort to not just contribute to the project, but help share and send your detailed feedback. This book exists because of all of you.

Table Of Contents

Chapter 1: Introduction

Prototype Driven Development with Data Oriented Design!

It's important that I prepare my mind for the material I'm about to review. This introduction provides thoughts and ideas to stimulate my initial understanding of the language, its roots, and general design philosophy. It's written as a set of notes and not fluid content like I will find in the remaining chapters.

Somewhere Along The Line
- We became impressed with programs that contain large amounts of code.
- We strived to create large abstractions in our code base.
- We forgot that the hardware is the platform.
- We lost the understanding that every decision comes with a cost.

These Days Are Gone
- We can throw more hardware at the problem.
- We can throw more developers at the problem.

Open My Mind
- Technology changes quickly but people's minds change slowly.
- Easy to adopt new technology but hard to adopt new ways of thinking.

Interesting Questions – What do they mean to me?
- Is it a good program?
- Is it an efficient program?
- Is it correct?
- Was it done on time?
- What did it cost?

Aspire To
- Be a champion for quality, efficiency and simplicity.
- Have a point of view.
- Value introspection and self-review.

1.1 Reading Code

Go is a language that focuses on code being readable as a first principle.

Quotes

- "If most computer people lack understanding and knowledge, then what they will select will also be lacking." - Alan Kay

- "The software business is one of the few places we teach people to write before we teach them to read." - Tom Love (inventor of Objective C)

- "Code is read many more times than it is written." - Dave Cheney

- "Programming is, among other things, a kind of writing. One way to learn writing is to write, but in all other forms of writing, one also reads. We read examples both good and bad to facilitate learning. But how many programmers learn to write programs by reading programs?" - Gerald M. Weinberg

- "Skill develops when we produce, not consume." - Katrina Owen

1.2 Legacy Software
Do I care about the legacy I'm leaving behind?

Quotes

- "There are two kinds of software projects: those that fail, and those that turn into legacy horrors." - Peter Weinberger (inventor of AWK)

- "Legacy software is an unappreciated but serious problem. Legacy code may be the downfall of our civilization." - Chuck Moore (inventor of Forth)

- "Few programmers of any experience would contradict the assertion that most programs are modified in their lifetime. Why then do we rarely find a program that contains any evidence of having been written with an eye to subsequent modification." - Gerald M. Weinberg

- "We think awful code is written by awful devs. But in reality, it's written by reasonable devs in awful circumstances." - Sarah Mei

- "There are many reasons why programs are built the way they are, although we may fail to recognize the multiplicity of reasons because we usually look at code from the outside rather than by reading it. When we do read code, we find that some of it gets written because of machine limitations, some because of language limitations, some because of programmer limitations, some because of historical accidents, and some because of specifications—both essential and inessential." - Gerald M. Weinberg

1.3 Mental Models
I must constantly make sure my mental model of the code I'm writing and maintaining is clear. When I can't remember where a piece of logic is or I can't remember how something works, I'm losing my mental model of the code. This is a clear indication that I need to refactor the code. Focus time on structuring code that provides the best mental model possible and during code reviews validate my mental models are still intact.

How much code do I think I can maintain in my head? I believe asking a single developer to maintain a mental model of more than one ream of copy paper (~10k lines of code) is asking a lot. If I do the math, it takes a team of 100 people to work on a code base that hits a million lines of code. That's 100 people that need to be coordinated, grouped, tracked and in a constant feedback loop of communication.

Quotes

- "Let's imagine a project that's going to end up with a million lines of code or more. The probability of those projects being successful in the United States these days is very low, well under 50%. That's debatable." - Tom Love (inventor of Objective C)

- "100k lines of code fit inside a box of paper." - Tom Love (inventor of Objective C)

- "One of our many problems with thinking is "cognitive load": the number of things we can pay attention to at once. The cliche is 7±2, but for many things it is even less. We make progress by making those few things be more powerful." - Alan Kay

- "The hardest bugs are those where your mental model of the situation is just wrong, so you can't see the problem at all." - Brian Kernighan

- "Everyone knows that debugging is twice as hard as writing a program in the first place. So if you're as clever as you can be when you write it, how will you ever debug it?" - Brian Kernighan

- "Debuggers don't remove bugs. They only show them in slow motion." - Unknown

- "Fixing bugs is just a side effect. Debuggers are for exploration." - @Deech (Twitter)

Reading

- The Magical Number Seven, Plus or Minus Two - Wikipedia
- Psychology of Code Readability - Egon Elbre

1.4 Productivity vs Performance

Productivity and performance both matter, but in the past I couldn't have both. I needed to choose one over the other. We naturally gravitated to productivity, with the idea or hope that the hardware would resolve our performance problems for free. This movement towards productivity has resulted in the design of programming languages that produce sluggish software that is outpacing the hardware's ability to make them faster.

By following Go's idioms and a few guidelines, I can write code that can be reasoned about by average developers. I can write software that simplifies, minimizes and reduces the amount of code we need to write to solve the problems we are working on. I don't have to choose productivity over performance or performance over productivity anymore. I can have both.

Quotes

- "The hope is that the progress in hardware will cure all software ills. However, a critical observer may observe that software manages to outgrow hardware in size and sluggishness. Other observers had noted this for some time before, indeed the trend was becoming obvious as early as 1987." - Niklaus Wirth

- "The most amazing achievement of the computer software industry is its continuing cancellation of the steady and staggering gains made by the computer hardware industry." - Henry Petroski (2015)

- "The hardware folks will not put more cores into their hardware if the software isn't going to use them, so, it is this balancing act of each other staring at each other, and we are hoping that Go is going to break through on the software side." - Rick Hudson (2015)

- "C is the best balance I've ever seen between power and expressiveness. You can do almost anything you want to do by programming fairly straightforwardly and you will have a very good mental model of what's going to happen on the machine; you can predict reasonably well how quickly it's going to run, you understand what's going on." - Brian Kernighan (2000)

- "The trend in programming language design has been to create languages that enhance software reliability and programmer productivity. What we should do is develop languages alongside sound software engineering practices so the task of developing reliable programs is distributed throughout the software lifecycle, especially into the early phases of system design." - Al Aho (2009)

1.5 Correctness vs Performance

I want to write code that is optimized for correctness. Don't make coding decisions based on what I think might perform better. I must benchmark or profile to know if code is not fast enough. Then and only then should I optimize for performance. This can't be done until I have something working.

Improvement comes from writing code and thinking about the code I write. Then refactoring the code to make it better. This requires the help of other people to also read the code I'm writing. Prototype ideas first to validate them. Try different approaches or ask others to attempt a solution. Then compare what I have learned.

Too many developers are not prototyping their ideas first before writing production code. It's through prototyping that I can validate my thoughts, ideas and designs. This is the time when I can break down walls and figure out how things work. Prototype in the concrete and consider contracts after I have a working prototype.

Refactoring must become part of the development cycle. Refactoring is the process of improving the code from the things that I learn on a daily basis. Without time to refactor, code will become impossible to manage and maintain over time. This creates the legacy issues we are seeing today.

Quotes

- "Make it correct, make it clear, make it concise, make it fast. In that order." - Wes Dyer

- "Make it work, then make it beautiful, then if you really, really have to, make it fast. 90 percent of the time, if you make it beautiful, it will already be fast. So really, just make it beautiful!" - Joe Armstrong

- "Good engineering is less about finding the "perfect" solution and more about understanding the tradeoffs and being able to explain them." - JBD

- "Choosing the right limitations for a certain problem domain is often much more powerful than allowing anything." - Jason Moiron

- "The correctness of the implementation is the most important concern, but there is no royal road to correctness. It involves diverse tasks such as thinking of invariants, testing and code reviews. Optimization should be done, but not prematurely." - Al Aho (inventor of AWK)

- "The basic ideas of good style, which are fundamental to write clearly and simply, are just as important now as they were 35 years ago. Simple, straightforward code is just plain easier to work with and less likely to have problems. As programs get bigger and more complicated, it's even more important to have clean, simple code." - Brian Kernighan

- "Problems can usually be solved with simple, mundane solutions. That means there's no glamorous work. You don't get to show off your amazing skills. You just build something that gets the job done and then move on. This approach may not earn you oohs and aahs, but it lets you get on with it." - Jason Fried

Reading
- Prototype your design! - Robert Griesemer

1.6 Understanding Rules
What should I understand about rules?

- Rules have costs.
- Rules must pull their weight - Don't be clever (high level).
- Value the standard, don't idolize it.
- Be consistent!
- Semantics convey ownership.

Quotes

- "An architecture isn't a set of pieces, it's a set of rules about what you can expect of them." - Michael Feathers

Reading

- The Philosophy of Google's C++ Code - Titus Winters

1.7 Differences Between Senior vs Junior Developers

What is the difference between a Senior and Junior developer?

Quotes

- "You are personally responsible for the software you write." - Stephen Bourne (Bourne shell)

- "And the difference between juniors+seniors to those who are in-between, is the confidence to ask "dumb" questions." - Natalie Pistunovich

- "Mistakes are an inevitable consequence of doing something new and, as such, should be seen as valuable; without them, we'd have no originality." - Ed Catmull (President of Pixar)

- "It takes considerable knowledge just to realize the extent of your own ignorance." - Thomas Sowell

- "If you don't make mistakes, you're not working on hard enough problems." - Frank Wilczek

- "Don't cling to a mistake because you spent so much time making it." - Aubrey de Grey

1.8 Design Philosophy

I can't look at a piece of code and determine if it smells good or bad without a design philosophy. These four major categories are the basis for code reviews and should be prioritized in this order: Integrity, Readability, Simplicity and then Performance. I must consciously and with great reason be able to explain the category I'm choosing.

1.8.1 Integrity

I need to become very serious about reliability.

There are two driving forces behind integrity:

- Integrity is about every allocation, read and write of memory being accurate, consistent and efficient. The type system is critical to making sure we have this micro level of integrity.
- Integrity is about every data transformation being accurate, consistent and efficient. Writing less code and error handling is critical to making sure we

have this macro level of integrity.

Write Less Code

There have been studies that have researched the number of bugs I can expect to have in my software. The industry average is around 15 to 50 bugs per 1000 lines of code. One simple way to reduce the number of bugs, and increase the integrity of my software, is to write less code.

Bjarne Stroustrup stated that writing more code than I need results in Ugly, Large and Slow code:

- Ugly: Leaves places for bugs to hide.
- Large: Ensures incomplete tests.
- Slow: Encourages the use of shortcuts and dirty tricks.

Error Handling

When error handling is treated as an exception and not part of the main code path, I can expect the majority of my critical failures to be due to error handling.

There was a study that looked at a couple hundred bugs in Cassandra, HBase, HDFS, MapReduce, and Redis. The study identified 48 critical failures that fell into these categories.

- 92%: Failures from bad error handling
  - 35%: Incorrect handling
    - 25%: Simply ignoring an error
    - 8%: Catching the wrong exception
    - 2%: Incomplete TODOs
  - 57% System specific
    - 23%: Easily detectable
    - 34%: Complex bugs
- 8%: Failures from latent human errors

Quotes

- "Failure is expected, failure is not an odd case. Design systems that help you identify failure. Design systems that can recover from failure." - JBD

- "Product excellence is the difference between something that only works under certain conditions, and something that only breaks under certain conditions". - Kelsey Hightower

- "Instability is a drag on innovation." - Yehudah Katz

Reading

- Software Development for Infrastructure - Bjarne Stroustrup
- Normalization of Deviance in Software - danluu.com
- Lessons learned from reading postmortems - danluu.com
- Technical Debt Quadrant - Martin Fowler
- Design Philosophy On Integrity - William Kennedy
- Ratio of bugs per line of code - Dan Mayer
- Developing Software The Right Way, with Intent and Carefulness - David Gee
- What bugs live in the Cloud – usenix.org
- Masterminds of Programming - Federico Biancuzzi and Shane Warden

1.8.2 Readability

I must structure my systems to be more comprehensible.

This is about writing simple code that is easier to read and understand without the need of mental exhaustion. Just as important, it's about not hiding the cost/impact of the code per line, function, package and the overall ecosystem it runs in.

Code Must Never Lie

It doesn't matter how fast the code might be if no one can understand or maintain it moving forward.

Average Developer

I must be aware of who I am on my team. When hiring new people, I must be aware of where the new person falls. Code must be written for the average developer to comprehend. If I'm below average for my team, I have the responsibility to work to be average. If I'm above average, I have the responsibility to reduce writing clever code and coach/mentor.

Real Machine

In Go, the underlying machine is a real machine, unlike what I would find in Java or C# with their virtual machine layer. The model of computation is that of the computer. Here is the key, Go gives me direct access to the machine while still providing abstraction mechanisms to allow higher-level ideas to be expressed.

Quotes

- "This is a cardinal sin amongst programmers. If code looks like it's doing one thing when it's actually doing something else, someone down the road will read that code and misunderstand it, and use it or alter it in a way that causes bugs. That someone might be you, even if it was your code in the first place." - Nate Finch

- "Can you explain it to the median user (developer)? as opposed to will the smartest user (developer) figure it out?" - Peter Weinberger (inventor of

AWK)

- "Making things easy to do is a false economy. Focus on making things easy to understand and the rest will follow." - Peter Bourgon

Reading
- Code Must Never Lie - Nate Finch

1.8.3 Simplicity

I must understand that simplicity is hard to design and complicated to build.

This is about hiding complexity. A lot of care and design must go into simplicity because it can cause more problems than it solves. It can create issues with readability and it can cause issues with performance.

Complexity Sells Better

Focus on encapsulation and validate that I'm not generalizing or even being too concise. I need to valid my code is still easy to use, understand, debug and maintain.

Encapsulation

Encapsulation is what the industry has been trying to figure out for 40+ years. Go is taking a slightly new approach with packaging. Bringing encapsulation up a level and providing richer support at the language level.

Quotes

- "Simplicity is a great virtue but it requires hard work to achieve it and education to appreciate it. And to make matters worse: complexity sells better." - Edsger W. Dijkstra

- "Everything should be made as simple as possible, but not simpler." - Albert Einstein

- "You wake up and say, I will be productive, not simple, today." - Dave Cheney

- Paraphrasing: "Encapsulation and the separation of concerns are drivers for designing software. This is largely based on how other industries handle complexity. There seems to be a human pattern of using encapsulation to wrestle complexity to the ground." - Brad Cox (inventor of Objective C)

- "The purpose of abstraction is not to be vague, but to create a new semantic level in which one can be absolutely precise." - Edsger W. Dijkstra

- "A proper abstraction decouples the code so that every change doesn't echo throughout the entire code base." - Ronna Steinburg

- "A good API is not just easy to use but also hard to misuse." - JBD

- "Computing is all about abstractions. Those below yours are just details. Those above yours are limiting complicated crazy town." - Joe Beda

Reading
- <u>Simplicity is Complicated</u> - Rob Pike
- <u>What did Alan Kay mean by, "Lisp is the greatest single programming language ever designed"?</u> - Alan Kay

1.8.4 Performance

I must compute less to get the results we need.

This is about not wasting effort and achieving execution efficiency. Writing code that is mechanically sympathetic with the runtime, operating system and hardware. Achieving performance by writing less and more efficient code, but staying within the idioms and framework of the language.

Rules of Performance
- Never guess about performance.
- Measurements must be relevant.
- Profile before I decide something is performance critical.
- Test to know I'm correct.

<u>Rules Of Optimization Club</u>

Broad Engineering
Performance is important but it can't be my priority unless the code is not running fast enough. I only know this once I have a working program and I have validated it. The industry places those who we think know how to write performant code on a pedestal. I need to put those who write code that is optimized for correctness and performs fast enough on those pedestals.

Quotes
- "Programmers waste enormous amounts of time thinking about, or worrying about, the speed of noncritical parts of their programs, and these attempts at efficiency actually have a strong negative impact when debugging and maintenance are considered. We should forget about small efficiencies, say about 97% of the time: premature optimization is the root of all evil. Yet we should not pass up our opportunities in that critical 3%." — Donald E. Knuth

- "I don't trust anything until it runs... In fact, I don't trust anything until it runs twice." - Andrew Gelman (one of the greatest living statisticians at Columbia University).

- "When we're computer programmers we're concentrating on the intricate little fascinating details of programming and we don't take a broad engineering point of view about trying to optimize the total system. You try to optimize the bits and bytes." - Tom Kurtz (inventor of BASIC)

1.8.5 Micro-Optimizations

Micro-Optimizations are about squeezing every ounce of performance out of the machine as possible. When code is written with this as the priority, it's very difficult to write code that is readable, simple or idiomatic.

1.8.6 Data-Orientation

Data oriented design is a core philosophy and concept with the language. I must embrace data oriented design with a prototype first approach.

- "Data dominates. If you've chosen the right data structures and organized things well, the algorithms will almost always be self-evident. Data structures, not algorithms, are central to programming." - Rob Pike

Design Philosophy
- If I don't understand the data, I don't understand the problem.
- All problems are unique and specific to the data I'm working with.
- Data transformations are at the heart of solving problems. Each function, method and work-flow must focus on implementing the specific data transformations required to solve the problems.
- If my data is changing, my problems are changing. When my problems are changing, the data transformations need to change with it.
- Uncertainty about the data is not a license to guess but a directive to STOP and learn more.
- Solving problems I don't have, creates more problems I now do.
- If performance matters, I must have mechanical sympathy for how the hardware and operating system work.
- Minimize, simplify and REDUCE the amount of code required to solve each problem. Do less work by not wasting effort.
- Code that can be reasoned about and does not hide execution costs can be better understood, debugged and performance tuned.
- Coupling data together and writing code that produces predictable access patterns to the data will be the most performant.
- Changing data layouts can yield more significant performance improvements than changing just the algorithms.
- Efficiency is obtained through algorithms but performance is obtained through data structures and layouts.

Reading
- Data-Oriented Design and C++ - Mike Acton
- Efficiency with Algorithms, Performance with Data Structures - Chandler Carruth

1.8.7 Interface And Composition

Here are design philosophies and guidelines I need to follow when it comes to interfaces and composition.

Design Philosophy
- Interfaces give programs structure.
- Interfaces encourage design by composition.
- Interfaces enable and enforce clean divisions between components.
  - The standardization of interfaces can set clear and consistent expectations.
- Decoupling means reducing the dependencies between components and the types they use.
  - This leads to correctness, quality and performance.
- Interfaces allow me to group concrete types by what they do.
  - Don't group types by a common DNA but by a common behavior.
  - Everyone can work together when we focus on what we do and not who we are.
- Interfaces help my code decouple itself from change.
  - I must do my best to understand what could change and use interfaces to decouple.
  - Interfaces with more than one method have more than one reason to change.
  - Uncertainty about change is not a license to guess but a directive to STOP and learn more.
- I must distinguish between code that:
  - Defends against fraud vs protects against accidents.

Validation

Use an interface when:
- Users of the API need to provide an implementation detail.
- API's have multiple implementations they need to maintain internally.
- Parts of the API that can change have been identified and require decoupling.

Don't use an interface:
- For the sake of using an interface.
- To generalize an algorithm.
- When users can declare their own interfaces.
- If it's not clear how the interface makes the code better.

Reading
- Methods, interfaces and Embedding - William Kennedy
- Composition with Go - William Kennedy
- Reducing type hierarchies - William Kennedy
- Application Focused API Design - William Kennedy
- Avoid interface pollution - William Kennedy
- Interface Values Are Valueless - William Kennedy

- <u>Interface Semantics</u> - William Kennedy

1.8.8 Writing Concurrent Software

Concurrency means undefined out of order execution. Taking a set of instructions that would otherwise be executed in sequence and finding a way to execute them out of order and still produce the same result. For the problem in front of me, it has to be obvious that out of order execution would add value.

When I say it adds value, I mean that it adds enough of a performance gain for the complexity cost. Depending on my problem, out of order execution may not be possible or even make sense.

It's also important to understand that concurrency is not the same as parallelism. Parallelism means executing two or more instructions at the same time. This is a different concept from concurrency. Parallelism is only possible when I have at least 2 cores or hardware threads available to me and I have at least 2 Goroutines, each executing instructions independently on each core/hardware thread.

Both me and the runtime have a responsibility of managing the concurrency of the application. I'm responsible for managing these three things when writing concurrent software:

Design Philosophy
- The application must startup and shutdown with integrity.
    - Know how and when every Goroutine I create terminates.
    - All Goroutines I create should terminate before main returns.
    - Applications should be capable of shutting down on demand, even under load, in a controlled way.
        - I want to stop accepting new requests and finish the requests I have (load shedding).
- Identify and monitor critical points of back pressure that can exist inside my application.
    - Channels, mutexes and atomic functions can create back pressure when Goroutines are required to wait.
    - A little back pressure is good, it means there is a good balance of concerns.
    - A lot of back pressure is bad, it means things are imbalanced.
    - Back pressure that is imbalanced will cause:
        - Failures inside the software and across the entire platform.
        - My application to collapse, implode or freeze.
    - Measuring back pressure is a way to measure the health of the application.
- Rate limit to prevent overwhelming back pressure inside my application.
    - Every system has a breaking point, I must know what it is for my

application.
- ○ Applications should reject new requests as early as possible once they are overloaded.
  - ▪ Don't take in more work than I can reasonably work on at a time.
  - ▪ Push back when I'm at critical mass. Create my own external back pressure.
- ○ Use an external system for rate limiting when it is reasonable and practical.
- Use timeouts to release the back pressure inside my application.
  - ○ No request or task is allowed to take forever.
  - ○ Identify how long users are willing to wait.
  - ○ Higher-level calls should tell lower-level calls how long they have to run.
  - ○ At the top level, the user should decide how long they are willing to wait.
  - ○ Use the Context package.
    - ▪ Functions that users wait for should take a Context.
      - ▪ These functions should select on <-ctx.Done() when they would otherwise block indefinitely.
    - ▪ Set a timeout on a Context only when I have good reason to expect that a function's execution has a real time limit.
    - ▪ Allow the upstream caller to decide when the Context should be canceled.
    - ▪ Cancel a Context whenever the user abandons or explicitly aborts a call.
- Architect applications to:
  - ○ Identify problems when they are happening.
  - ○ Stop the bleeding.
  - ○ Return the system back to a normal state.

Reading
Scheduling In Go - Chapter 14

1.8.9 Signaling and Channels

Channels allow Goroutines to communicate with each other through the use of signaling semantics. Channels accomplish this signaling through the use of sending/receiving data or by identifying state changes on individual channels. Don't architect software with the idea of channels being queues, focus on signaling and the semantics that simplify the orchestration required.

Depending on the problem I'm solving, I may require different channel semantics. Depending on the semantics I need, different architectural choices must be taken.

Language Mechanics
- Use channels to orchestrate and coordinate Goroutines.
  - Focus on the signaling semantics and not the sharing of data.
  - Signaling with data or without data.
  - Question their use for synchronizing access to shared state.
    - There are cases where channels can be simpler for this but initially question.
- Unbuffered channels:
  - Receive happens before the Send.
  - Benefit: 100% guarantee the signal being sent has been received.
  - Cost: Unknown latency on when the signal will be received.
- Buffered channels:
  - Send happens before the Receive.
  - Benefit: Reduce blocking latency between signaling.
  - Cost: No guarantee when the signal being sent has been received.
    - The larger the buffer, the less guarantee.
- Closing channels:
  - Close happens before the Receive. (like Buffered)
  - Signaling without data.
  - Perfect for signaling cancellations and deadlines.
- NIL channels:
  - Send and Receive block.
  - Turn off signaling
  - Perfect for rate limiting or short-term stoppages.

Design Philosophy
- If any given Send on a channel CAN cause the sending Goroutine to block:
  - Be careful with Buffered channels larger than 1.
    - Buffers larger than 1 must have reason/measurements.
  - Must know what happens when the sending Goroutine blocks.
- If any given Send on a channel WON'T cause the sending Goroutine to block:
  - I have the exact number of buffers for each send.
    - Fan Out pattern
  - I have the buffer measured for max capacity.
    - Drop pattern
- Less is more with buffers.
  - Don't think about performance when thinking about buffers.
  - Buffers can help to reduce blocking latency between signaling.
    - Reducing blocking latency towards zero does not necessarily mean better throughput.
    - If a buffer of one is giving me good enough throughput then keep it.
    - Question buffers that are larger than one and measure for size.
    - Find the smallest buffer that provides good enough throughput.

Chapter 2: Language Mechanics

In this chapter, I will learn about the basic language mechanics, idioms, and guidelines around types and memory management. I will learn the data semantics behind the built-in types.

2.1 Built-in Types

Types provide integrity and readability by asking 2 questions:

- What is the amount of memory to allocate? (e.g. 1, 2, 4, 8 bytes)
- What does that memory represent? (e.g. int, uint, bool,..)

Types can be specific to a precision such as int32 or int64:

- uint8 represents an unsigned integer with 1 byte of allocation
- int32 represents a signed integer with 4 bytes of allocation

When I declare a type using a non-precision based type (unit, int) the size of the value is based on the architecture being used to build the program:

- 32 bit arch: int represents a signed int at 4 bytes of memory allocation
- 64 bit arch: int represents a signed int at 8 bytes of memory allocation

2.2 Word Size

The word size represents the amount of memory allocation required to store integers and pointers for a given architecture. For example:

- 32 bit arch: word size is 4 bytes of memory allocation
- 64 bit arch: word size is 8 bytes of memory allocation

This is important because Go has internal data structures (maps, channels, slices, interfaces, and functions) that store integers and pointers. The size of these data structures will be based on the architecture being used to build the program.

In Go, the amount of memory allocated for a value of type int, a pointer, or a word will always be the same on the same architecture.

2.3 Zero Value Concept

Every single value I construct in Go is initialized at least to its zero value state unless I specify the initialization value at construction. The zero value is the setting of every bit in every byte to zero.

This is done for data integrity and it's not free. It takes time to push electrons through the machine to reset those bits, but I should always take integrity over performance.

Listing 2.1

Type	Zero Value
Boolean	false
Integer	0
Float	0
Complex	0i
String	"" (empty)
Pointer	nil

2.4 Declare and Initialize

The keyword var can be used to construct values to their zero value state for all types.

Listing 2.2

```
var a int
var b string
var c float64
var d bool

fmt.Printf("var a int \t %T [%v]\n", a, a)
fmt.Printf("var b string \t %T [%v]\n", b, b)
fmt.Printf("var c float64 \t %T [%v]\n", c, c)
fmt.Printf("var d bool \t %T [%v]\n\n", d, d)

Output:
var a int        int [0]
var b string     string []
var c float64    float64 [0]
var d bool       bool [false]
```

Strings use the UTF8 character set, but are really just a collection of bytes.

A string is a two-word internal data structure in Go:

- The first word represents a pointer to a backing array of bytes
- The second word represents the length or the number of bytes in the backing array
- If the string is set to its zero value state, then the first word is nil and the second word is 0.

Using the short variable declaration operator, I can declare, construct, and initialize a value all at the same time.

26

Listing 2.3

```
aa := 10        // int [10]
bb := "hello"   // string [hello]
cc := 3.14159   // float64 [3.14159]
dd := true      // bool [true]

fmt.Printf("aa := 10 \t %T [%v]\n", aa, aa)
fmt.Printf("bb := \"hello\" \t %T [%v]\n", bb, bb)
fmt.Printf("cc := 3.14159 \t %T [%v]\n", cc, cc)
fmt.Printf("dd := true \t %T [%v]\n\n", dd, dd)

Output:
aa := 10        int [10]
bb := "hello"   string [hello]
cc := 3.14159   float64 [3.14159]
dd := true      bool [true]
```

2.5 Conversion vs Casting

Go doesn't have casting, but conversion. Instead of telling the compiler to map a set of bytes to a different representation, the bytes need to be copied to a new memory location for the new representation.

Listing 2.4

```
aaa := int32(10)
fmt.Printf("aaa := int32(10) %T [%v]\n", aaa, aaa)

Output:
aaa := int32(10) int32 [10]
```

Go does have a package in the standard library called unsafe if I need to perform an actual casting operation. I should really avoid that and be honest with myself why I am considering using it. Performing a conversion provides the highest level of integrity for these types of operations.

2.6 Struct and Construction Mechanics

This declaration represents a concrete user-defined type as a composite of different fields and types.

Listing 2.5

```
type example struct {
    flag    bool
    counter int16
    pi      float32
}
```

Declare a variable of type example and initialize it to its zero value state.

Listing 2.6

```
var e1 example

fmt.Printf("%+v\n", e1)

Output:
{flag:false counter:0 pi:0}
```

Declare a variable of type example not set to its zero value state by using literal construction syntax.

Listing 2.7

```
e2 := example{
    flag:    true,
    counter: 10,
    pi:      3.141592,
}

fmt.Println("Flag", e2.flag)
fmt.Println("Counter", e2.counter)
fmt.Println("Pi", e2.pi)

Output:
Flag true
Counter 10
Pi 3.141592
```

Declare a variable of an unnamed literal type set to its non-zero value state using literal construction syntax. This is a one-time thing.

Listing 2.8

```
e3 := struct {
    flag    bool
    counter int16
    pi      float32
}{
    flag:    true,
    counter: 10,
    pi:      3.141592,
}

fmt.Println("Flag", e3.flag)
fmt.Println("Counter", e3.counter)
fmt.Println("Pi", e3.pi)

Output:
Flag true
Counter 10
Pi 3.141592
```

The idea of literal construction is just that, to construct something literally and not to its zero value state. Because of this, I should use var for zero value and the short variable declaration operator with the { } syntax for non-zero value construction.

2.7 Padding and Alignment

How much memory is allocated for a value of type example?

Listing 2.9

```
type example struct {
    flag     bool
    counter  int16
    pi       float32
}
```

A bool is 1 byte, int16 is 2 bytes, and float32 is 4 bytes. Add that all together and I get 7 bytes. However, the actual answer is 8 bytes. Why, because there is a padding byte sitting between the flag and counter fields for the reason of alignment.

Figure 2.1

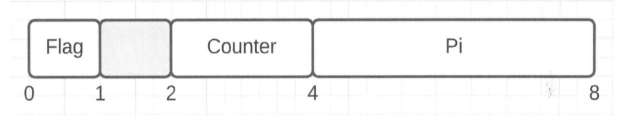

The idea of alignment is to allow the hardware to read memory more efficiently by placing memory on specific alignment boundaries. The compiler takes care of the alignment boundary mechanics so I don't have to.

Depending on the size of a particular field and its placement in the struct, Go determines the padding I need.

Listing 2.10

```
type example2 struct {
    flag     bool
    counter  int16
    flag2    bool
    pi       float32
}
```

In this example, I've added a new field called flag2 between the counter and pi fields. This causes more padding inside the struct.

Listing 2.11

```
type example2 struct {
    flag    bool      // 0xc000100020 <- Starting Address
            byte      // 0xc000100021 <- 1 byte padding
    counter int16     // 0xc000100022 <- 2 byte alignment
    flag2   bool      // 0xc000100024 <- 1 byte alignment
            byte      // 0xc000100025 <- 1 byte padding
            byte      // 0xc000100026 <- 1 byte padding
            byte      // 0xc000100027 <- 1 byte padding
    pi      float32   // 0xc000100028 <- 4 byte alignment
}
```

This is how the alignment and padding play out if a value of type example2 starts at address 0xc000100020. The flag field represents the starting address and is only 1 byte in size. Since the counter field requires 2 bytes of allocation, it must be placed in memory on a 2-byte alignment, meaning it needs to fall on an address that is a multiple of 2. This requires the counter field to start at address 0xc000100022. This creates a 1-byte gap between the flag and counter fields.

Figure 2.2

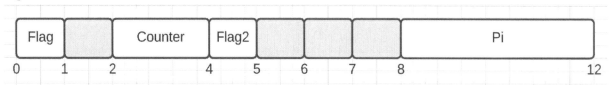

The flag2 field is a bool and can fall at the next address 0xc000100024. The final field is pi and requires 4 bytes of allocation so it needs to fall on a 4-byte alignment. The next address for a 4 byte value is at 0xc000100028. That means 3 more padding bytes are needed to maintain a proper alignment. This results in a value of type example2 requiring 12 bytes of total memory allocation.

The largest field in a struct represents the alignment boundary for the entire struct. In this case, the largest field is 4 bytes so the starting address for this struct value must be a multiple of 4. I can see the address 0xc000100020 is a multiple of 4.

If I need to minimize the amount of padding bytes, I must lay out the fields from highest allocation to lowest allocation. This will push any necessary padding bytes down to the bottom of the struct and reduce the total number of padding bytes necessary.

Listing 2.12

```
type example struct {
    pi      float32   // 0xc000100020 <- Starting Address
    counter int16     // 0xc000100024 <- 2 byte alignment
    flag    bool      // 0xc000100026 <- 1 byte alignment
    flag2   bool      // 0xc000100027 <- 1 byte alignment
}
```

After the reordering of the fields, the struct value only requires 8 bytes of allocation and not 12 bytes. Since all the fields allow the struct value to fall on a 4-byte alignment, no extra padding bytes are necessary.

Figure 2.3

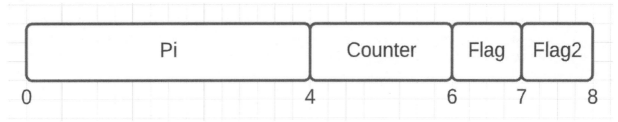

2.8 Assigning Values

If I have two different named types that are identical in structure, I can't assign a value of one to the other.

For example, if the types example1 and example2 are declared using the same exact declaration and we initialize two variables.

Listing 2.13

```
var ex1 example1
var ex2 example2
```

I can't assign these two variables to each other since they are of different named types. The fact that they are identical in structure is irrelevant.

Listing 2.14

```
ex1 = ex2  // Not allowed, compiler error
```

To perform this assignment, I would have to use conversion syntax and since they are identical in structure, the compiler will allow this.

Listing 2.15

```
ex1 = example1(ex2)   // Allowed, NO compiler error
```

However, if ex2 was changed to be declared as an unnamed type using the same exact declaration as ex1, no conversion syntax would be required.

Listing 2.16

```
var ex2 struct {
    flag     bool
    counter  int16
    pi       float32
}

ex1 = ex2  // Allowed, NO need for conversion syntax
```

The compiler will allow this assignment without the need for conversion.

2.9 Pointers

Pointers serve the purpose of sharing values across program boundaries. There are several types of program boundaries. The most common one is between function calls. There is also a boundary between Goroutines which I have notes for later.

When a Go program starts up, the Go runtime creates a Goroutine. Goroutines are lightweight application level threads with many of the same semantics as operating system threads. Their job is to manage the physical execution of a distinct set of instructions. Every Go program has at least 1 Goroutine that I call the main Goroutine.

Each Goroutine is given its own block of memory called a stack. Each stack starts out as a 2048 byte (2k) allocation. It's very small, but stacks can grow in size over time.

Figure 2.4

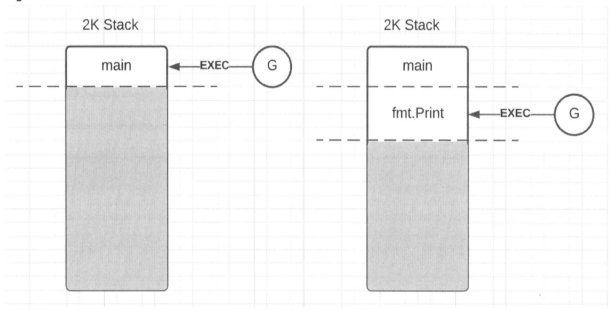

Every time a function is called, a block of stack space is taken to help the Goroutine execute the instructions associated with that function. Each individual block of memory is called a frame.

The size of a frame for a given function is calculated at compile time. No value can be constructed on the stack unless the compiler knows the size of that value at compile time. If the compiler doesn't know the size of a value at compile time, the value has to be constructed on the heap.

Stacks are self cleaning and zero value helps with the initialization of the stack. Every time I make a function call, and a frame of memory is blocked out, the memory for that frame is initialized, which is how the stack is self cleaning. On a function return, the memory for the frame is left alone since it's unknown if that memory will be needed again. It would be inefficient to initialize memory on returns.

2.10 Pass By Value

All data is moved around the program by value. This means as data is being passed across program boundaries, each function or Goroutine is given its own copy of the data. There are two types of data I work with, the value itself (int, string, user) or the value's address. Addresses are data that need to be copied and stored across program boundaries.

The following code attempts to explain this more.

Listing 2.17

```
func main() {

    // Declare variable of type int with a value of 10.
    count := 10

    // To get the address of a value, use the & operator.
    println("count:\tValue Of[", count, "]\tAddr Of[", &count, "]")

    // Pass a copy of the "value of" count (what's in the box)
    // to the increment1 function.
    increment1(count)

    // Print out the "value of" and "address of" count.
    // The value of count will not change after the function call.
    println("count:\tValue Of[", count, "]\tAddr Of[", &count, "]")

    // Pass a copy of the "address of" count (where is the box)
    // to the increment2 function. This is still considered a pass by
    // value and not a pass by reference because addresses are values.
    increment2(&count)

    // Print out the "value of" and "address of" count.
    // The value of count has changed after the function call.
    println("count:\tValue Of[", count, "]\tAddr Of[", &count, "]")
}

// increment1 declares the function to accept its own copy of
// and integer value.
func increment1(inc int) {

    // Increment the local copy of the caller's int value.
    inc++
    println("inc1:\tValue Of[", inc, "]\tAddr Of[", &inc, "]")
}

// increment2 declares the function to accept its own copy of
// an address that points to an integer value.
// Pointer variables are literal types and are declared using *.
func increment2(inc *int) {

    // Increment the caller's int value through the pointer.
    *inc++
    println("inc2:\tValue Of[", inc, "]\tAddr Of[", &inc, "]\tPoints To[",
*inc, "]")
```

```
}
Output:
count:   Value Of[ 10 ]   Addr Of[ 0xc000050738 ]
inc1:    Value Of[ 11 ]   Addr Of[ 0xc000050730 ]
count:   Value Of[ 10 ]   Addr Of[ 0xc000050738 ]
inc2:    Value Of[ 0xc000050738 ] Addr Of[ 0xc000050748 ] Points To[ 11 ]
count:   Value Of[ 11 ]   Addr Of[ 0xc000050738 ]
```

There are lots of little details related to the stacks and pointers, so to learn more read the post in chapter 14 titled, Stacks and Pointer Mechanics.

2.11 Escape Analysis

The algorithm the compiler uses to determine if a value should be constructed on the stack or heap is called "escape analysis". The name of the algorithm makes it sound like values are constructed on the stack first and then escape (or move) to the heap when necessary. This is NOT the case. The construction of a value only happens once, and the escape analysis algorithm decides where that will be (stack or heap). Only construction on the heap is called an allocation in Go.

Understanding escape analysis is about understanding value ownership. The idea is, when a value is constructed within the scope of a function, then that function owns the value. From there ask the question, does the value being constructed still have to exist when the owning function returns? If the answer is no, the value can be constructed on the stack. If the answer is yes, the value must be constructed on the heap.

Note: The ownership rule is a good base rule for identifying code that causes allocations. However, I must appreciate that escape analysis has flaws that can result in non-obvious allocations. Also, the algorithm takes opportunities to leverage compiler optimizations to save on allocations.

Listing 2.18

```
// user represents a user in the system.
type user struct {
    name  string
    email string
}

func stayOnStack() user {
    u := user{
        name:  "Bill",
        email: "bill@email.com",
    }

    return u
}
```

The stayOnStack function is using value semantics to return a user value back to the caller. In other words, the caller gets their own copy of the user value being

34

constructed.

When the stayOnStack function is called and returns, the user value it constructs no longer needs to exist, since the caller is getting their own copy. Therefore, the construction of the user value inside of stayOnStack can happen on the stack. No allocation.

Listing 2.19

```
type user struct {
    name  string
    email string
}

func escapeToHeap() *user {
    u := user{
        name:  "Bill",
        email: "bill@email.com",
    }

    return &u
}
```

The escapeToHeap function is using pointer semantics to return a user value back to the caller. In other words, the caller gets shared access (an address) to the user value being constructed.

When the escapeToHeap function is called and returns, the user value it constructs does still need to exist, since the caller is getting shared access to the value. Therefore, the construction of the user value inside of escapeToHeap can't happen on the stack, it must happen on the heap. Yes allocation.

Think about what would happen if the user value in the last example was constructed on the stack when using pointer semantics on the return.

Figure 2.5

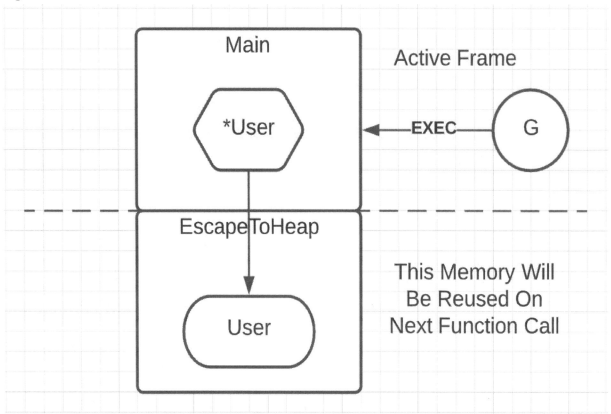

The caller would get a copy of a stack address from the frame below and integrity would be lost. Once control goes back to the calling function, the memory on the stack where the user value exists is reusable again. The moment the calling function makes another function call, a new frame is sliced and the memory will be overridden, destroying the shared value.

This is why I think about the stack being self cleaning. Zero value initialization helps every stack frame that I need to be cleaned without the use of GC. The stack is self cleaning since a frame is taken and initialized for the execution of each function call. The stack is cleaned during function calls and not on returns because the compiler doesn't know if that memory on the stack will ever be needed again.

Escape analysis decides if a value is constructed on the stack (the default) or the heap (the escape). With the stayOnStack function, I'm passing a copy of the value back to the caller, so it's safe to keep the value on the stack. With the escapeToHeap function, I'm passing a copy of the value's address back to the caller (sharing up the stack) so it's not safe to keep the value on the stack.

There are lots of little details related to the escape analysis, so to learn more read the post in chapter 14 titled, Escape Analysis Mechanics.

Note: As of version 1.17, Go changed the ABI (application binary interface) to implement a new way of passing function input and output arguments using registers instead of memory on the stack. This is enabled for Linux, MacOS, and

Windows on the 64-bit x86 architectures. This means that some function arguments won't be copied on the stack, but some may depending on the viability of using registers. This doesn't change any of the semantics described in this chapter.

2.12 Stack Growth

The size of each frame for every function is calculated at compile time. This means, if the compiler doesn't know the size of a value at compile time, the value must be constructed on the heap. An example of this is using the built-in function make to construct a slice whose size is based on a variable.

Listing 2.20

```
b := make([]byte, size) // Backing array allocates on the heap.
```

Go uses a contiguous stack implementation to determine how stacks grow and shrink. One alternative Go could have used is a segmented stack implementation, which is used by some operating systems.

Every function call comes with a little preamble that asks, "Is there enough stack space for this new frame?". If yes, then no problem and the frame is taken and initialized. If not, then a new larger stack must be constructed and the memory on the existing stack must be copied over to the new one. This requires changes to pointers that reference memory on the stack. The benefits of contiguous memory and linear traversals with modern hardware is the tradeoff for the cost of the copy.

Because of the use of contiguous stacks, no Goroutine can have a pointer to some other Goroutine's stack. There would be too much overhead for the runtime to keep track of every pointer to every stack and readjust those pointers to the new location.

2.13 Garbage Collection

Once a value is constructed on the heap, the Garbage Collector (GC) has to get involved. The most important part of the GC is the pacing algorithm. It determines the frequency/pace that the GC has to run in order to maintain the smallest heap possible in conjunction with the best application throughput.

There are lots of little details related to the GC, so to learn more read the post in chapter 14 titled, Garbage Collection Semantics.

2.14 Constants

One of the more unique features of Go is how the language implements constants. The rules for constants in the language specification are unique to Go. They provide the flexibility Go needs to make the code we write readable and intuitive while still maintaining type safety.

Constants can be typed or untyped. When a constant is untyped, it's considered to be of a kind. Constants of a kind can be implicitly converted by the compiler. This all happens at compile time and not at runtime.

Listing 2.21

```
const ui = 12345      // kind: integer
const uf = 3.141592   // kind: floating-point
```

Untyped numeric constants have a precision of 256 bits as stated by the specification. They are based on a kind.

Listing 2.22

```
const ti int     = 12345     // type: int
const tf float64 = 3.141592  // type: float64
```

Typed constants still use the constant type system, but their precision is restricted.

Listing 2.23

```
const myUint8 uint8 = 1000 // Compiler Error: constant 1000 overflows uint8
```

This doesn't work because the number 1000 is too large to store in an uint8.

Listing 2.24

```
var answer = 3 * 0.333   // float64 = KindFloat(3) * KindFloat(0.333)
```

Constant arithmetic supports the use of different kinds of constants. Kind Promotion is used to handle these different scenarios. All of this happens implicitly. The answer variable in this example will be of type float64 and represent 0.999 at a precision of 64 bits.

Listing 2.25

```
const third = 1 / 3.0   // KindFloat = KindFloat(1) / KindFloat(3.0)
```

The third constant will be of kind float and represent 1/3 at a precision of 256 bits.

Listing 2.26

```
const zero = 1 / 3   // KindInt = KindInt(1) / KindInt(3)
```

The zero constant will be of kind integer and set to 0 since integer division has no remainder.

Listing 2.27

```
const one int8 = 1
const two = 2 * one  // int8(2) * int8(1)
```

This is an example of constant arithmetic between typed and untyped constants. In this case, a constant of a type promotes over a constant of a kind. The two constant will be of type int8 and set to 2.

Listing 2.28

```
const maxInt = 9223372036854775807
```

This is the max integer value for a 64 bit integer.

Listing 2.27

```
const bigger = 9223372036854775808543522345
```

The bigger constant is a much larger value than a 64 bit integer, but it can be stored in a constant of kind int since constants of kind int are not limited to 64 bits of precision.

Listing 2.29

```
const bigger int64 = 9223372036854775808543522345

Compiler Error:
    constant 9223372036854775808543522345 overflows int64
```

However, if bigger was a constant of type int64, this would not compile.

2.15 IOTA

IOTA provides support for setting successive integer constants. It's possible the name comes from the integer function ι from the programming language APL. In APL, the ι function (represented with the ninth letter of the Greek alphabet, iota) is used to create a zero-based array of consecutive, ascending integers of a specified length.

Listing 2.30

```
const (
    A1 = iota    // 0 : Start at 0
    B1 = iota    // 1 : Increment by 1
    C1 = iota    // 2 : Increment by 1
)
fmt.Println(A1, B1, C1)

Output:
0 1 2
```

The iota keyword works within a constant block and starts with the value of 0. Then for each successive constant declared in the block, iota increments by 1.

Listing 2.31

```
const (
    A2 = iota  // 0 : Start at 0
    B2         // 1 : Increment by 1
    C2         // 2 : Increment by 1
)
fmt.Println(A2, B2, C2)

Output:
0 1 2
```

I don't need to repeat the use of the iota keyword. The successive nature of the integer constants are assumed once applied.

Listing 2.32

```
const (
    A3 = iota + 1  // 1 : 0 + 1
    B3             // 2 : 1 + 1
    C3             // 3 : 2 + 1
)
fmt.Println(A3, B3, C3)

Output:
1 2 3
```

If I didn't want to apply a mathematical pattern, I can perform some math and the math is reapplied with an increasing value of iota.

Listing 2.33

```
const (
    Ldate= 1 << iota  //  1 : Shift 1 to the left 0.   0000 0001
    Ltime             //  2 : Shift 1 to the left 1.   0000 0010
    Lmicroseconds     //  4 : Shift 1 to the left 2.   0000 0100
    Llongfile         //  8 : Shift 1 to the left 3.   0000 1000
    Lshortfile        // 16 : Shift 1 to the left 4.   0001 0000
    LUTC              // 32 : Shift 1 to the left 5.   0010 0000
)

fmt.Println(Ldate, Ltime, Lmicroseconds, Llongfile, Lshortfile, LUTC)

Output:
1 2 4 8 16 32
```

I can use this feature like the Log package does for setting flags. In this case, bit operations are being applied with increasing values of iota to calculate flag values.

Chapter 3: Data Structures

In this chapter, I will learn about Go's data structures and the mechanical sympathy behind them.

3.1 CPU Caches

There are lots of mechanical differences between processors and their design. In this section, I will talk at a high level about processors and the semantics that are relatively the same between them all. This semantic understanding will provide me a good mental model for how the processor works and the sympathy I can provide.

Each core inside the processor has its own local cache of memory (L1 and L2) and a common cache of memory (L3) used to store/access data and instructions. The hardware threads in each core can access their local L1 and L2 caches. Data from L3 or main memory needs to be copied into the L1 or L2 cache for access.

Figure 3.1

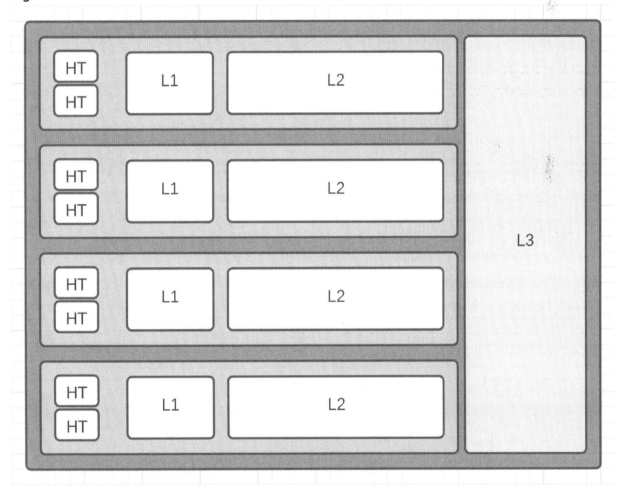

The latency cost of accessing data that exists in the different caches changes from least to most: L1 -> L2 -> L3 -> main memory. As Scott Meyers said, "If performance matters then the total amount of memory I have is the total amount of cache. Main memory is so slow to access, practically speaking, it might as well not even be there."

Performance today is about how efficiently data flows through the hardware. If every piece of data the hardware needs (at any given time) exists only in main memory, my programs will run slower as compared to the data already being present in the L1 or L2 caches.

Listing 3.1

```
3GHz(3 clock cycles/ns) * 4 instructions per cycle = 12 instructions per ns!

1 ns ............. 1 ns ............. 12 instructions   (one)
1 μs ......... 1,000 ns ......... 12,000 instructions   (thousand)
1 ms ..... 1,000,000 ns ...... 12,000,000 instructions  (million)
1 s .. 1,000,000,000 ns .. 12,000,000,000 instructions  (billion)


Industry Defined Latencies
L1 cache reference ......................... 0.5 ns ................... 6
ins
L2 cache reference ......................... 7 ns ................... 84
ins
Main memory reference ..................... 100 ns ................ 1200
ins
```

How do I write code that guarantees the data that is needed to execute an instruction is always present in the L1 or L2 caches? I need to write code that is mechanically sympathetic with the processor's prefetcher. The prefetcher attempts to predict what data is needed before instructions request the data so it's already present in either the L1 or L2 cache.

There are different granularities of memory access depending on where the access is happening. My code can read/write a byte of memory as the smallest unit of memory access. However, from the caching systems point of view, the granularity is 64 bytes. This 64 byte block of memory is called a cache line.

The Prefetcher works best when the instructions being executed create predictable access patterns to memory. One way to create a predictable access pattern to memory is to construct a contiguous block of memory and then iterate over that memory performing a linear traversal with a predictable stride.

The array is the most important data structure to the hardware because it supports predictable access patterns. However, the slice is the most important data structure in Go. Slices in Go use an array underneath.

Once I construct an array, every element is equally distant from the next or previous element. As I iterate over an array, I begin to walk cache line by connected cache line in a predictable stride. The Prefetcher will pick up on this predictable data access pattern and begin to efficiently pull the data into the processor, thus reducing data access latency costs.

Imagine I have a big square matrix of memory and a linked list of nodes that match the number of elements in the matrix. If I perform a traversal across the linked list, and then traverse the matrix in both directions (Column and Row), how will the performance of the different traversals compare?

Listing 3.2

```
func RowTraverse() int {
    var ctr int
    for row := 0; row < rows; row++
        for col := 0; col < cols; col++ {
            if matrix[row][col] == 0xFF {
                ctr++
            }
        }
    }
    return ctr
}
```

Row traverse will have the best performance because it walks through memory, cache line by connected cache line, which creates a predictable access pattern. Cache lines can be prefetched and copied into the L1 or L2 cache before the data is needed.

Listing 3.3

```
func ColumnTraverse() int {
    var ctr int
    for col := 0; col < cols; col++ {
        for row := 0; row < rows; row++ {
            if matrix[row][col] == 0xFF {
                ctr++
            }
        }
    }
    return ctr
}
```

Column Traverse is the worst by an order of magnitude because this access pattern crosses over OS page boundaries on each memory access. This causes no predictability for cache line prefetching and becomes essentially random access memory.

Listing 3.4

```
func LinkedListTraverse() int {
    var ctr int
    d := list
    for d != nil {
        if d.v == 0xFF {
            ctr++
        }
        d = d.p
    }
    return ctr
}
```

The linked list is twice as slow as the row traversal mainly because there are cache line misses but fewer TLB (Translation Lookaside Buffer) misses. A bulk of the nodes connected in the list exist inside the same OS pages.

Listing 3.5

```
BenchmarkLinkListTraverse-16    128    28738407 ns/op
BenchmarkColumnTraverse-16       30   126878630 ns/op
BenchmarkRowTraverse-16         310    11060883 ns/op
```

I can see this is true from the benchmark results. I will learn about benchmarking later.

3.2 Translation Lookaside Buffer (TLB)

Each running program is given a full memory map of virtual memory by the OS and that running program thinks they have all of the physical memory on the machine. However, physical memory needs to be shared with all the running programs. The operating system shares physical memory by breaking the physical memory into pages and mapping pages to virtual memory for any given running program. Each OS can decide the size of a page, but 4k, 8k, 16k are reasonable and common sizes.

The TLB is a small cache inside the processor that helps to reduce latency on translating a virtual address to a physical address within the scope of an OS page and offset inside the page. A miss against the TLB cache can cause large latencies because now the hardware has to wait for the OS to scan its page table to locate the right page for the virtual address in question. If the program is running on a virtual machine (like in the cloud) then the virtual machine paging table needs to be scanned first.

Remember when I said:

The linked list is twice as slow as the row traversal mainly because there are cache line misses but fewer TLB misses (explained next). A bulk of the nodes connected in the list exist inside the same OS pages.

The LinkedList is orders of magnitude faster than the column traversal because of TLB access. Even though there are cache line misses with the linked list traversal, since a majority of the memory for a group of nodes will land inside the same page, TLB latencies are not affecting performance. This is why for programs that use a large amount of memory, like DNA based applications, I may want to use a distribution of Linux that is configured with page sizes in the order of a megabyte or two of memory.

All that said, data-oriented design matters. Writing an efficient algorithm has to take into account how the data is accessed. Remember, performance today is about how efficiently I can get data into the processor.

3.3 Declaring and Initializing Values

Declare an array of five strings initialized to its zero value state.

Listing 3.6

```
var strings [5]string
```

A string is an immutable, two word, data structure representing a pointer to a backing array of bytes and the total number of bytes in the backing array. Since this array is set to its zero value state, every element is set to its zero value state. This means that each string has the first word set to nil and the second word set to 0.

Figure 3.2

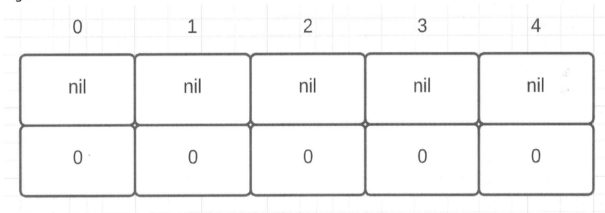

3.4 String Assignments

What happens when a string is assigned to another string?

Listing 3.7

```
strings[0] = "Apple"
```

When a string is assigned to another string, the two word value is copied, resulting in two different string values both sharing the same backing array.

Figure 3.3

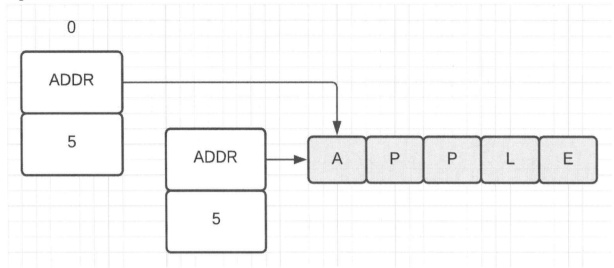

The cost of copying a string is the same regardless of the size of a string, a two word copy.

3.5 Iterating Over Collections

Go provides two different semantics for iterating over a collection. I can iterate using value semantics or pointer semantics.

Listing 3.8

```
// Value Semantic Iteration
for i, fruit := range strings {
    println(i, fruit)
}


// Pointer Semantic Iteration
for i := range strings {
    println(i, strings[i])
}
```

When using value semantic iteration, two things happen. First, the collection I'm iterating over is copied and I iterate over the copy. In the case of an array, the copy could be expensive since the entire array is copied. In the case of a slice, there is no real cost since only the internal slice value is copied and not the backing array. Second, I get a copy of each element being iterated on.

When using pointer semantic iteration, I iterate over the original collection and I access each element associated with the collection directly.

3.6 Value Semantic Iteration

Given the following code and output.

Listing 3.9

```
strings := [5]string{"Apple", "Orange", "Banana", "Grape", "Plum"}
for i, fruit := range strings {
    println(i, fruit)
}

Output:
0 Apple
1 Orange
2 Banana
3 Grape
4 Plum
```

The strings variable is an array of 5 strings. The loop iterates over each string in the collection and displays the index position and the string value. Since this is value semantic iteration, the for range is iterating over its own shallow copy of the array and on each iteration the fruit variable is a copy of each string (the two word data structure).

Notice how the fruit variable is passed to the print function using value semantics. The print function is getting its own copy of the string value as well. By the time the string is passed to the print function, there are 4 copies of the string value (array, shallow copy, fruit variable and the print function's copy). All 4 copies are sharing the same backing array of bytes.

Figure 3.4

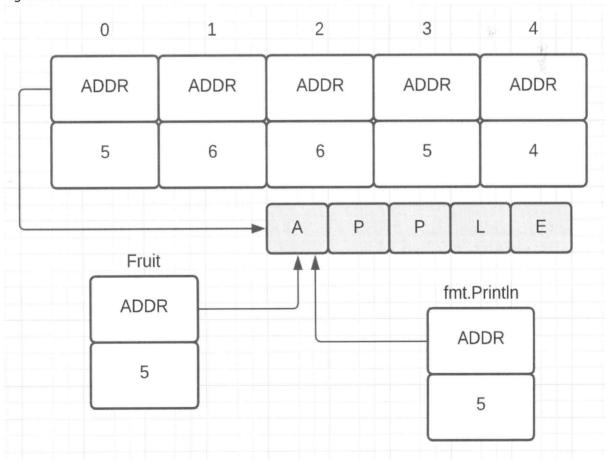

Making copies of the string value is important because it prevents the string value from ever escaping to the heap. This eliminates non-productive allocation on the heap.

3.7 Pointer Semantic Iteration

Given the following code and output.

Listing 3.10

```
strings := [5]string{"Apple", "Orange", "Banana", "Grape", "Plum"}
for i := range strings {
    println(i, strings[i])
}

Output:
0 Apple
1 Orange
2 Banana
3 Grape
4 Plum
```

Once again, the strings variable is an array of 5 strings. The loop iterates over each string in the collection and displays the index position and the string value. Since this is pointer semantic iteration, the for range is iterating over the strings array directly and on each iteration, the string value for each index position is accessed directly for the print call.

3.8 Data Semantic Guideline For Built-In Types

As a guideline, if the data I'm working with is a numeric, string, or bool, then use value semantics to move the data around my program. This includes declaring fields on a struct type.

Listing 3.11

```
func Foo(x int, y string, z bool) (int, string, bool)

type Foo struct {
    X int
    Y string
    Z bool
}
```

One reason I might take an exception and use pointer semantics is if I need the semantics of NULL (absence of value). Then using pointers of these types is an option, but document this if it's not obvious.

The nice thing about using value semantics for these types is that I'm guaranteed that each function is operating on its own copy. This means reads and writes to this data are isolated to that function. This helps with integrity and identifying bugs related to data corruption.

3.9 Different Type Arrays

It's interesting to see what the compiler provides as an error when assigning arrays of the same types that are of different lengths.

Listing 3.12

```
var five [5]int
four := [4]int{10, 20, 30, 40}

five = four

Compiler Error:
cannot use four (type [4]int) as type [5]int in assignment
```

Here I declare an array of 4 and 5 integers initialized to its zero value state. Then try to assign them to each other and the compiler says, "cannot use four (type [4]int) as type [5]int in assignment".

It's important to be clear about what the compiler is saying. It's saying that an array of 4 integers and an array of 5 integers represent data of different types. The size of an array is part of its type information. In Go, the size of an array has to be known at compile time.

3.10 Contiguous Memory Construction

I want to prove that an array provides a contiguous layout of memory.

Listing 3.13

```
five := [5]string{"Annie", "Betty", "Charley", "Doug", "Bill"}

for i, v := range five {
    fmt.Printf("Value[%s]\tAddress[%p]   IndexAddr[%p]\n",
        v, &v, &five[i])
}

Output:
Value[Annie]      Address[0xc000010250]    IndexAddr[0xc000052180]
Value[Betty]      Address[0xc000010250]    IndexAddr[0xc000052190]
Value[Charley]    Address[0xc000010250]    IndexAddr[0xc0000521a0]
Value[Doug]       Address[0xc000010250]    IndexAddr[0xc0000521b0]
Value[Bill]       Address[0xc000010250]    IndexAddr[0xc0000521c0]
```

Here I declare an array of 5 strings initialized with values. Then use value semantic iteration to display information about each string. The output shows each individual string value, the address of the v variable and the address of each element in the array.

I can see how the array is a contiguous block of memory and how a string is a two word or 16 byte data structure on my 64 bit architecture. The address for each element is distanced on a 16 byte stride.

The fact that the v variable has the same address on each iteration strengthens the understanding that v is a local variable of type string which contains a copy of each string value during iteration.

3.11 Constructing Slices

The slice is Go's most important data structure and it's represented as a three word data structure.

Figure 3.5

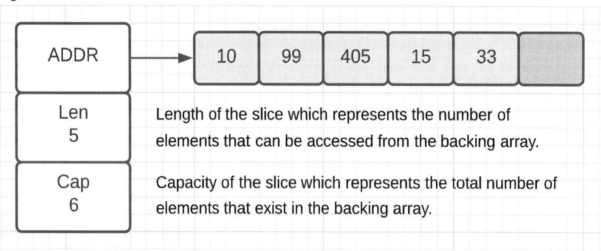

Constructing a slice can be done in several ways.

Listing 3.14

```
// Slice of string set to its zero value state.
var slice []string

// Slice of string set to its empty state.
slice := []string{}

// Slice of string set with a length and capacity of 5.
slice := make([]string, 5)

// Slice of string set with a length of 5 and capacity of 8.
slice := make([]string, 5, 8)

// Slice of string set with values with a length and capacity of 5.
slice := []string{"A", "B", "C", "D", "E"}
```

I can see the built-in function make allows me to pre-allocate both length and capacity for the backing array. If the compiler knows the size at compile time, the backing array could be constructed on the stack.

3.12 Slice Length vs Capacity

The length of a slice represents the number of elements that can be read and written to. The capacity represents the total number of elements that exist in the backing array from that pointer position.

Because of syntactic sugar, slices look and feel like an array.

Listing 3.15

```
slice := make([]string, 5)
slice[0] = "Apple"
slice[1] = "Orange"
slice[2] = "Banana"
slice[3] = "Grape"
slice[4] = "Plum"
```

I can tell the difference between slice and array construction since an array has a known size at compile time and slices necessarily don't.

If I try to access an element beyond the slice's length, I will get a runtime error.

Listing 3.16

```
slice := make([]string, 5)
slice[5] = "Raspberry"

Compiler Error:
Error: panic: runtime error: index out of range slice[5] = "Runtime error"
```

In this example, the length of the slice is 5 and I'm attempting to access the 6th element, which does not exist.

3.13 Data Semantic Guideline For Slices

As a guideline, if the data I'm working with is a slice, then use value semantics to move the data around my program. This includes declaring fields on a type.

Listing 3.17

```
func Foo(data []byte) []byte

type Foo struct {
    X []int
    Y []string
    Z []bool
}
```

This goes for all of Go's internal data structures (slices, maps, channels, interfaces, and functions).

One reason to switch to pointer semantics is if I need to share the slice for a decoding or unmarshaling operation. Using pointers for these types of operations are ok, but document this if it's not obvious.

3.14 Contiguous Memory Layout

The idea behind the slice is to have an array, which is the most efficient data structure as it relates to the hardware. However, I still need the ability to be dynamic and efficient with the amount of data I need at runtime and future growth.

Listing 3.18

```
func main() {
    slice := make([]string, 5, 8)
    slice[0] = "Apple"
    slice[1] = "Orange"
    slice[2] = "Banana"
    slice[3] = "Grape"
    slice[4] = "Plum"

    inspectSlice(slice)
}

func inspectSlice(slice []string) {
    fmt.Printf("Length[%d] Capacity[%d]\n", len(slice), cap(slice))
    for i := range slice {
        fmt.Printf("[%d] %p %s\n", i, &slice[i], slice[i])
    }
}

Output:
Length[5] Capacity[8]
[0] 0xc00007e000 Apple
[1] 0xc00007e010 Orange
[2] 0xc00007e020 Banana
[3] 0xc00007e030 Grape
[4] 0xc00007e040 Plum
```

The inspectSlice function shows how a slice does have a contiguous backing array with a predictable stride. It also shows how a slice has a length and capacity which may be different. Notice how the print function only iterates over the length of a slice.

3.15 Appending With Slices

The language provides a built-in function called append to add values to an existing slice.

Listing 3.19

```
var data []string

for record := 1; record <= 102400; record++ {
    data = append(data, fmt.Sprintf("Rec: %d", record))
}
```

The append function works with a slice even when the slice is initialized to its zero value state. The API design of append is what's interesting because it uses value semantic mutation. Append gets its own copy of a slice value, it mutates its own copy, then it returns a copy back to the caller.

Why is the API designed this way? This is because the idiom is to use value semantics to move a slice value around a program. This must still be respected even with a mutation operation. Plus, value semantic mutation is the safest way to perform mutation since the mutation is being performed on the function's own copy of the data in isolation.

Append always maintains a contiguous block of memory for the slice's backing array, even after growth. This is important for the hardware.

Figure 3.6

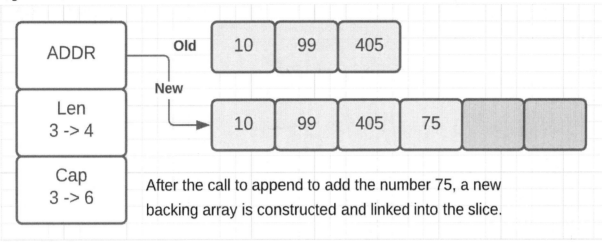

After the call to append to add the number 75, a new backing array is constructed and linked into the slice.

Every time the append function is called, the function checks if the length and capacity of the slice is the same or not. If it's the same, it means there is no more room in the backing array for the new value. In this case, append creates a new backing array (doubling or growing by 25%) and then copies the values from the old array into the new one. Then the new value can be appended.

Figure 3.7

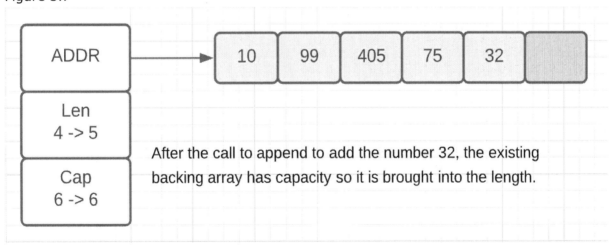

After the call to append to add the number 32, the existing backing array has capacity so it is brought into the length.

If it's not the same, it means that there is an extra element of capacity existing for the append. An element is taken from capacity and added to the length of the slice. This makes an append operation very efficient.

When the backing array has 1024 elements of capacity or less, new backing arrays are constructed by doubling the size of the existing array. Once the backing array grows past 1024 elements, growth happens at 25%.

3.16 Slicing Slices

Slices provide the ability to avoid extra copies and heap allocations of the backing array when needing to isolate certain elements of the backing array for different operations.

The slicing syntax represents the list notation [a:b) which means, include elements from index a through b, but not including b.

Listing 3.20

```
slice1 := []string{"A", "B", "C", "D", "E"}
slice2 := slice1[2:4]
```

The variable slice2 is a new slice value that is now sharing the same backing array that slice1 is using. However, slice2 only allows me to access the elements at index 2 and 3 (C and D) of the original slice's backing array. The length of slice2 is 2 and not 5 like in slice1 and the capacity is 3 since there are now 3 elements from that pointer position.

Figure 3.8

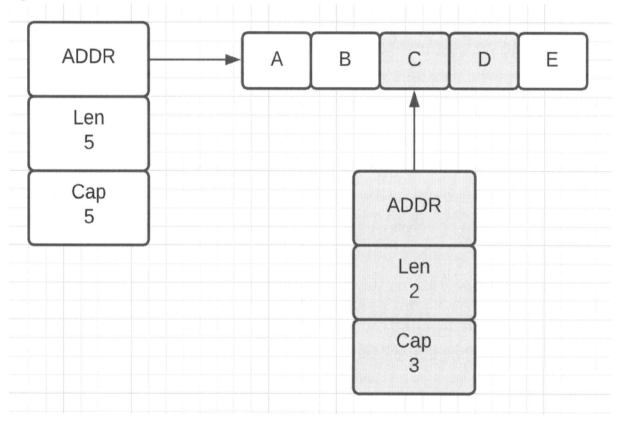

A better way to think about slicing is to focus on the length using this notation [a:a+len] index a through a plus the length. This will reduce errors in calculating new slices.

Using this inspect function.

Listing 3.21

```
func inspectSlice(slice []string) {
    fmt.Printf("Length[%d] Capacity[%d]\n", len(slice), cap(slice))
    for i, s := range slice {
        fmt.Printf("[%d] %p %s\n",
            i,
            &slice[i],
            s)
        }
    }
}
```

I can see this in action.

Listing 3.22

```
slice1 := []string{"A", "B", "C", "D", "E"}
slice2 := slice1[2:4]
inspectSlice(slice1)
inspectSlice(slice2)

Output:
Length[5] Capacity[5]
[0] 0xc00007e000 A
[1] 0xc00007e010 B
[2] 0xc00007e020 C
[3] 0xc00007e030 D
[4] 0xc00007e040 E
Length[2] Capacity[3]
[0] 0xc00007e020 C    <-- SAME AS INDEX 2 IN SLICE 1
[1] 0xc00007e030 D    <-- SAME AS INDEX 3 IN SLICE 1
```

Notice how the two different slices are sharing the same backing array. I can see this by comparing addresses.

The nice thing here is there are no allocations. The compiler knows the size of the backing array for slice1 at compile time. Passing a copy of the slice value down into the inspectSlice function keeps everything on the stack.

3.17 Mutations To The Backing Array

When I use slice2 to change the value of the string at index 0, any slice value that is sharing the same backing array (where the address for that index is part of that slice's length) will see the change.

Listing 3.23

```
slice1 := []string{"A", "B", "C", "D", "E"}
slice2 := slice1[2:4]
slice2[0] = "CHANGED"
inspectSlice(slice1)
inspectSlice(slice2)

Output:
Length[5] Capacity[5]
[0] 0xc00007e000 A
[1] 0xc00007e010 B
[2] 0xc00007e020 CHANGED
[3] 0xc00007e030 D
[4] 0xc00007e040 E
Length[2] Capacity[3]
[0] 0xc00007e020 CHANGED
[1] 0xc00007e030 D
```

I always have to be aware when I am modifying a value at an index position if the backing array is being shared with another slice.

Figure 3.9

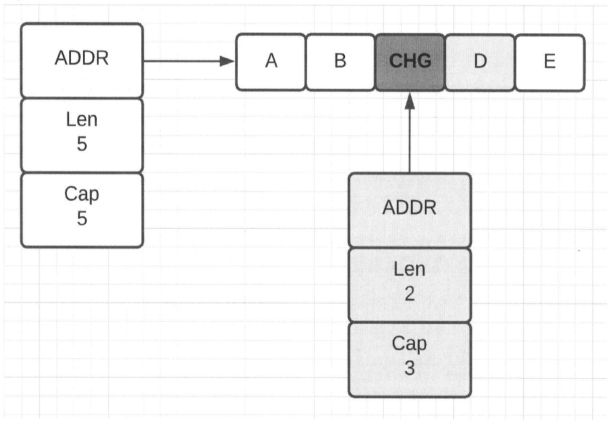

What if I use the built-in function append instead?

Listing 3.24

```
slice1 := []string{"A", "B", "C", "D", "E"}
slice2 := slice1[2:4]
slice2 = append(slice2, "CHANGED")
inspectSlice(slice1)
inspectSlice(slice2)

Output:
Length[5] Capacity[5]
[0] 0xc00007e000 A
[1] 0xc00007e010 B
[2] 0xc00007e020 C
[3] 0xc00007e030 D
[4] 0xc00007e040 CHANGED
Length[3] Capacity[3]
[0] 0xc00007e020 C
[1] 0xc00007e030 D
[2] 0xc00007e040 CHANGED
```

The append function creates the same side effect, but it's hidden. In this case, bringing in more length from capacity for slice2 has caused the value at address 0xc00007e040 to be changed. Unfortunately, slice1 had this address already as part of its length.

Figure 3.10

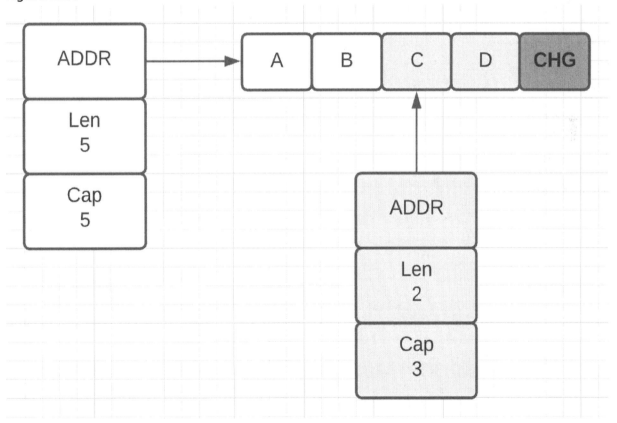

One way to avert the side effect is to use a three index slice when constructing slice2 so the length and capacity is the same at 2.

Listing 3.25

```
slice1 := []string{"A", "B", "C", "D", "E"}
slice2 := slice1[2:4:4]
inspectSlice(slice1)
inspectSlice(slice2)

Output:
Length[5] Capacity[5]
[0] 0xc00007e000 A
[1] 0xc00007e010 B
[2] 0xc00007e020 C
[3] 0xc00007e030 D
[4] 0xc00007e040 E
Length[2] Capacity[2]
[0] 0xc00007e020 C
[1] 0xc00007e030 D
```

The syntax for a three index slice is [a:b:c] when b and c should be the same since [a-b] sets the length and [a-c] sets the capacity. Now the length and capacity of slice2 is the same.

Now I use the built-in function append again like before.

Listing 3.26

```
slice1 := []string{"A", "B", "C", "D", "E"}
slice2 := slice1[2:4:4]
slice2 = append(slice2, "CHANGED")
inspectSlice(slice1)
inspectSlice(slice2)

Output:
Length[5] Capacity[5]
[0] 0xc00007e000 A
[1] 0xc00007e010 B
[2] 0xc00007e020 C
[3] 0xc00007e030 D
[4] 0xc00007e040 E
Length[3] Capacity[4]
[0] 0xc000016080 C
[1] 0xc000016090 D
[2] 0xc0000160a0 CHANGED
```

Notice after the call to append, slice2 has a new backing array.

Figure 3.11

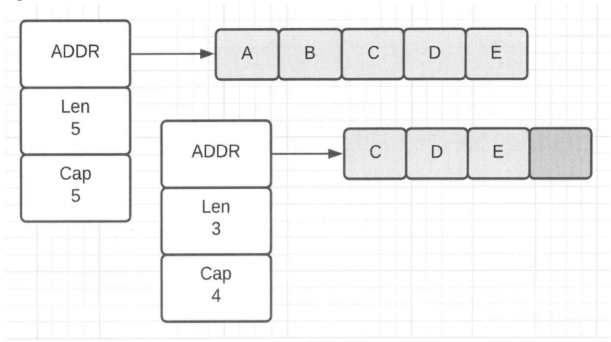

This can be seen by comparing the addresses of each slice. In this case, the mutation against slice2 didn't cause a side effect against slice1.

3.18 Copying Slices Manually

There is a built-in function named copy that will allow for the shallow copying of slices. Since a string has a backing array of bytes that are immutable, it can be used as a source but never a destination.

Listing 3.27

```
slice1 := []string{"A", "B", "C", "D", "E"}
slice3 := make([]string, len(slice1))
copy(slice3, slice1)

inspectSlice(slice1)
inspectSlice(slice3)

Output:
Length[5] Capacity[5]
[0] 0xc00005c050 A
[1] 0xc00005c060 B
[2] 0xc00005c070 C
[3] 0xc00005c080 D
[4] 0xc00005c090 E
Length[5] Capacity[5]
[0] 0xc00005c0a0 A
[1] 0xc00005c0b0 B
[2] 0xc00005c0c0 C
[3] 0xc00005c0d0 D
[4] 0xc00005c0e0 E
```

As long as the destination slice has the proper type and length, the built-in function copy can perform a shallow copy.

3.19 Slices Use Pointer Semantic Mutation

It's important to remember that even though I use value semantics to move a slice around the program, when reading and writing a slice, I am using pointer semantics. Sharing individual elements of a slice with different parts of my program can cause unwanted side effects.

Listing 3.28

```
// Construct a slice of 1 user, set a pointer to that user,
// use the pointer to update likes.

users := make([]user, 1)
ptrUsr0 := &users[0]
ptrUsr0.likes++

for i := range users {
    fmt.Printf("User: %d Likes: %d\n", i, users[i].likes)
}

Output:
User: 0 Likes: 1
```

A slice is used to maintain a collection of users. Then a pointer is set to the first user and used to update likes. The output shows that using the pointer is working.

Figure 3.12

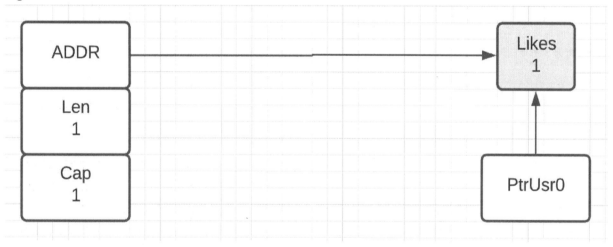

Then a new user is appended to the collection and the pointer is used again to add a like to the first user.

Listing 3.29

```
// Append a new user to the collection. Use the pointer again
// to update likes.

users = append(users, user{})
ptrUsr0.likes++

for i := range users {
    fmt.Printf("User: %d Likes: %d\n", i, users[i].likes)
}

Output:
User: 0 Likes: 1
User: 1 Likes: 0
```

However, since the append function replaced the backing array with a new one, the pointer is updating the old backing array and the likes are lost. The output shows the likes for the first user did not increase.

Figure 3.13

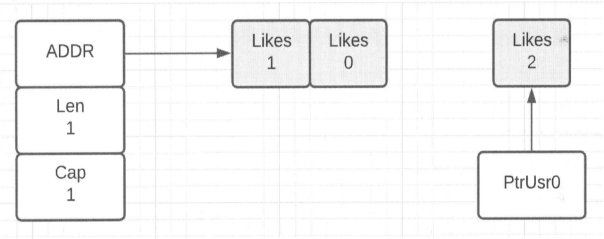

I have to be careful to know if a slice is going to be used in an append operation during the course of a running program. How I share the slice needs to be considered. Sharing individual indexes may not be the best idea. Sharing an entire slice value may not work either when appending is in operation. Probably using a slice as a field in a struct, and sharing the struct value is a better way to go.

3.20 Linear Traversal Efficiency

The beauty of a slice is its ability to allow for performing linear traversals that are mechanically sympathetic while sharing data using value semantics to minimize heap allocations.

Listing 3.30

```
x := []byte{0x0A, 0x15, 0x0e, 0x28, 0x05, 0x96, 0x0b, 0xd0, 0x0}

a := x[0]
b := binary.LittleEndian.Uint16(x[1:3])
c := binary.LittleEndian.Uint16(x[3:5])
d := binary.LittleEndian.Uint32(x[5:9])

println(a, b, c, d)
```

The code is performing a linear traversal by creating slice values that read different sections of the byte array from beginning to end.

Figure 3.14

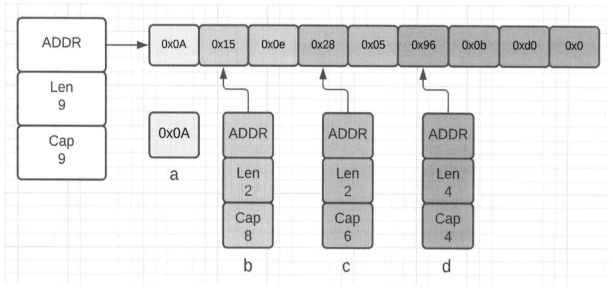

All the data in this code stays on the stack. No extra copies of the data inside the byte slice are copied.

3.21 UTF-8

Go's compiler expects all code to be encoded in the UTF-8 character set. Make sure any file with source code is saved with this encoding or literal strings may be wrong when the program runs.

UTF-8 is a character set where I have bytes, code points, and then characters. One to four bytes of data can represent a code point (int32) and one to many code points can represent a character.

Listing 3.31

```
s := "世界 means world"
```

The string above represents 18 bytes, 14 code points, and 14 characters. Each Chinese character I see requires 3 bytes to represent the code point/character I see.

Listing 3.32

```
var buf [utf8.UTFMax]byte
```

There is a utf8 package in the standard library that declares a constant named UTFMax. This constant represents the max number of bytes a code point could require, which is 4.

Listing 3.33

```
for i, r := range s {
```

When iterating over a string, the iteration moves code point by code point. Go has an alias type named rune (alias of int32) that represents a code point. Hence the use of the variable r as the value being copied.

On the first iteration, i will equal 0. On the next iteration, i will equal 3. Then in the next iteration, i will equal 6. All subsequent iterations will increment i by 1.

Listing 3.34

```
rl := utf8.RuneLen(r)
```

The RuneLen function returns the number of bytes required to store the rune value. For the first two iterations, rl will equal 3.

Listing 3.35

```
si := i + rl
copy(buf[:], s[i:si])
```

The si variable represents the index position for the slice operation to slice the bytes associated with the rune. Then the built-in function copy is used to copy the bytes for the rune into the array. Notice how an array can be sliced. This proves that every array in Go is just a slice waiting to happen.

Listing 3.36

```
fmt.Printf("%2d: %q; codepoint: %#6x; encoded bytes: %#v\n",
    i, r, r, buf[:rl])
}
```

The print statement displays each character, code point, and the set of bytes.

Listing 3.37

```
Output:
 0: '世'; codepoint: 0x4e16; encoded bytes: []byte{0xe4, 0xb8, 0x96}
 3: '界'; codepoint: 0x754c; encoded bytes: []byte{0xe7, 0x95, 0x8c}
 6: ' '; codepoint:   0x20; encoded bytes: []byte{0x20}
 7: 'm'; codepoint:   0x6d; encoded bytes: []byte{0x6d}
 8: 'e'; codepoint:   0x65; encoded bytes: []byte{0x65}
 9: 'a'; codepoint:   0x61; encoded bytes: []byte{0x61}
10: 'n'; codepoint:   0x6e; encoded bytes: []byte{0x6e}
11: 's'; codepoint:   0x73; encoded bytes: []byte{0x73}
12: ' '; codepoint:   0x20; encoded bytes: []byte{0x20}
13: 'w'; codepoint:   0x77; encoded bytes: []byte{0x77}
14: 'o'; codepoint:   0x6f; encoded bytes: []byte{0x6f}
15: 'r'; codepoint:   0x72; encoded bytes: []byte{0x72}
16: 'l'; codepoint:   0x6c; encoded bytes: []byte{0x6c}
17: 'd'; codepoint:   0x64; encoded bytes: []byte{0x64}
```

3.22 Declaring And Constructing Maps

A map is a data structure that provides support for storing and accessing data based on a key. It uses a hash map and bucket system that maintains a contiguous block of memory underneath.

Listing 3.38

```
type user struct {
    name     string
    username string
}

// Construct a map set to its zero value,
// that can store user values based on a key of type string.
// Trying to use this map will result in a runtime error (panic).
var users map[string]user

// Construct a map initialized using make,
// that can store user values based on a key of type string.
users := make(map[string]user)

// Construct a map initialized using empty literal construction,
// that can store user values based on a key of type string.
users := map[string]user{}
```

There are several ways to construct a map for use. A map set to its zero value is not usable and will result in my program panicking. The use of the built-in function make and literal construction constructs a map ready for use.

Listing 3.39

```
func main() {
    users := make(map[string]user)

    users["Roy"] = user{"Rob", "Roy"}
    users["Ford"] = user{"Henry", "Ford"}
    users["Mouse"] = user{"Mickey", "Mouse"}
    users["Jackson"] = user{"Michael", "Jackson"}

    for key, value := range users {
        fmt.Println(key, value)
    }
}

Output:
Roy {Rob Roy}
Ford {Henry Ford}
Mouse {Mickey Mouse}
Jackson {Michael Jackson}
```

If the built-in function make is used to construct a map, then the assignment operator can be used to add and update values in the map. The order of how keys/values are returned when ranging over a map is undefined by the spec and up to the compiler to implement.

Listing 3.40

```
func main() {
    users := map[string]user{
        "Roy":     {"Rob", "Roy"},
        "Ford":    {"Henry", "Ford"},
        "Mouse":   {"Mickey", "Mouse"},
        "Jackson": {"Michael", "Jackson"},
    }

    for key, value := range users {
        fmt.Println(key, value)
    }
}

Output:
Ford {Henry Ford}
Jackson {Michael Jackson}
Roy {Rob Roy}
Mouse {Mickey Mouse}
```

In this case, the output was returned in a different order from how they are listed in the construction. The current algorithm for 1.16 will return the results in a random order once the number of values reaches a certain limit. Once again, this is a compiler implementation that is allowed to change. I can't depend on it.

3.23 Lookups and Deleting Map Keys

Once data is stored inside of a map, to extract any data a key lookup is required.

Listing 3.41

```
user1, exists1 := users["Bill"]
user2, exists2 := users["Ford"]

fmt.Println("Bill:", exists1, user1)
fmt.Println("Ford:", exists2, user2)

Output:
Bill: false { }
Ford: true {Henry Ford}
```

To perform a key lookup, square brackets are used with the map variable. Two values can be returned from a map lookup, the value and a boolean that represents if the value was found or not. If I don't need to know this, I can leave the "exists" variable out.

When a key is not found in the map, the operation returns a value of the map type set to its zero value state. I can see this with the "Bill" key lookup. Don't use zero value to determine if a key exists in the map or not since zero value may be valid and what was actually stored for the key.

Listing 3.42

```
delete(users, "Roy")
```

There is a built-in function named delete that allows for the deletion of data from the map based on a key.

3.24 Key Map Restrictions
Not all types can be used as a key.

Listing 3.43

```
type slice []user
Users := make(map[slice]user)

Compiler Error:
invalid map key type users
```

A slice is a good example of a type that can't be used as a key. Only values that can be run through the hash function are eligible. A good way to recognize types that can be a key is if the type can be used in a comparison operation. I can't compare two slice values.

Chapter 4: Decoupling

In this chapter, I will learn about the mechanics and semantics for decoupling code from change. I will learn how to extend behavior to data, what polymorphism really is about, and how it is applied in the language.

4.1 Methods

A method provides data the ability to exhibit behavior.

A function is called a method when that function has a receiver declared. The receiver is the parameter that is declared between the keyword func and the function name. There are two types of receivers, value receivers for implementing value semantics and pointer receivers for implementing pointer semantics.

Listing 4.1

```
type user struct {
      name  string
      email string
}

func (u user) notify() {
      fmt.Printf("Sending User Email To %s<%s>\n", u.name, u.email)
}

func (u *user) changeEmail(email string) {
      u.email = email
      fmt.Printf("Changed User Email To %s\n", email)
}
```

The notify function is implemented with a value receiver. This means the method operates under value semantics and will operate on its own copy of the value used to make the call.

The changeEmail function is implemented with a pointer receiver. This means the method operates under pointer semantics and will operate on shared access to the value used to make the call.

Outside of a few exceptions, a method set for a type should not contain a mix of value and pointer receivers. Data semantic consistency is critically important and this includes declaring methods.

4.2 Method Calls

When making a method call, the compiler doesn't care if the value used to make the call matches the receiver's data semantics exactly. The compiler just wants a value or pointer of the same type.

Listing 4.2

```
bill := user{"Bill", "bill@email.com"}
bill.notify()
bill.changeEmail("bill@hotmail.com")
```

I can see that a value of type user is constructed and assigned to the bill variable. In the case of the notify call, the bill variable matches the receiver type which is using a value receiver. In the case of the changeEmail call, the bill variable doesn't match the receiver type which is using a pointer receiver. However, the compiler accepts the method call and shares the bill variable with the method. Go will adjust to make the call.

This works the same when the variable used to make the call is a pointer variable.

Listing 4.3

```
bill := &user{"Bill", "bill@email.com"}
bill.notify()
bill.changeEmail("bill@hotmail.com")
```

In this case, the bill variable is a pointer variable to a value of type user. Once again, Go adjusts to make the method call when calling the notify method.

If Go didn't adjust, then this is what I would have to do to make those same method calls.

Listing 4.4

```
bill := user{"Bill", "bill@email.com"}
(&bill).changeEmail("bill@hotmail.com")

bill := &user{"Bill", "bill@email.com"}
(*bill).notify()
```

I'm glad I don't have to do that to make method calls in Go.

4.3 Data Semantic Guideline For Internal Types

As a guideline, if the data I'm working with is an internal type (slice, map, channel, function, interface) then use value semantics to move the data around my program. This includes declaring fields on a type. However, when I'm reading and writing I need to remember I'm using pointer semantics.

Listing 4.5

```
type IP []byte
type IPMask []byte
```

These types are declared in the net package that is part of the standard library. They are declared with an underlying type which is a slice of bytes. Because of this, these types follow the guidelines for internal types.

Listing 4.6

```
func (ip IP) Mask(mask IPMask) IP {
    if len(mask) == IPv6len && len(ip) == IPv4len && allFF(mask[:12]) {
        mask = mask[12:]
    }
    if len(mask) == IPv4len && len(ip) == IPv6len &&
        bytesEqual(ip[:12], v4InV6Prefix) {
        ip = ip[12:]
    }
    n := len(ip)
    if n != len(mask) {
        return nil
    }
    out := make(IP, n)
    for i := 0; i < n; i++ {
        out[i] = ip[i] & mask[i]
    }
    return out
}
```

With the Mask method, value semantics are in play for both the receiver, parameter, and return argument. This method accepts its own copy of a Mask value, it mutates that value and then it returns a copy of the mutation. This method is using value semantic mutation. This is not an accident or random.

A function can decide what data input and output it needs. What it can't decide is the data semantics for how the data flows in or out. The data drives that decision and the function must comply. This is why Mask implements a value semantic mutation api. It must respect how a slice is designed to be moved around the program.

Listing 4.7

```
func ipEmptyString(ip IP) string {
    if len(ip) == 0 {
        return ""
    }
    return ip.String()
}
```

The ipEmptyString function is also using value semantics for the input and output. This function accepts its own copy of an IP value and returns a string value. No use of pointer semantics because the data dictates the data semantics and not the function.

One exception to using value semantics is when I need to share a slice or map with a function that performs unmarshaling or decoding.

4.4 Data Semantic Guideline For Struct Types

As a guideline, if the data I'm working with is a struct type then I have to think about what the data represents to make a decision. Though it would be great to choose value semantics for everything, when I'm not sure, evaluate if the data is safe to be copied. If it's safe to be copied, start with value semantics. If it's not safe for copying or that's not even clear, start with pointer semantics.

After some time working with a new data type, the data semantic could become self-evident and refactoring the data semantic is what I want to do. Don't become paralyzed if it's not self-evident from the start.

Listing 4.8

```
type Time struct {
    sec  int64
    nsec int32
    loc  *Location
}
```

Here is the Time struct from the time package. If I was being asked to implement the API for this data structure, what should I choose, value or pointer semantics?

Sometimes I can ask these question:

- Does a change in the data completely create a new data point?
- Is the data specific to a context, and are mutations isolated to that context?
- Should there only ever be one instance of this data?

If I'm looking at an existing code base and I want to know what data semantic was chosen, look for a factory function. The return type of a factory function should dictate the data semantics.

Listing 4.9

```
func Now() Time {
    sec, nsec := now()
    return Time{sec + unixToInternal, nsec, Local}
}
```

This is the factory function for constructing Time values. Look at the return, it's using value semantics. This tells me that I should be using value semantics for Time values which means every function gets its own copy of a Time value and fields in a struct should be declared as values of type Time.

Listing 4.10

```go
func (t Time) Add(d Duration) Time {
    t.sec += int64(d / 1e9)
    nsec := int32(t.nsec) + int32(d%1e9)
    if nsec >= 1e9 {
        t.sec++
        nsec -= 1e9
    } else if nsec < 0 {
        t.sec--
        nsec += 1e9
    }
    t.nsec = nsec
    return t
}
```

Add is a method that needs to perform a mutation operation. If I look closely, I will see the function is using value semantic mutation. The Add method gets its own copy of the Time value used to make the call, it mutates its own copy, then it returns a copy back to the caller. Once again, this is the safest way to perform a mutation operation.

Listing 4.11

```go
func div(t Time, d Duration) (qmod2 int, r Duration) {}
```

Here is another example where the div function accepts a value of type Time and Duration (int64), then returns values of type int and Duration. Value semantics for the Time type and for all the built-in types. Duration has an underlying type of int64.

Listing 4.12

```go
func (t *Time) UnmarshalBinary(data []byte) error {}
func (t *Time) GobDecode(data []byte) error {}
func (t *Time) UnmarshalJSON(data []byte) error {}
func (t *Time) UnmarshalText(data []byte) error {}
```

These four methods from the Time package seem to break the rules for data semantic consistency. They are using pointer semantics, why? Because they are implementing an interface where the method signature is locked in. Since the implementation requires a mutation, pointer semantics are the only choice.

Here is a guideline: If value semantics are at play, I can switch to pointer semantics for some functions as long as I don't let the data in the remaining call chain switch back to value semantics. Once I switch to pointer semantics, all future calls from that point need to stick to pointer semantics. I can never, ever, never, go from pointer to value. It's never safe to make a copy of a value that a pointer points to.

Listing 4.13

```
func Open(name string) (file *File, err error) {
    return OpenFile(name, O_RDONLY, 0)
}
```

The Open function from the os package shows that when using a value of type File, pointer semantics are at play. File values need to be shared and should never be copied.

Listing 4.14

```
func (f *File) Chdir() error {
    if f == nil {
        return ErrInvalid
    }
    if e := syscall.Fchdir(f.fd); e != nil {
        return &PathError{"chdir", f.name, e}
    }
    return nil
}
```

The method Chdir is using a pointer receiver even though this method does not mutate the File value. This is because File values need to be shared and can't be copied.

Listing 4.15

```
func epipecheck(file *File, e error) {
    if e == syscall.EPIPE {
        if atomic.AddInt32(&file.nepipe, 1) >= 10 {
            sigpipe()
        }
    } else {
        atomic.StoreInt32(&file.nepipe, 0)
    }
}
```

The epipecheck function as well accepts File values using pointer semantics.

4.5 Methods Are Just Functions

Methods are really just functions that provide syntactic sugar to provide the ability for data to exhibit behavior.

Listing 4.16

```
type data struct {
    name string
    age  int
}

func (d data) displayName() {
    fmt.Println("My Name Is", d.name)
}

func (d *data) setAge(age int) {
    d.age = age
    fmt.Println(d.name, "Is Age", d.age)
}
```

A type and two methods are declared. The displayName method is using value semantics and setAge is using pointer semantics.

Note: Do not implement setters and getters in Go. These are not apis with purpose and in these cases it's better to make those fields exported.

Listing 4.17

```
d := data{
    name: "Bill",
}

d.displayName()
d.setAge(21)
```

A value of type data is constructed and method calls are made.

Listing 4.18

```
data.displayName(d)
(*data).setAge(&d, 21)
```

Since methods are really just functions with syntactic sugar, the methods can be executed like functions. I can see that the receiver is really a parameter, it's the first parameter. When I call a method, the compiler converts that to a function call underneath.

Note: Do not execute methods like this, but I may see this syntax in tooling messages.

4.6 Know The Behavior of the Code

If I know the data semantics at play, then I know the behavior of the code. If I know the behavior of the code, then I know the cost of the code. Once I know the cost, I'm engineering.

Given this type and method set.

Listing 4.19

```go
type data struct {
    name string
    age  int
}

func (d data) displayName() {
    fmt.Println("My Name Is", d.name)
}

func (d *data) setAge(age int) {
    d.age = age
    fmt.Println(d.name, "Is Age", d.age)
}
```

I can write the following code.

Listing 4.20

```go
func main() {
    d := data{
        name: "Bill",
    }

    f1 := d.displayName
    f1()
    d.name = "Joan"
    f1()
}

Output:
My Name Is Bill
My Name Is Bill
```

I start with constructing a value of type Data assigning it to the variable d. Then I take the method displayName, bound to d, and assign that to a variable named f1. This is not a method call but an assignment which creates a level of indirection. Functions are values in Go and belong to the set of internal types.

After the assignment, I can call the method indirectly through the use of the f1 variable. This displays the name Bill. Then I change the data so the name is now Joan, and call the method once again through the f1 variable. I don't see the change. Bill is the output once again. So Why?

Figure 4.1

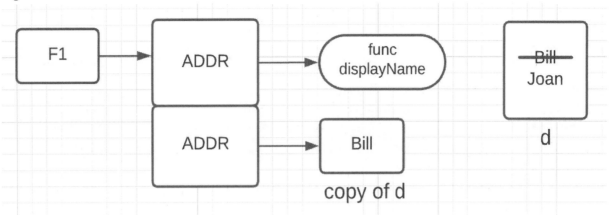

It has to do with the data semantics at play. The displayName method is using a value receiver so value semantics are at play.

Listing 4.21

```
func (d data) displayName() {
    fmt.Println("My Name Is", d.name)
}
```

This means that the f1 variable maintains and operates against its own copy of d. So calling the method through the f1 variable, will always use the copy and that copy is protected against change. This is what I want with value semantics.
Now I will do the same thing but with the setAge method.

Listing 4.22

```
func main() {
    d := data{
        name: "Bill",
    }

    f2 := d.setAge
    f2(45)
    d.name = "Sammy"
    f2(45)
}

Output:
Bill Is Age 45
Sammy Is Age 45
```

This time the setAge method is assigned to the variable f2. Once again, the method is executed indirectly through the f2 variable passing 45 for Bill's age. Then Bill's name is changed to Sammy and the f2 variable is used again to make the call. This time I see the name has changed.

Figure 4.2

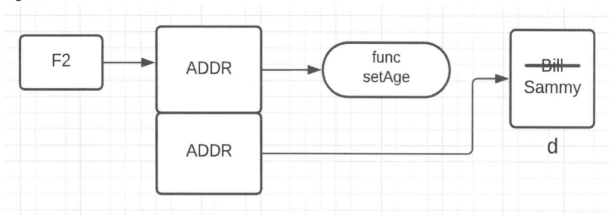

The setAge function is using a pointer receiver so setAge doesn't operate on its own copy of the d variable, but is operating directly on the d variable. Therefore, f2 is operating on shared access and I see the change.

Listing 4.23

```
func (d *data) setAge(age int) {
    d.age = age
    fmt.Println(d.name, "Is Age", d.age)
}
```

Without knowing the data semantics at play, I won't know the behavior of the code. These data semantics are real and affect the behavior.

4.7 Interfaces

Interfaces give programs structure and encourage design by composition. They enable and enforce clean divisions between components. The standardization of interfaces can set clear and consistent expectations. Decoupling means reducing the dependencies between components and the types they use. This leads to correctness, quality and maintainability.

Interfaces allow me to group concrete data together by what the data can do. It's about focusing on what data can do and not what the data is. Interfaces also help my code decouple itself from change by asking for concrete data based on what it can do. It's not limited to one type of data.

I must do my best to understand what data changes are coming and use interfaces to decouple my program from that change. Interfaces should describe behavior and not state. They should be verbs and not nouns.

Generalized interfaces that focus on behavior are best. Interfaces with more than one method have more than one reason to change. Interfaces that are based on nouns, tend to be less reusable, are more susceptible to change, and defeat the purpose of the interface.

Uncertainty about change is not a license to guess but a directive to STOP and learn more. I must distinguish between code that defends against fraud vs protects against accidents.

Use an interface when:

- Users of the API need to provide an implementation detail.
- API's have multiple implementations they need to maintain internally.
- Parts of the API that can change have been identified and require decoupling.

Don't use an interface:

- For the sake of using an interface.
- To generalize an algorithm.
- When users can declare their own interfaces.
- If it's not clear how the interface makes the code better.

4.8 Interfaces Are Valueless

The first important thing to understand is that an interface type declares a valueless type.

Listing 4.24

```
type reader interface {
    read(b []byte) (int, error)
}
```

Type reader is not a struct type, but an interface type. Its declaration is not based on state, but behavior. Interface types declare a method-set of behavior that concrete data must exhibit in order to satisfy the interface. There is nothing concrete about interface types, therefore they are valueless.

Listing 4.25

```
var r reader
```

Because they are valueless, the construction of a variable (like r) is odd because in our programming model, r does not exist, it's valueless. There is nothing about r itself that I can manipulate or transform. This is a critical concept to understand. I'm never working with interface values, only concrete values. An interface has a compiler representation (internal type), but from our programming model, interfaces are valueless.

4.9 Implementing Interfaces

Go is a language that is about convention over configuration. When it comes to a concrete type implementing an interface, there is no exception.

Listing 4.26

```go
type reader interface {
     read(b []byte) (int, error)
}

type file struct {
    name string
}

func (file) read(b []byte) (int, error) {
    s := "<rss><channel><title>Going Go</title></channel></rss>"
    copy(b, s)
    return len(s), nil
}
```

The code declares a type named file and then declares a method named read. Because of these two declarations, I can say the following:

"The concrete type file now implements the reader interface using value semantics"

Every word I just said is important. In Go, all I have to do is declare the full method-set of behavior defined by an interface to implement that interface. In this case, that is what I've done since the reader interface only declares a single act of behavior named read.

Listing 4.27

```go
type reader interface {
     read(b []byte) (int, error)
}

type pipe struct {
    name string
}

func (pipe) read(b []byte) (int, error) {
    s := `{name: "Bill", title: "developer"}`
    copy(b, s)
    return len(s), nil
}
```

This code declares a type named pipe and then declares a method name read. Because of these two declarations, I can say the following:

"The concrete type pipe now implements the reader interface using value semantics"

Now I have two concrete types implementing the reader interface. Two concrete types each with their unique implementation. One type is reading file systems and the other networks.

4.10 Polymorphism

Polymorphism means that a piece of code changes its behavior depending on the concrete data it's operating on. This was said by Tom Kurtz, who is the inventor of BASIC. This is the definition we will use moving forward.

Listing 4.28

```
// retrieve can read any device and process the data.
func retrieve(r reader) error {
    data := make([]byte, 100)

    len, err := r.read(data)
    if err != nil {
        return err
    }

    fmt.Println(string(data[:len]))
    return nil
}
```

Take a look at the type of data this function accepts. It wants a value of type reader. That's impossible since reader is an interface and interfaces are valueless types. It can't be asking for a reader value, they don't exist.

If the function is not asking for a reader value then what is the function asking for? It is asking for the only thing it can ask for, concrete data.

The function retrieve is a polymorphic function because it's asking for concrete data not based on what the data is (concrete type), but based on what the data can do (interface type).

Listing 4.29

```
f := file{"data.json"}
p := pipe{"cfg_service"}

retrieve(f)
retrieve(p)
```

I can construct two concrete values, one of type file and one of type pipe. Then I can pass a copy of each value to the polymorphic function. This is because each of these values implement the full method set of behavior defined by the reader interface.

When the concrete file value is passed into retrieve, the value is stored inside a two word internal type representing the interface value.

Figure 4.3

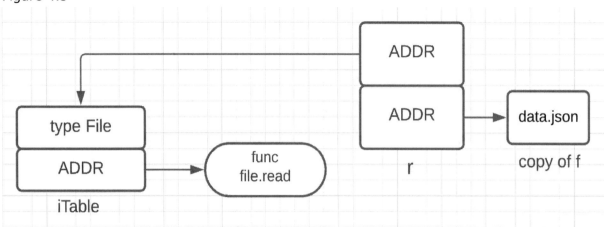

The second word of the interface value points to the value being stored. In this case, it's a copy of the file value since value semantics are at play. The first word points to a special data structure that is called the iTable.

The iTable serves 2 purposes:

- It describes the type of value being stored. In my case, it's a file value.
- It provides function pointers to the concrete implementations of the method set for the type of value being stored.

When the read call is made against the interface value, an iTable lookup is performed to find the concrete implementation of the read method associated with the type. Then the method call is made against the value being stored in the second word.

I can say retrieve is a polymorphic function because the concrete value pipe can be passed into retrieve and now the call to read against the interface value changes its behavior. This time that call to read is reading a network instead of reading a file.

4.11 Method Set Rules

Implementing an interface using pointer semantics applies some constraints on interface compliance.

Listing 4.30

```
type notifier interface {
    notify()
}

type user struct {
    name  string
    email string
}

func (u *user) notify() {
    fmt.Printf("Sending User Email To %s<%s>\n", u.name, u.email)
}

func sendNotification(n notifier) {
    n.notify()
}

func main() {
    u := user{"Bill", "bill@email.com"}
    sendNotification(u)
}
```

The notifier interface is implemented by the user type using pointer semantics. When value semantics are used to make the polymorphic call, the following compiler message is produced.

> *"cannot use u (type user) as type notifier in argument to sendNotification:*
> *user does not implement notifier (notify method has pointer receiver)"*

This is because there is a special set of rules in the specification about method sets. These rules define what methods are attached to values and pointers of a type. They are in place to maintain the highest level of integrity in my program.

These are the rules defined in the specification:

- For any value of type T, only those methods implemented with a value receiver for that type belong to the method set of that value.
- For any address of type T, all methods implemented for that type belong to the method set of that value.

In other words, when working with an address (pointer), all methods implemented are attached and available to be called. When working with a value, only those methods implemented with value receivers are attached and available to be called.

In the previous lesson about methods, I was able to call a method against a concrete piece of data regardless of the data semantics declared by the receiver. This is because the compiler can adjust to make the call. In this case, a value is being stored inside an interface and the methods must exist. No adjustments can be made.

The question now becomes: Why can't methods implemented with pointer receivers be attached to values of type T? What is the integrity issue here?

One reason is because I can't guarantee that every value of type T is addressable. If a value doesn't have an address, it can't be shared.

Listing 4.31

```
type duration int

func (d *duration) notify() {
        fmt.Println("Sending Notification in", *d)
}

func main() {
    duration(42).notify()
}

Compiler Error:
cannot call pointer method on duration(42)
cannot take the address of duration(42)
```

In this example, the value of 42 is a constant of kind int. Even though the value is converted into a value of type duration, it's not being stored inside a variable. This means the value is never on the stack or heap. There isn't an address. Constants only live at compile time.

The second reason is the bigger reason. The compiler is telling me that I am not allowed to use value semantics if I have chosen to use pointer semantics. In other words, I am being forced to share the value with the interface since it's not safe to make a copy of a value that a pointer points to. If I chose to implement the method with pointer semantics, I am stating that a value of this type isn't safe to be copied.

Listing 4.32

```
func main() {
    u := user{"Bill", "bill@email.com"}
    sendNotification(&u)
}
```

To fix the compiler message, I must use pointer semantics on the call to the polymorphic function and share u. The answer is not to change the method to use value semantics.

4.12 Slice of Interface

When I declare a slice of an interface type, I'm capable of grouping different concrete values together based on what they can do. This is why Go doesn't need the concept of sub-typing. It's not about a common DNA, it's about a common behavior.

Listing 4.33

```go
type printer interface {
    print()
}

type canon struct {
    name string
}

func (c canon) print() {
    fmt.Printf("Printer Name: %s\n", c.name)
}

type epson struct {
    name string
}

func (e *epson) print() {
    fmt.Printf("Printer Name: %s\n", e.name)
}

func main() {
    c := canon{"PIXMA TR4520"}
    e := epson{"WorkForce Pro WF-3720"}

    printers := []printer{
        c,
        &e,
    }
    c.name = "PROGRAF PRO-1000"
    e.name = "Home XP-4100"

    for _, p := range printers {
        p.print()
    }
}

Output:
Printer Name: PIXMA TR4520
Printer Name: Home XP-4100
```

The code shows how a slice of the interface type printer allows me to create a collection of different concrete printer types. Iterating over the collection and leveraging polymorphism since the call to p.print changes its behavior depending on the concrete value the code is operating against.

The example also shows how the choice of data semantics changes the behavior of the program. When storing the data using value semantics, the change to the original value is not seen. This is because a copy is stored inside the interface. When pointer semantics are used, any changes to the original value are seen.

4.13 Embedding

This first example does not show embedding, just the declaration of two struct types working together as a field from one type to the other.

Listing 4.34

```
type user struct {
    name  string
    email string
}

type admin struct {
    person user        // NOT Embedding
    level  string
}
```

This is embedding.

Listing 4.35

```
type user struct {
    name  string
    email string
}

type admin struct {
    user               // Value Semantic Embedding
    level  string
}
```

The person field is removed and just the type name is left. I can also embed a type using pointer semantics.

Listing 4.36

```
type user struct {
    name  string
    email string
}

type admin struct {
    *user              // Pointer Semantic Embedding
    level  string
}
```

In this case, a pointer of the type is embedded. In either case, accessing the embedded value is done through the use of the type's name.

The best way to think about embedding is to view the user type as an inner type and admin as an outer type. It's this inner/outer type relationship that is magical because with embedding, everything related to the inner type (both fields and methods) can be promoted up to the outer type.

Listing 4.37

```go
type user struct {
    name    string
    email   string
}

func (u *user) notify() {
    fmt.Printf("Sending user email To %s<%s>\n",
        u.name,
        u.email)
}

type admin struct {
    *user                   // Pointer Semantic Embedding
    level   string
}

func main() {
    ad := admin{
        user: &user{
            name:  "john smith",
            email: "john@yahoo.com",
        },
        level: "super",
    }

    ad.user.notify()
    ad.notify() // Outer type promotion
}

Output:
Sending user email To john smith<john@yahoo.com>
Sending user email To john smith<john@yahoo.com>
```

Once I add a method named notify for the user type and then a small main function, I can see the output is the same whether I call the notify method through the inner pointer value directly or through the outer type value. The notify method declared for the user type is accessible directly by the admin type value.

Though this looks like inheritance, I must be careful. This is not about reusing state, but about promoting behavior.

Listing 4.38

```go
type notifier interface {
    notify()
}

func sendNotification(n notifier) {
    n.notify()
}
```

Now I add an interface and a polymorphic function that accepts any concrete value that implements the full method set of behavior defined by the notifier interface. Which is just a method named notify.

Because of embedding and promotion, values of type admin now implement the notifier interface.

Listing 4.39

```
func main() {
    ad := admin{
        user: &user{
            name:  "john smith",
            email: "john@yahoo.com",
        },
        level: "super",
    }

    sendNotification(&ad)
}

Output:
Sending user email To john smith<john@yahoo.com>
```

I can send the address of the admin value into the polymorphic function since embedding promotes the notify behavior up to the admin type.

Listing 4.40

```
type admin struct {
    *user  // Pointer Semantic Embedding
    level  string
}

func (a *admin) notify() {
    fmt.Printf("Sending admin Email To %s<%s>\n",
        a.name,
        a.email)
}
```

When the outer type implements a method already implemented by the inner type, the promotion doesn't take place.

Listing 4.41

```
func main() {
    ad := admin{
        user: &user{
            name:  "john smith",
            email: "john@yahoo.com",
        },
        level: "super",
    }

    sendNotification(&ad)
}

Output:
Sending admin email To john smith<john@yahoo.com>
```

I can see the outer type's method is now being executed.

4.14 Exporting

Exporting provides the ability to declare if an identifier is accessible to code outside of the package it's declared in. A package is the basic unit of compiled code in Go. It represents a physical compiled unit of code, usually as a compiled library on the host operating system. Exporting determines access to identifiers across package boundaries.

Listing 4.42

```
package counters

type AlertCounter int
```

In this case, since a capital letter is being used to name the type AlterCounter, the type is exported and can be referenced directly by code outside of the counters package.

Listing 4.43

```
package counters

type alertCounter int
```

Now that I changed the type's name to start with a lowercase letter, the type is unexported. This means only code inside the counters package can reference this type directly.

Listing 4.44

```
package counters

type alertCounter int

func New(value int) alertCounter {
    return alertCounter(value)
}
```

Even though the code above is legal syntax and will compile, there is no value in it. Returning a value of an unexported type is confusing since the caller (who will probably exist in a different package) can't reference the type name directly.

Listing 4.45

```
package main

import (
    "fmt"

    "github.com/ardanlabs/.../exporting/example3/counters"
)

func main() {
    counter := counters.New(10)
    fmt.Printf("Counter: %d\n", counter)
}
```

In this case, the main function in package main calls the counters.New function successfully and the compiler can declare and construct a variable of the unexported type. This doesn't mean I should do this nor does it mean I'm getting any real protections for this. This should be avoided, and if New will return a value, it should be of an exported type.

Listing 4.46

```
package users

type User struct {
    Name string
    ID   int

    password string
}
```

When it comes to fields in a struct, the first letter declares if the field is accessible to code outside of the package it's declared in. In this case, Name and ID are accessible, but password is not. It's an idiom to separate exported and unexported fields in this manner if this is reasonable or practical to do. Normally all fields would be one or the other.

Listing 4.47

```
package users

type user struct {
    Name string
    ID   int
}

type Manager struct {
    Title string

    user
}
```

In this scenario, even though the user type is unexported, it has two exported fields. This means that when the user type is embedded in the exported Manager type, the user fields promote and are accessible. It's common to have types that are unexported with exported fields because the reflection package can only operate on exported fields. Marshallers won't work otherwise.

The example creates a bad situation where code outside of package users can construct a Manager, but since the embedded type user is unexported, the fields for those type can be initialized. This creates partial construction problems that will lead to bugs. I need to be consistent with exporting and unexporting.

Chapter 5: Software Design

In this chapter, I will learn about the mechanics and semantics behind error handling and an important design pattern in Go called composition. Along the way, I will learn how to group data of different types and learn about precision based semantics.

5.1 Grouping Different Types of Data

It's important to remember that in Go the concepts of sub-typing or sub-classing really don't exist and these design patterns should be avoided.

The following is an anti-pattern I shouldn't follow or implement.

Listing 5.1

```
type Animal struct {
    Name     string
    IsMammal bool
}
```

The Animal type is being declared as a base type that tries to define data that is common to all animals. I also attempt to provide some common behavior to an animal as well.

Listing 5.2

```
func (a *Animal) Speak() {
    fmt.Println("UGH!",
        "My name is", a.Name, ", it is", a.IsMammal, "I am a mammal")
}
```

Most animals have the ability to speak in one way or the other. However, trying to apply this common behavior to just an animal doesn't make any sense. At this point, I have no idea what sound this animal makes, so I wrote UGH.

Listing 5.3

```
type Dog struct {
    Animal
    PackFactor int
}
```

Now the real problems begin. I'm attempting to use embedding to make a Dog everything an Animal is plus more. On the surface this will seem to work, but there will be problems. With that being said, a Dog does have a specific way they speak.

Listing 5.4

```
func (d *Dog) Speak() {
    fmt.Println("Woof!",
        "My name is", d.Name,
        ", it is", d.IsMammal,
        "I am a mammal with a pack factor of", d.PackFactor)
}
```

In the implementation of the Speak method, I can change out UGH for Woof. This is specific to how a dog speaks.

Listing 5.5

```
type Cat struct {
    Animal
    ClimbFactor int
}
```

If I'm going to have a Dog that represents an Animal, then I have to have a Cat. Using embedding, a Cat is everything an Animal is plus more.

Listing 5.6

```
func (c *Cat) Speak() {
    fmt.Println("Meow!",
        "My name is", c.Name,
        ", it is", c.IsMammal,
        "I am a mammal with a climb factor of", c.ClimbFactor)
}
```

In the implementation of the Speak method, I can change out UGH for Meow. This is specific to how a cat speaks.

Everything seems fine and it looks like embedding is providing the same functionality as inheritance does in other languages. Then I try to go ahead and group dogs and cats by the fact they have a common DNA of being an Animal.

Listing 5.7

```
animals := []Animal{
    Dog{
        Animal: Animal{
            Name:      "Fido",
            IsMammal: true,
        },
        PackFactor: 5,
},
    Cat{
        Animal: Animal{
            Name:      "Milo",
            IsMammal: true,
        },
        ClimbFactor: 4,
    },
}

for _, animal := range animals {
    animal.Speak()
}
```

When I try to do this, the compiler complains that a Dog and Cat are not an Animal and this is true. Embedding isn't the same as inheritance and this is the pattern I need to stay away from. A Dog is a Dog, a Cat a Cat, and an Animal an Animal. I can't pass Dog's and Cat's around as if they are Animals because they are not.

This kind of mechanic is also not very flexible. It requires configuration by the developer and unless I have access to the code, I can't make configuration changes over time.

If this is not how we can construct a collection of Dog's and Cat's, how can we do this in Go? It's not about grouping through common DNA, it's about grouping through common behavior. Behavior is the key.

Listing 5.8

```
type Speaker interface {
    Speak()
}
```

If I use an interface, then I can define the common method set of behavior that I want to group different types of data against.

Listing 5.9

```
speakers := []Speaker{
    &Dog{
        Animal: Animal{
            Name:     "Fido",
            IsMammal: true,
        },
        PackFactor: 5,
},
    &Cat{
        Animal: Animal{
            Name:     "Milo",
            IsMammal: true,
        },
        ClimbFactor: 4,
    },
}

for _, speaker := range speakers {
    speaker.Speak()
}
```

In the new code, I can now group Dogs and Cats together based on their common set of behavior, which is the fact that Dogs and Cats can speak.

In fact, the Animal type is really type pollution because declaring a type just to share a set of common states is a smell and should be avoided.

Listing 5.10

```
type Dog struct {
    Name       string
    IsMammal   bool
    PackFactor int
}

type Cat struct {
    Name        string
    IsMammal    bool
    ClimbFactor int
}
```

In this particular case, I would rather see the Animal type removed and the fields copied and pasted into the Dog and Cat types. Later I will have notes about better patterns that eliminate these scenarios from happening.

Here are the code smells from the original code:

- The Animal type provides an abstraction layer of reusable state.
- The program never needs to create or solely use a value of Animal type.
- The implementation of the Speak method for the Animal type is generalized.
- The Speak method for the Animal type is never going to be called.

Guidelines around declaring types:

- Declare types that represent something new or unique.
- Don't create aliases just for readability.
- Validate that a value of any type is created or used on its own.
- Embed types not because I need the state, but because we need the behavior.
- If I am not thinking about behavior, I'm locking myself into the design that I can't grow in the future without cascading code changes.
- Question types that are aliases or abstractions for an existing type.
- Question types whose sole purpose is to share a common set of states.

5.2 Don't Design With Interfaces

Unfortunately, too many developers attempt to solve problems in the abstract first. They focus on interfaces right away and this leads to interface pollution. As a developer, I exist in one of two modes: a programmer and then an engineer.

When I am programming, I am focused on getting a piece of code to work. Trying to solve the problem and break down walls. Prove that my initial ideas work. That is all I care about. This programming should be done in the concrete and is never production ready.

Once I have a prototype of code that solves the problem, I need to switch to engineering mode. I need to focus on how to write the code at a micro-level for data semantics and readability, then at a macro-level for mental models and maintainability. I also need to focus on errors and failure states.

This work is done in a cycle of refactoring. Refactoring for readability, efficiency, abstraction, and for testability. Abstracting is only one of a few refactors that need to be performed. This works best when I start with a piece of concrete code and then DISCOVER the interfaces that are needed. Don't apply abstractions unless they are absolutely necessary.

Every problem I solve with code is a data problem requiring me to write data transformations. If I don't understand the data, I don't understand the problem. If I don't understand the problem, I can't write any code. Starting with a concrete solution that is based on the concrete data structures is critical. As Rob Pike said,

"Data dominates. If you've chosen the right data structures and organized things well, the algorithms will almost always be self-evident". - Rob Pike

When is abstraction necessary? When I see a place in the code where the data could change and I want to minimize the cascading code effects that would result. I might use abstraction to help make code testable, but I should try to avoid this if possible. The best testable functions are functions that take raw data in and send raw data out. It shouldn't matter where the data is coming from or going.

In the end, start with a concrete solution to every problem. Even if the bulk of that is just programming. Then discover the interfaces that are absolutely required for the code today.

"Don't design with interfaces, discover them". - Rob Pike

5.3 Composition

The best way to take advantage of embedding is through the compositional design pattern. The idea is to compose larger types from smaller types and focus on the composition of behavior.

Listing 5.11

```
type Xenia struct {
    Host     string
    Timeout time.Duration
}

func (*Xenia) Pull(d *Data) error {
    switch rand.Intn(10) {
    case 1, 9:
        return io.EOF
    case 5:
        return errors.New("Error reading data from Xenia")
    default:
        d.Line = "Data"
        fmt.Println("In:", d.Line)
        return nil
    }
}
```

The Xenia type represents a system that I need to pull data from. The implementation is not important. What is important is that the method Pull can succeed, fail, or not have any data to pull.

Listing 5.12

```
type Pillar struct {
    Host     string
    Timeout time.Duration
}

func (*Pillar) Store(d *Data) error {
    fmt.Println("Out:", d.Line)
    return nil
}
```

The Pillar type represents a system that I need to store data into. What is important again is that the method Store can succeed or fail.

These two types represent a primitive layer of code that provides the base behavior required to solve the business problem of pulling data out of Xenia and storing that data into Pillar.

Listing 5.13

```
func Pull(x *Xenia, data []Data) (int, error) {
    for i := range data {
        if err := x.Pull(&data[i]); err != nil {
            return i, err
        }
    }

    return len(data), nil
}

func Store(p *Pillar, data []Data) (int, error) {
    for i := range data {
        if err := p.Store(&data[i]); err != nil {
            return i, err
        }
    }

    return len(data), nil
}
```

The next layer of code is represented by these two functions, Pull and Store. They build on the primitive layer of code by accepting a collection of data values to pull or store in the respective systems. These functions focus on the concrete types of Xenia and Pillar since those are the systems the program needs to work with at this time.

Listing 5.14

```
func Copy(sys *System, batch int) error {
    data := make([]Data, batch)

    for {
        i, err := Pull(&sys.Xenia, data)
        if i > 0 {
            if _, err := Store(&sys.Pillar, data[:i]); err != nil {
                return err
            }
        }

        if err != nil {
            return err
        }
    }
}
```

The Copy function builds on top of the Pull and Store functions to move all the data that is pending for each run. If I notice the first parameter to Copy, it's a type called System.

Listing 5.15

```
type System struct {
    Xenia
    Pillar
}
```

The initial idea of the System type is to compose a system that knows how to Pull and Store. In this case, composing the ability to Pull and Store from Xenia and Pillar.

Listing 5.16

```
func main() {
    sys := System{
        Xenia: Xenia{
            Host:    "localhost:8000",
            Timeout: time.Second,
        },
        Pillar: Pillar{
            Host:    "localhost:9000",
            Timeout: time.Second,
        },
    }

    if err := Copy(&sys, 3); err != io.EOF {
        fmt.Println(err)
    }
}
```

Finally, the main function can be written to construct a Xenia and Pillar within the composition of a System. Then the System can be passed to the Copy function and data can begin to flow between the two systems.

With all this code, I now have my first draft of a concrete solution to a concrete problem.

5.4 Decoupling With Interfaces

The next step is to understand what could change in the program. In this case, what can change is the systems themselves. Today it's Xenia and Pillar, tomorrow it could be Alice and Bob. With this knowledge, I want to decouple the existing concrete solution from this change. To do that, I want to change the concrete functions to be polymorphic functions.

Listing 5.17

```go
func Pull(p Puller, data []Data) (int, error) {
    for i := range data {
        if err := p.Pull(&data[i]); err != nil {
            return i, err
        }
    }

    return len(data), nil
}

func Store(s Storer, data []Data) (int, error) {
    for i := range data {
        if err := s.Store(&data[i]); err != nil {
            return i, err
        }
    }

    return len(data), nil
}
```

Currently, the Pull function accepts a Xenia value and the Store function accepts a Pillar value. In the end, it wasn't Xenia and Pillar that was important, what's important is a concrete value that knows how to Pull and Store. I can change these concrete functions to be polymorphic by asking for data based on what it can do instead of what it is.

Listing 5.18

```go
type Puller interface {
    Pull(d *Data) error
}

type Storer interface {
    Store(d *Data) error
}
```

These two interfaces describe what concrete data must do and it's these types that are replaced in the declaration of the Pull and Store functions. Now these functions are polymorphic. When Alice and Bob are declared and implemented as a Puller and a Storer, they can be passed into the functions.

I am not done yet. The Copy function needs to be polymorphic as well.

Listing 5.19

```
func Copy(ps PullStorer, batch int) error {
    data := make([]Data, batch)

    for {
        i, err := Pull(ps, data)
        if i > 0 {
            if _, err := Store(ps, data[:i]); err != nil {
                return err
            }
        }

        if err != nil {
            return err
        }
    }
}
```

The Copy function is no longer asking for a System value, but any concrete value that knows how to both Pull and Store.

Listing 5.20

```
type PullStorer interface {
    Puller
    Storer
}
```

The PullStorer interface is declared through the use of composition. It's composed of the Puller and Storer interfaces. Work towards composing larger interfaces from smaller ones.

Notice how the PullStorer variable is now being passed into the Pull and Store functions. How is this possible when the type information is different?

Listing 5.21

```
// func Pull(p Puller, data []Data) (int, error) {
i, err := Pull(ps, data)

// func Store(s Storer, data []Data) (int, error) {
if _, err := Store(ps, data[:i]); err != nil {
```

I always need to remember, I am never passing an interface value around my program since they don't exist and are valueless. I can only pass concrete data. So the concrete data stored inside of the interface ps variable is what's being passed to Pull and Store. Isn't it true, the concrete value stored inside of ps must know how to Pull and Store?

Figure 5.1

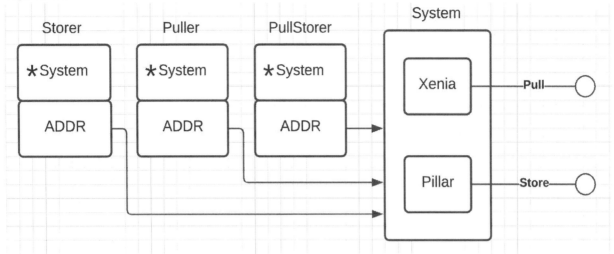

Since a System is composed from a Xenia and Pillar, System implements the PullStorer interface. With these changes, I can now create new concrete types that implement the PullStorer interface.

Listing 5.22

```
type System1 struct {
    Xenia
    Pillar
}

type System2 struct {
    Alice
    Bob
}

type System3 struct {
    Xenia
    Bob
}

type System4 struct {
    Alice
    Pillar
}
```

When I think about this more, declaring different System types for all the possible combinations is not realistic. This will work, but the maintenance nightmare requires a better solution.

5.5 Interface Composition

What if I decided to compose my concrete system type from two interface types?

Listing 5.23

```
type System struct {
    Puller
    Storer
}
```

This is an interesting solution. This would allow the application to inject the concrete Puller or Storer into the system at application startup.

Listing 5.24

```
func main() {
    sys := System{
        Puller: &Xenia{
            Host:    "localhost:8000",
            Timeout: time.Second,
        },
        Storer: &Pillar{
            Host:    "localhost:9000",
            Timeout: time.Second,
        },
    }

    if err := Copy(&sys, 3); err != io.EOF {
        fmt.Println(err)
    }
}
```

This one system type implements the PullStorer interface for all possible combinations of concrete types.

Figure 5.2

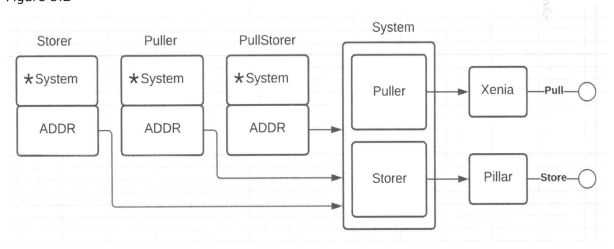

With this change, the application is fully decoupled from changes to a new system that may come online over time.

5.6 Precision Review

The next question to ask is, are the polymorphic functions as precise as they otherwise could be? This is a part of the engineering process that can't be skipped. The answer is no, two changes can be made.

Listing 5.25

```
func Copy(sys *System, batch int) error {
```

The Copy function doesn't need to be polymorphic anymore since there will only be a single System type. The PullStorer interface type can be removed from the program. Remember, I moved the polymorphism inside the type when I used composition with the interface types.

Listing 5.26

```
func Copy(p Puller, s Storer, batch int) error {
```

This is another change that can be made to the Copy function. This change makes the function more precise and polymorphic again. Now the function is asking for exactly what it needs based on what the concrete data can do.

Figure 5.3

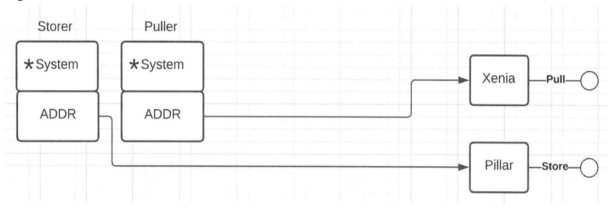

With that change the System struct type can be removed from the program as well.

Listing 5.25

```
func main() {
    x := Xenia{
        Host:    "localhost:8000",
        Timeout: time.Second,
    }

    p := Pillar{
        Host:    "localhost:9000",
        Timeout: time.Second,
    }

    if err := Copy(&x, &p, 3); err != io.EOF {
        fmt.Println(err)
    }
}
```

By removing the PullStorer and System types, the program simplifies. The main function can focus on constructing the concrete Puller and Storer values necessary for that moving data. The type system and APIs are more precise.

This idea of precision comes from Edsger W. Dijkstra

"The purpose of abstraction is not to be vague, but to create a new semantic level in which one can be absolutely precise". - Edsger W. Dijkstra

5.7 Implicit Interface Conversions

As I saw in the last example, An interface value of one type can be passed for a different interface type if the concrete value stored inside the interface implements both behaviors. This could be considered an implicit interface conversion, but it's better to think about how concrete data is being moved through interfaces in a decoupled state.

Listing 5.26

```
type Mover interface {
    Move()
}

type Locker interface {
    Lock()
    Unlock()
}

type MoveLocker interface {
    Mover
    Locker
}
```

Given these three interfaces, where MoveLocker is the composition of Mover and Locker.

Listing 5.27

```
type bike struct{}

func (bike) Move() {
    fmt.Println("Moving the bike")
}

func (bike) Lock() {
    fmt.Println("Locking the bike")
}

func (bike) Unlock() {
    fmt.Println("Unlocking the bike")
}
```

And given this concrete type bike that implements all three interfaces. What can I do?

Listing 5.28

```
var ml MoveLocker
var m Mover
```

I can construct a value of type MoveLocker and Mover to its zero value state. These are interface values that are truly valueless.

Listing 5.29

```
ml = bike{}
```

Then I can construct a value of type bike to its zero value state and assign a copy to the MoveLocker variable ml. This is possible because a bike implements all three behaviors, and the compiler can see that the implementation exists.

Listing 5.30

```
m = ml
```

I can then assign the MoveLocker variable ml to the Mover variable m. This is possible because I'm not assigning the interface value ml but the concrete value stored inside of ml which is a bike value. The compiler knows that any concrete value stored inside of ml must also implement the Mover interface.

This assignment however is not valid.

Listing 5.31

```
ml = m

cannot use m (type Mover) as type MoveLocker in assignment:
    Mover does not implement MoveLocker (missing Lock method)
```

I can't assign the Mover variable m back to the MoverLocker variable ml because the compiler can only guarantee that the concrete value stored inside of m knows how to Move. It doesn't know at compile time if the concrete value also knows how to Lock and Unlock.

5.8 Type assertions

With all that being said, there is a way at runtime to test if the assignment is legal and then make it happen. That is by using a type assertion.

Listing 5.32

```
b := m.(bike)
ml = b
```

A type assertion allows me at runtime to ask a question, is there a value of the given type stored inside the interface. I see that with the m.(bike) syntax. In this case, I am asking if there is a bike value stored inside of m at the moment the code is executed. If there is, then the variable b is given a copy of the bike value stored. Then the copy can be copied inside of the ml interface variable.

If there isn't a bike value stored inside of the interface value, then the program panics. I want this if there absolutely should have been a bike value stored. What if there is a chance there isn't and that is valid? Then I need the second form of the type assertion.

Listing 5.33

```
b, ok := m.(bike)
```

In this form, if ok is true, there is a bike value stored inside of the interface. If ok is false, then there isn't and the program does not panic. The variable b however is still of type bike, but it is set to its zero value state.

Listing 5.34

```
func main() {
    rand.Seed(time.Now().UnixNano())

    mvs := []fmt.Stringer{
        Car{},
        Cloud{},
    }

    for i := 0; i < 10; i++ {
        rn := rand.Intn(2)

        if v, is := mvs[rn].(Cloud); is {
            fmt.Println("Got Lucky:", v)
            continue
        }

        fmt.Println("Got Unlucky")
    }
}
```

Assuming the program does declare two types named Car and Cloud that each implement the fmt.Stringer interface, I can construct a collection that allows me to store a value of both Car and Cloud. Then 10 times, I randomly choose a number from 0 to 1, and perform a type assertion to see if the value at that random index contains a Cloud value. Since it's possible it's not of type Cloud, the second form of the type assertion is critical here.

5.9 Interface Pollution

I can spot interface pollution from a mile away. It mostly comes from the fact that people are designing software with interfaces instead of discovering them. I should design a concrete solution to the problem first. Then I can discover where the program needs to be polymorphic, if at all.

These are things I've heard from other developers.

"I'm using interfaces because we have to use interfaces".

No. We don't have to use interfaces. We use interfaces when it's practical and reasonable to do so. There is a cost of using interfaces: a level of indirection and allocation when we store concrete values inside of them. Unless the cost of the allocation is worth what I'm gaining by decoupling, I shouldn't be using interfaces.

"I need to be able to test my code so I need to use interfaces".

No. I must design my API for the user first, not my test. If the API is not testable, I should question if it's usable. There are different layers of API's as well. The lower level unexported API's can and should focus on testability. The higher level exported API's need to focus on usability.

Functions that accept raw data in and return raw data out are the most testable. Separate the data transformation from where the data comes from and where it is going. This is a refactoring exercise I need to perform during the engineering coding cycle.

Below is an example that creates interface pollution by improperly using an interface when one is not needed.

Listing 5.35

```
type Server interface {
    Start() error
    Stop() error
    Wait() error
}
```

The Server interface defines a contract for TCP servers. The problem here is I don't need a contract, I need an implementation. There will only be one implementation as well, especially since I am the one implementing it. I do not need someone else to implement this for me.

Plus, this interface is based on a noun and not a verb. Concrete types are nouns since they represent the concrete problem. Interfaces describe the behavior and Server is not behavior.

Here are some ways to identify interface pollution:

- A package declares an interface that matches the entire API of its own concrete type.
- The interfaces are exported but the concrete types implementing the interface are unexported.

- The factory function for the concrete type returns the interface value with the unexported concrete type value inside.
- The interface can be removed and nothing changes for the user of the API.
- The interface is not decoupling the API from change.

Guidelines around interface pollution:

Use an interface:
- When users of the API need to provide an implementation detail.
- When APIs have multiple implementations that need to be maintained.
- When parts of the APIs that can change have been identified and require decoupling.

Question an interface:
- When its only purpose is for writing testable API's (write usable APIs first).
- When it's not providing support for the API to decouple from change.
- When it's not clear how the interface makes the code better.

5.10 Interface Ownership

One thing that is different about Go from other languages is the idea of convention over configuration. This really shows itself with how Go handles interface compliance. Because the compiler can perform static code analysis to determine if a concrete value implements an interface, the developer declaring the concrete type doesn't need to provide interfaces as well.

Listing 5.36

```
package pubsub

type PubSub struct {
    host string
}

func New(host string) *PubSub {
    return &PubSub{
        host: host,
    }
}

func (ps *PubSub) Publish(key string, v interface{}) error {
    // PRETEND THERE IS A SPECIFIC IMPLEMENTATION.
    return nil
}

func (ps *PubSub) Subscribe(key string) error {
    // PRETEND THERE IS A SPECIFIC IMPLEMENTATION.
    return nil
}
```

I've just implemented a new API that provides a concrete implementation for publish and subscribe. There are no interfaces being provided because this API does not need one. This is a single concrete implementation.

What if the application developer wanting to use this new API needs an interface because they have the need to mock this implementation during tests? In Go, that developer can declare the interface and the compiler can identify the compliance.

Listing 5.37

```
package main

type publisher interface {
    Publish(key string, v interface{}) error
    Subscribe(key string) error
}

type mock struct{}

func (m *mock) Publish(key string, v interface{}) error {
    // ADD MY MOCK FOR THE PUBLISH CALL.
    return nil
}

func (m *mock) Subscribe(key string) error {
    // ADD MY MOCK FOR THE SUBSCRIBE CALL.
    return nil
}
```

This code in the main package is declaring an interface. This interface represents the API that the application is using from the pubsub package. The developer has implemented their own pubsub implementation for testing. The key here is that this application developer doesn't use any concrete implementation directly, but decouples themselves through their own interface.

Listing 5.38

```
func main() {
    pubs := []publisher{
        pubsub.New("localhost"),
        &mock{},
    }

    for _, p := range pubs {
        p.Publish("key", "value")
        p.Subscribe("key")
    }
}
```

To provide an example, the main function constructs a collection that is initialized with the pubsub implementation and the mock implementation. The publisher interface allows this. Then a for range loop is implemented to show how the application code is abstracted from any concrete implementation.

5.11 Error Handling

Integrity matters and it's a big part of the engineering process. At the heart of integrity is error handling. When it comes to Go, error handling is not an exception to be handled later or somewhere else in the code. It's a part of the main path and needs to be a main focus.

Developers have the responsibility to return enough context about any error so a user can make an informed decision about how to proceed. Handling an error is about three things: logging the error, not propagating the error any further, and determining if the Goroutine/program needs to be terminated.

In Go, errors are just values so they can be anything I need them to be. They can maintain any state or behavior.

Listing 5.39

```
// http://golang.org/pkg/builtin/#error
type error interface {
    Error() string
}
```

This is the error interface and it's an interface that is built into the language. This is why it appears to be an unexported identifier. Any concrete value that implements this interface can be used as an error value.

One important aspect of Go is that error handling is done in a decoupled state through this interface. A key reason for this is because error handling is an aspect of my application that is more susceptible to change and improvement. This interface is the type Go applications must use as the return type for error handling.

Listing 5.40

```
// http://golang.org/src/pkg/errors/errors.go
type errorString struct {
    s string
}

// http://golang.org/src/pkg/errors/errors.go
func (e *errorString) Error() string {
    return e.s
}
```

This is the most commonly used error value in Go programs. It's declared in the errors package from the standard library. Notice how the type is unexported and it has one unexported field which is a string. I can also see how pointer semantics are used to implement the error interface. This means only addresses to values of this type can be shared and stored inside the interface. The method just returned the error string.

It's important to remember, the implementation of the Error method serves the purpose of implementing the interface and for logging. If any user needs to parse the string returned from this method, I have failed to provide the user the right amount of context to make an informed decision.

Listing 5.41

```
// http://golang.org/src/pkg/errors/errors.go
func New(text string) error {
    return &errorString{text}
}
```

The New function is how an error using the concrete type errorString is constructed. Notice how the function returns the error using the error interface. Also notice how pointer semantics are being used.

Listing 5.42

```
func main() {
    if err := webCall(); err != nil {
        fmt.Println(err)
        return
    }
    fmt.Println("Life is good")
}

func webCall() error {
    return New("bad request")
}
```

Context is everything with errors. Each error must provide enough context to allow the caller to make an informed decision about the state of the goroutine/application. In this example, the webCall function returns an error with the message Bad Request. In the main function, a call is made to webCall and then a check is made to see if an error has occurred with the call.

Listing 5.43

```
if err := webCall(); err != nil {
    fmt.Println(err)
    return
}
```

The key to the check is err != nil. What this condition is asking is, is there a concrete value stored inside the err interface value. When the interface value is storing a concrete value, there is an error. In this case, the context is literally just the fact that a concrete value exists, it's not important what the concrete value is.

What if it's important to know what error value exists inside the err interface variable? Then error variables are a good option.

Listing 5.44

```
var (
    ErrBadRequest = errors.New("Bad Request")
    ErrPageMoved = errors.New("Page Moved")
)
```

Error variables provide a mechanic to identify what specific error is being returned. They have an idiom of starting with the prefix Err and are based on the concrete type errorString from the errors package.

Listing 5.45

```
func webCall(b bool) error {
    if b {
        return ErrBadRequest
    }
    return ErrPageMoved
}
```

In this new version of webCall, the function returns one or the other error variable. This allows the caller to determine which error took place.

Listing 5.46

```
func main() {
    if err := webCall(true); err != nil {
        switch err {
        case ErrBadRequest:
            fmt.Println("Bad Request Occurred")
            return

        case ErrPageMoved:
            fmt.Println("The Page moved")
            return

        default:
            fmt.Println(err)
            return
        }
    }

    fmt.Println("Life is good")
}
```

In the application after the call to webCall is made, a check can be performed to see if there is a concrete value stored inside the err interface variable. If there is, then a switch statement is used to determine which error it was by comparing err to the different error variables.

In this case, the context of the error is based on which error variable was returned. What if an error variable is not enough context? What if some special state needs to be checked, like with networking errors? In these cases, a custom concrete error type is the answer.

Listing 5.47

```
type UnmarshalTypeError struct {
    Value string
    Type  reflect.Type
}

func (e *UnmarshalTypeError) Error() string {
    return "json: cannot unmarshal " + e.Value +
            " into Go value of type " + e.Type.String()
}
```

This is a custom concrete error type implemented in the json package. Notice the name has a suffix of Error in the naming of the type. Also notice the use of pointer semantics for the implementation of the error interface. Once again the implementation is for logging and should display information about all the fields being captured.

Listing 5.48

```
type InvalidUnmarshalError struct {
    Type reflect.Type
}

func (e *InvalidUnmarshalError) Error() string {
    if e.Type == nil {
        return "json: Unmarshal(nil)"
    }
    if e.Type.Kind() != reflect.Ptr {
        return "json: Unmarshal(non-pointer " + e.Type.String() + ")"
    }
    return "json: Unmarshal(nil " + e.Type.String() + ")"
}
```

This is a second custom concrete error type found in the json package. The implementation of the Error method is a bit more complex, but once again just for logging and using pointer semantics.

Listing 5.49

```
func Unmarshal(data []byte, v interface{}) error {
    rv := reflect.ValueOf(v)
    if rv.Kind() != reflect.Ptr || rv.IsNil() {
        return &InvalidUnmarshalError{reflect.TypeOf(v)}
    }
    return &UnmarshalTypeError{"string", reflect.TypeOf(v)}
}
```

Here is a portion of the Unmarshal function. Notice how it constructs the concrete error values in the return, passing them back to the caller through the error interface. Pointer semantic construction is being used because pointer semantics were used in the declaration of the Error method.

The context of the error here is more about the type of error stored inside the error interface. There needs to be a way to determine that.

Listing 5.50

```
func main() {
    var u user
    err := Unmarshal([]byte(`{"name":"bill"}`), u)
    if err != nil {
        switch e := err.(type) {
        case *UnmarshalTypeError:
            fmt.Printf("UnmarshalTypeError: Value[%s] Type[%v]\n",
                e.Value, e.Type)
        case *InvalidUnmarshalError:
            fmt.Printf("InvalidUnmarshalError: Type[%v]\n", e.Type)
        default:
            fmt.Println(err)
        }
        return
    }
    fmt.Println("Name:", u.Name)
}
```

A generic type assertion within the scope of the switch statement is how I can write code to test what type of value is being stored inside the err interface value. Type is the context here and now I can test and take action with access to all the states of the error.

However, this poses one problem. I'm no longer decoupled from the concrete error value. This means if the concrete error value is changed, my code can break. The beautiful part of using an interface for error handling is being decoupled from breaking changes.

If the concrete error value has a method set, then I can use an interface for the type check. As an example, the net package has many concrete error types that implement different methods. One common method is called Temporary. This method allows the user to test if the networking error is critical or just something that can recover on its own.

Listing 5.51

```go
type temporary interface {
    Temporary() bool
}

func (c *client) BehaviorAsContext() {
    for {
        line, err := c.reader.ReadString('\n')
        if err != nil {
            switch e := err.(type) {
            case temporary:
                if !e.Temporary() {
                    log.Println("Temporary: Client leaving chat")
                    return
                }
            default:
                if err == io.EOF {
                    log.Println("EOF: Client leaving chat")
                    return
                }
                log.Println("read-routine", err)
            }
        }
        fmt.Println(line)
    }
}
```

In this code, the call to ReadString could fail with an error from the net package. In this case, an interface is declared that represents the common behavior a given concrete error value could implement. Then with a generic type assertion, I test if that behavior exists and I can call into it. The best part, I stay in a decoupled state with my error handling.

5.12 Always Use The Error Interface

One mistake Go developers can make is when they use the concrete error type and not the error interface for the return type for handling errors. If I were to do this, bad things could happen.

Listing 5.52

```
type customError struct{}

func (c *customError) Error() string {
    return "Find the bug."
}

func fail() ([]byte, *customError) {
    return nil, nil
}

func main() {
    var err error
    if _, err = fail(); err != nil {
        log.Fatal("Why did this fail?")
    }
    log.Println("No Error")
}

Output:
Why did this fail?
```

Why does this code think there is an error when the fail function returns nil for the error? It's because the fail function is using the concrete error type and not the error interface. In this case, there is a nil pointer of type customError stored inside the err variable. That is not the same as a nil interface value of type error.

5.13 Handling Errors

Handling errors is more of a macro level engineering conversation. In my world, error handling means the error stops with the function handling the error, the error is logged with full context, and the error is checked for its severity. Based on the severity and ability to recover, a decision to recover, move on, or shutdown is made.

One problem is that not all functions can handle an error. One reason could be because not all functions are allowed to log. What happens when an error is being passed back up the call stack and can't be handled by the function receiving it? An error needs to be wrapped in context so the function that eventually handles it, can properly do so.

There are two options for wrapping extra context around an error. I can use Dave Cheney's errors package or I can use standard library support that can be found in the errors and fmt packages. Whatever I decide, it's important to annotate errors for enough context to help identify and fix problems. Both at runtime and after.

Using Dave Cheney's package:

Listing 5.53

```
package main

import (    .
    "fmt"

    "github.com/pkg/errors"
)

type AppError struct {
    State int
}

func (c *AppError) Error() string {
    return fmt.Sprintf("App Error, State: %d", c.State)
}

func main() {
    if err := firstCall(10); err != nil {
        switch v := errors.Cause(err).(type) {
        case *AppError:
            fmt.Println("Custom App Error:", v.State)
        default:
            fmt.Println("Default Error")
        }

        fmt.Printf("%v\n", err)
    }
}

func firstCall(i int) error {
    if err := secondCall(i); err != nil {
        return errors.Wrapf(err, "secondCall(%d)", i)
    }
    return nil
}

func secondCall(i int) error {
    return &AppError{99}
}

Output:
Custom App Error: 99
secondCall(10): App Error, State: 99
```

What's nice about this package is the errors.Wrap and errors.Cause API's. They make the code a bit more readable.

Using the standard library:

Listing 5.54

```go
package main

import (
    "errors"
    "fmt"
)

type AppError struct {
    State int
}

func (c *AppError) Error() string {
    return fmt.Sprintf("App Error, State: %d", c.State)
}

func Cause(err error) error {
    root := err
    for {
        if err = errors.Unwrap(root); err == nil {
            return root
        }
        root = err
    }
}

func main() {
    if err := firstCall(10); err != nil {
        var ap *AppError
        if errors.As(err, &ap) {
            fmt.Println("As says it is an AppError")
        }

        switch v := Cause(err).(type) {
        case *AppError:
            fmt.Println("Custom App Error:", v.State)
        default:
            fmt.Println("Default Error")
        }

        fmt.Printf("%v\n", err)
    }
}

func firstCall(i int) error {
    if err := secondCall(i); err != nil {
        return fmt.Errorf("secondCall(%d) : %w", i, err)
    }
    return nil
}

func secondCall(i int) error {
    return &AppError{99}
}

Output:
As says it is an AppError
Custom App Error: 99
secondCall(10): App Error, State: 99
```

117

To use the standard library in a similar way, the Cause function needed to be written. In this example, I can see the use of the errors.As function.

Chapter 6: Concurrency

In this chapter, I will learn about the mechanics and semantics behind writing multithreaded code in Go. I will learn what concurrency is and how to apply it safely by understanding the concepts of synchronization and orchestration.

6.1 Scheduler Semantics

When a Go program starts up, the Go runtime asks the machine (virtual or physical) how many operating system threads can run in parallel. This is based on the number of cores that are available to the program. For each thread that can be run in parallel, the runtime creates an operating system thread (M) and attaches that to a data structure that represents a logical processor (P) inside the program. This P and M represent the compute power or execution context for running the Go program.

Also, an initial Goroutine (G) is created to manage the execution of instructions on a selected M/P. Just like an M manages the execution of instructions on the hardware, a G manages the execution of instructions on the M. This creates a new layer of abstraction above the operating system, but it moves execution control to the application level.

Figure 6.1

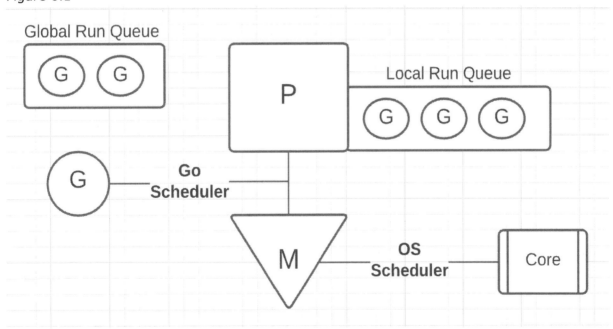

Since the Go scheduler sits on top of the operating system scheduler, it's important to have some semantic understanding of the operating system scheduler and the constraints it applies to the Go scheduler and applications.

The operating system scheduler has the job of creating the illusions that multiple pieces of work are being executed at the same time. Even when this is physically impossible. This requires some tradeoffs in the design of the scheduler. Before I go any further, it's important to define some words.

Work: A set of instructions to be executed for a running application. This is accomplished by threads and an application can have 1 to many threads.

Thread: A path of execution that is scheduled and performed. Threads are responsible for the execution of instructions on the hardware.

Thread States: A thread can be in one of three states: Running, Runnable, or Waiting. Running means the thread is executing its assigned instructions on the hardware by having a G placed on the M. Runnable means the thread wants time on the hardware to execute its assigned instructions and is sitting in a run queue. Waiting means the thread is waiting for something before it can resume its work. Waiting threads are not a concern of the scheduler.

Concurrency: This means undefined out of order execution. In other words, given a set of instructions that would be executed in the order provided, they are executed in a different undefined order, but all executed. The key is, the result of executing the full set of instructions in any undefined order produces the same result. I will say work can be done concurrently when the order the work is executed in doesn't matter, as long as all the work is completed.

Parallelism: This means doing a lot of things at once. For this to be an option, I need the ability to physically execute two or more operating system threads at the same time on the hardware.

CPU Bound Work: This is work that does not cause the thread to naturally move into a waiting state. Calculating fibonacci numbers would be considered CPU-Bound work.

I/O Bound Work: This is work that does cause the thread to naturally move into a waiting state. Fetching data from different URLs would be considered I/O-Bound work.

Synchronization: When two or more Goroutines will need to access the same memory location potentially at the same time, they need to be synchronized and take turns. If this synchronization doesn't take place, and at least one Goroutine is performing a write, I can end up with a data race. Data races are a cause of data corruption bugs that can be difficult to find.

Orchestration: When two or more Goroutines need to signal each other, with or without data, orchestration is the mechanic required. If orchestration does not take place, guarantees about concurrent work being performed and completed will be missed. This can cause all sorts of data corruption bugs.

There are lots of little details related to the scheduling semantics, so to learn more read the three posts in chapter 14 titled, Scheduling In Go.

6.2 Concurrency Basics

Starting with a basic concurrency problem that requires orchestration.

Listing 6.1

```
func init() {
    runtime.GOMAXPROCS(1)
}
```

The call to GOMAXPROCS is being used to run the Go program as a single threaded Go program. This program will be single threaded and have a single P/M to execute all Goroutines. The function is capitalized because it's also an environment variable. Though this function call will overwrite the variable.

Listing 6.2

```
g := runtime.GOMAXPROCS(0)
```

This function is an important function when I set CPU quotas to a container configuration. When passing 0, the number of threads the Go program will be using is reported. I must make sure that number matches the number of operating system threads I have available in my containerized environment. If the numbers are not the same, the Go program won't run as well as it otherwise could. I might want to use the environment variable or this call to match things up.

Listing 6.3

```
func main() {
    var wg sync.WaitGroup
    wg.Add(2)

    go func() {
        lowercase()
        wg.Done()
    }()

    go func() {
        uppercase()
        wg.Done()
    }()

    fmt.Println("Waiting To Finish")
    wg.Wait()

    fmt.Println("\nTerminating Program")
}
```

This program has to solve an orchestration problem. The main Goroutine can't allow the main function to return until there is a guarantee the two Goroutines being created finish their work first. A WaitGroup is a perfect tool for orchestration problems that don't require data to be passed between Goroutines. The signaling here is performed through an API that allows a Goroutine to wait for other Goroutines to signal they're done.

In this code, a WaitGroup is constructed to its zero value state and then immediately the Add method is called to set the WaitGroup to 2, which will match the number of Goroutines to be created. When I know how many Goroutines upfront that will be created, I should call Add once with that number. When I don't know (like in a streaming service) then calling Add(1) is acceptable.

At the end of main is the call to Wait. Wait holds the main Goroutine from causing the function to return. When the main function returns, the Go program is shut down with extreme prejudice. This is why managing the orchestration with the proper guarantees is important. The Wait call will block until the WaitGroup is set back to 0.

In the middle of the program, I have the creation of the two Goroutines.

Listing 6.4

```
func main() {
    . . .

    go func() {
        lowercase()
        wg.Done()
    }()

    go func() {
        uppercase()
        wg.Done()
    }()

    . . .
}
```

Literal functions are declared and executed with the use of the keyword go. At this point, I am telling the Go scheduler to execute these functions concurrently. To execute them in an undefined order. Inside the implementation of each Goroutine is the call to Done. That call is what decrements the WaitGroup by 1. Once both calls to Done are made, the WaitGroup will change from 2 to 0, and then the main Goroutine will be allowed to be unblocked from the call to Wait, terminating the program.

Listing 6.5

```
func main() {
    var wg sync.WaitGroup
    wg.Add(2)

    go func() {
        lowercase()
        wg.Done()
    }()

    . . .
}
```

An important part of this orchestration pattern is keeping the Add and Done calls in the same line of sight. Try not to pass the WaitGroup as a function parameter where the calls get lost. This will help to reduce bugs.

Listing 6.6

```
Output:

Start Goroutines
Waiting To Finish
A B C D E F G H I J K L M N O P Q R S T U V W X Y Z A B C D E F G H I J K L
M N O P Q R S T U V W X Y Z A B C D E F G H I J K L M N O P Q R S T U V W X
Y Z a b c d e f g h i j k l m n o p q r s t u v w x y z a b c d e f g h i j
k l m n o p q r s t u v w x y z a b c d e f g h i j k l m n o p q r s t u v
w x y z
Terminating Program
```

When I build and run this program, I see how this program runs concurrently. The second Goroutine created was scheduled first. It got to finish its work and then the other Goroutine ran. Both ran to completion before the program terminated. The next time I run this program, there is no guarantee I see the same output. The only guarantee in this program is that the program won't terminate until the two Goroutines are done.

Even if I run this program 100 times and see the same output, there is no guarantee it will happen again. It may be highly probable, but not guaranteed. Especially not guaranteed across different versions, operating systems and architectures.

Listing 6.7

```
func main() {
    . . .

    fmt.Println("Waiting To Finish")
    // wg.Wait()                              <-- CHANGED

    fmt.Println("\nTerminating Program")
}
```

If I comment the call to Wait what will happen when I run this program? Once again, there is no guarantee at all anymore with what will happen, but there are different possibilities.

The program could behave as before since calls to Println are system calls that do allow the scheduler to make a context switch. The program could execute just one of the two Goroutines or possibly terminate immediately.

Listing 6.8

```
func main() {
    var wg sync.WaitGroup
    wg.Add(2)

    go func() {
        lowercase()
        // wg.Done()                           <-- CHANGED
    }()


    . . .
}
```

What happens if I forget to call Done in one of the Goroutines? In this case, the program would deadlock since the WaitGroup can't get back down to 0. The Wait call will block forever.

Listing 6.9

```
Output:

Start Goroutines
Waiting To Finish
A B C D E F G H I J K L M N O P Q R S T U V W X Y Z A B C D E F G H I J K L
M N O P Q R S T U V W X Y Z A B C D E F G H I J K L M N O P Q R S T U V W X
Y Z a b c d e f g h i j k l m n o p q r s t u v w x y z a b c d e f g h i j
k l m n o p q r s t u v w x y z a b c d e f g h i j k l m n o p q r s t u v
w x y z fatal error: all goroutines are asleep - deadlock!

goroutine 1 [semacquire]:
sync.runtime_Semacquire(0xc00001a0a8)
    /usr/local/go/src/runtime/sema.go:56 +0x45
sync.(*WaitGroup).Wait(0xc00001a0a0)
    /usr/local/go/src/sync/waitgroup.go:130 +0x65
main.main()
    /Users/bill/code/go/src/github.com/ardanlabs/gotraining/topics/go/
concurrency/goroutines/example1/example1.go:42 +0x145
exit status 2
```

I can see how the Go Runtime identifies the program is deadlocked on line 42 where the call to Wait is happening. I shouldn't get too excited about deadlock detection since every single Goroutine needs to be blocked with no way out. This shows why keeping the Add and Done call together is so important.

Listing 6.10

```go
func main() {
    var wg sync.WaitGroup
    wg.Add(1)                      <-- CHANGED, Number Too Small

    go func() {
        lowercase()
        wg.Done()
    }()

    go func() {
        uppercase()
        wg.Done()
    }()

    . . .
}
```

What happens if I don't give the WaitGroup the correct number of Goroutines to wait on? If the number is too large, I will have another deadlock. If the number is too small, there are no guarantees that the work is done before the program moves on. The output of the program is undefined.

6.3 Preemptive Scheduler

Even though the scheduler runs within the scope of the application, it's important to see how the schedule is preemptive. This means I can't predict when a context switch will take place and this will change every time I run the program.

Listing 6.11

```go
func main() {
    var wg sync.WaitGroup
    wg.Add(2)

    go func() {
        printHashes("A")
        wg.Done()
    }()

    go func() {
        printHashes("B")
        wg.Done()
    }()

    fmt.Println("Waiting To Finish")
    wg.Wait()

    fmt.Println("\nTerminating Program")
}
```

Using the same orchestration pattern as before, this program has each Goroutine doing a lot more work. Work that the scheduler won't give a Goroutine enough time to finish completely in one time slice.

125

Listing 6.12

```go
func printHashes(prefix string) {
    for i := 1; i <= 50000; i++ {
        num := strconv.Itoa(i)
        sum := sha1.Sum([]byte(num))
        fmt.Printf("%s: %05d: %x\n", prefix, i, sum)
    }
    fmt.Println("Completed", prefix)
}
```

This function is performing a lot of I/O bound work that has the potential of being context switched.

Listing 6.13

```
$ ./example2 | cut -c1 | grep '[AB]' | uniq
B
A
B
A
B
A
B
A
B
A  9 Context Switches

$ ./example2 | cut -c1 | grep '[AB]' | uniq
B
A
B
A  3 Context Switches
```

As I can see, every time I run the program, there are a different number of context switches. This is a great thing because a scheduler shouldn't be predictable. Concurrency needs to remain undefined and I must remember that when I use concurrency to solve my performance problems.

Listing 6.14

```go
func init() {
    runtime.GOMAXPROCS(2)
}
```

What happens if I go back to the original program but change GOMAXPROCS so the program runs as a two threaded Go program?

Listing 6.15

```
Output:

Start Goroutines
Waiting To Finish
A B C D E F G H I J K L M N O P Q R S T U V W X Y Z A B C D E F G H I J K L
M N a b c d e f g h i j k l m n o O P Q R S T U V W X Y Z A B C D E F G H I
J K L M N O P Q R S T U V W X Y Z p q r s t u v w x y z a b c d e f g h i j
k l m n o p q r s t u v w x y z a b c d e f g h i j k l m n o p q r s t u v
w x y z
Terminating Program
```

What I see is that the concurrency of the program is now more fine grained. The output to the letter is undefined and out of order.

6.4 Data Races

A data race is when two or more Goroutines are trying to access the same memory location at the same time where at least one Goroutine is performing a write. When this happens it is impossible to predict the result. These types of bugs are difficult to find because they cause issues that always appear random.

These ~8 minutes from Scott Meyers is great to listen to here:

CPU Caches and Why You Care 30:09-38:30
https://youtu.be/WDIkqP4JbkE?t=1809

6.5 Data Race Example

This is a great example of a data race and how they can be hidden for years and eventually show up at odd times and cause data corruption.

Listing 6.16

```
var counter int

func main() {
    const grs = 2

    var wg sync.WaitGroup
    wg.Add(grs)

    for g := 0; g < grs; g++ {
        go func() {
            for i := 0; i < 2; i++ {
                value := counter
                value++
                counter = value
            }
            wg.Done()
        }()
    }

    wg.Wait()
    fmt.Println("Counter:", counter)
}
```

This program creates two Goroutines that each access the same integer variable, incrementing the variable twice. The Goroutine performs a read, modify, and write operation against the shared state manually.

Listing 6.17

```
var counter int

func main() {
    . . .

    go func() {
        for i := 0; i < 2; i++ {
            value := counter
            value++
            counter = value
        }
        wg.Done()
    }()

    . . .
}
```

I can see the access to the shared state inside the for loop. When I build and run this program I get the right answer of 4 each and every time.

Listing 6.18

```
$ ./example1
Final Counter: 4

$ ./example1
Final Counter: 4

$ ./example1
Final Counter: 4
```

How is this working?

Listing 6.19

```
G1                                      Shared State: 0
G2
-------------------------------------------------------------------------
Read:   0
Modify: 1
Write:  1                               Shared State: 1
Context Switch

Read: 1

Modify: 2
                                        Shared State: 2

Write: 2
                                                                  Context
Switch
Read:   2
Modify: 3
Write:  3                               Shared State: 3
Terminate

Read: 3

Modify: 4
                                        Shared State: 4

Write: 4

Terminate
-------------------------------------------------------------------------
```

The read, modify and write operations are happening uninterrupted. Just because I am getting the right answer doesn't mean there isn't a problem. What happens if I add a log statement in the middle of the read, modify, and write operation?

Listing 6.20

```
var counter int

func main() {
    . . .

    go func() {
        for i := 0; i < 2; i++ {
            value := counter
            value++
            log.Println("logging")      <-- Add Logging Here
            counter = value
        }
        wg.Done()
    }()

    . . .
}
```

If I run this program I no longer get the same result of 4, now I get the answer of 2.

Listing 6.21

```
$ ./example1
Final Counter: 2

$ ./example1
Final Counter: 2

$ ./example1
Final Counter: 2
```

What is happening? I am running into a data race bug that did exist before, but wasn't happening. The call to log is now causing the scheduler to make a context switch between the two Goroutines at a bad time.

Listing 6.22

```
G1                                  Shared State: 0                                 G2
---------------------------------------------------------------------------------------
Read:    0
Modify:  1
Context Switch
                                                                              Read:
0

Modify: 1
                                                                            Context
Switch
Write:   1                          Shared State: 1
Read:    1
Modify:  2
Context Switch
                                    Shared State: 1                           Write:
1
                                                                              Read:
1

Modify: 2
                                                                            Context
Switch
Write:   2                          Shared State: 2
Terminate
                                    Shared State: 2                           Write:
2

Terminate
---------------------------------------------------------------------------------------
```

After the modify operation a context switch is taking place. The three operations are no longer uninterrupted and Goroutine 2 ends up with its local value being wrong by the time it completes the write operation. I am very lucky this is happening every time and I can see it. But normally a data race like this happens "randomly" and is impossible to know about until it's too late. Luckily Go has a race detector to help find data races.

6.6 Race Detection

There are several ways to engage the race detector. I can use it with the run, build and test command. If I use it with the build command, I have to remember to run the program. They say an instrumented binary can slow my program down by ~20%.

Listing 6.23

```
$ go build -race
$ ./example1
```

The -race flag is how to instrument the build with the race detector. I will probably use it more with "go test", but for this example I am instrumenting the binary and then running it.

Listing 6.24

```
2021/02/01 17:30:52 logging
2021/02/01 17:30:52 logging
2021/02/01 17:30:52 logging
==================
WARNING: DATA RACE
Write at 0x000001278d88 by goroutine 8:
  main.main.func1()
      /data_race/example1/example1.go:41 +0xa6

Previous read at 0x000001278d88 by goroutine 7:
  main.main.func1()
      /data_race/example1/example1.go:38 +0x4a

Goroutine 8 (running) created at:
  main.main()
      /data_race/example1/example1.go:36 +0xaf

Goroutine 7 (finished) created at:
  main.main()
      /data_race/example1/example1.go:36 +0xaf
==================
2021/02/01 17:30:52 logging
Final Counter: 2
Found 1 data race(s)
```

I can see a race was detected when running the program. This would happen with or without the log statement inserted. When a race is detected, the program panics and provides this trace. The trace shows where there was unsynchronized access to the same shared state where at least one access was a write.

In this trace, a Goroutine performed a write at address 0x000001278d88 on line 41, and there was an unsynchronized read at the same address by another Goroutine on line 38. Both Goroutines were created on line 36.

Listing 6.25

```
36 go func() {
37     for i := 0; i < 2; i++ {
38         value := counter
39         value++
40         log.Println("logging")
41         counter = value
42     }
43     wg.Done()
44 }()
```

I can clearly see the unsynchronized read and write. As a side note, the plus plus operation on line 39 would also be a data race if the code was accessing the counter variable. The plus plus operation is a read, modify, and write operation underneath and the operating system could easily context switch in the middle of that.

So how can I fix the code to make sure that I remove the data race? There are two tools I can use, atomic instructions and mutexes.

6.7 Atomics

Atomics provide synchronization at the hardware level. Because of this, it's limited to words and half-words of data. So they're great for counters or fast switching mechanics. The WaitGroup API's use atomics.

What changes do I need to make to apply atomics to the code?

Listing 6.26

```
var counter int32                              <-- CHANGED

func main() {
    const grs = 2

    var wg sync.WaitGroup
    wg.Add(grs)

    for g := 0; g < grs; g++ {
        go func() {
            for i := 0; i < 2; i++ {
                atomic.AddInt32(&counter, 1)      <-- CHANGED
            }
            wg.Done()
        }()
    }

    wg.Wait()
    fmt.Println("Counter:", counter)
}
```

I only need to do a couple things. First, change the counter variable to be a precision based integer. I can see that at the top of the code listing. The atomic functions only work with precision based integers. Second, remove the manually read, modify, and write code for one call to atomic.AddInt32. That one call handles it all.

All of the functions associated with the atomic package take the address to the shared state to be synchronized. Synchronization only happens at the address level. So different Goroutines calling the same function, but at a different address, won't be synchronized.

The API for atomics looks like this:

Listing 6.27

```
func AddInt32(addr *int32, delta int32) (new int32)
func AddInt64(addr *int64, delta int64) (new int64)
func AddUint32(addr *uint32, delta uint32) (new uint32)
func AddUint64(addr *uint64, delta uint64) (new uint64)
func AddUintptr(addr *uintptr, delta uintptr) (new uintptr)

func CompareAndSwapInt32(addr *int32, old, new int32) (swapped bool)
func CompareAndSwapInt64(addr *int64, old, new int64) (swapped bool)
func CompareAndSwapPointer(addr *unsafe.Pointer, old, new unsafe.Pointer)
(swapped bool)
func CompareAndSwapUint32(addr *uint32, old, new uint32) (swapped bool)
func CompareAndSwapUint64(addr *uint64, old, new uint64) (swapped bool)
func CompareAndSwapUintptr(addr *uintptr, old, new uintptr) (swapped bool)

func LoadInt32(addr *int32) (val int32)
func LoadInt64(addr *int64) (val int64)
func LoadPointer(addr *unsafe.Pointer) (val unsafe.Pointer)
func LoadUint32(addr *uint32) (val uint32)
func LoadUint64(addr *uint64) (val uint64)
func LoadUintptr(addr *uintptr) (val uintptr)

func StoreInt32(addr *int32, val int32)
func StoreInt64(addr *int64, val int64)
func StorePointer(addr *unsafe.Pointer, val unsafe.Pointer)
func StoreUint32(addr *uint32, val uint32)
func StoreUint64(addr *uint64, val uint64)
func StoreUintptr(addr *uintptr, val uintptr)

func SwapInt32(addr *int32, new int32) (old int32)
func SwapInt64(addr *int64, new int64) (old int64)
func SwapPointer(addr *unsafe.Pointer, new unsafe.Pointer) (old
unsafe.Pointer)
func SwapUint32(addr *uint32, new uint32) (old uint32)
func SwapUint64(addr *uint64, new uint64) (old uint64)
func SwapUintptr(addr *uintptr, new uintptr) (old uintptr)

type Value
    func (v *Value) Load() (x interface{})
    func (v *Value) Store(x interface{})
```

I can see that the first parameter is always the address to a precision based integer or pointer. There is also a type named Value that provides a synchronous value with a small API.

6.8 Mutexes

What if I wanted to keep the three lines of code I had. Then atomics aren't going to work. What I need then is a mutex. A mutex lets me box a group of code so only one Goroutine at a time can execute that code.

Listing 6.28

```
var counter int

func main() {
    const grs = 2

    var wg sync.WaitGroup
    wg.Add(grs)

    var mu sync.Mutex                        <-- CHANGED

    for g := 0; g < grs; g++ {
        go func() {
            for i := 0; i < 2; i++ {
                mu.Lock()                    <-- CHANGED
                {
                    value := counter
                    value++
                    counter = value
                }
                mu.Unlock()                  <-- CHANGED
            }
            wg.Done()
        }()
    }

    wg.Wait()
    fmt.Println("Counter:", counter)
}
```

There are several changes to this code from the original. I added the construction of the mu variable to be a mutex set to its zero value. Then inside the for loop, I added calls to Lock and Unlock with an artificial code block. Inside the code block I have the code that needs to be synchronized. The code block is used for readability.

With this code in place, the scheduler will only allow one Goroutine to enter the code block at a time. It's important to understand that a mutex is not a queue. The first Goroutine that calls Lock isn't necessarily the first Goroutine who gets the Lock. There is a fairness based algorithm but this is done on purpose so people don't use mutexes as queues.

It's important to remember the Lock creates back pressure, so the longer it takes to get from the Lock to the Unlock, the more chance of Goroutines waiting for their turn. If I forget to call Unlock, then all Goroutines waiting will deadlock. This is why it's critical that the call to Lock and Unlock happen in the same function. Make sure I'm doing the bare minimum synchronization I need in the code block, but at least the minimum.

This is very bad code where someone is trying to get in and out of the Lock so quickly they actually lose the synchronization and the race detector can't even discover the problem.

Listing 6.29

```
var counter int

func main() {
    const grs = 2

    var wg sync.WaitGroup
    wg.Add(grs)

    var mu sync.Mutex

    for g := 0; g < grs; g++ {
        go func() {
            for i := 0; i < 2; i++ {
                var value int
                mu.Lock()                    <-- Bad Use Of Mutex
                {
                    value = counter
                }
                mu.Unlock()

                value++

                mu.Lock()                    <-- Bad Use Of Mutex
                {
                    counter = value
                }
                mu.Unlock()
            }
            wg.Done()
        }()
    }

    wg.Wait()
    fmt.Println("Counter:", counter)
}
```

As a general guideline, if I see a call to Lock from the same mutex twice in the same function, stop the code review. There is probably a mistake or over complication. In this case the calls to read and write are being synchronized, however, two Goroutines can end up at the value++ line of code with the same value. The data race still exists and the race detector is helpless in finding it.

6.9 Read/Write Mutexes

There is a second type of mutex called a read/write mutex. It allows me to separate the locks around reads and writes. This is important since reading data doesn't pose a threat unless a Goroutine is attempting to write at the same time. So this type of mutex allows multiple Goroutines to read the same memory at the same time. As soon as a write lock is requested, the reads are no longer issued, the write takes place, the reads can start again.

Listing 6.30

```go
package main

import (
    "fmt"
    "math/rand"
    "sync"
    "time"
)

var data []string
var rwMutex sync.RWMutex

func main() {
    var wg sync.WaitGroup
    wg.Add(1)

    go func() {
        for i := 0; i < 10; i++ {
            writer(i)
        }
        wg.Done()
    }()

    for i := 0; i < 8; i++ {
        go func(id int) {
            for {
                reader(id)
            }
        }(i)
    }

    wg.Wait()
    fmt.Println("Program Complete")
}

func writer(i int) {
    rwMutex.Lock()
    {
        time.Sleep(time.Duration(rand.Intn(100)) * time.Millisecond)
        fmt.Println("****> : Performing Write")
        data = append(data, fmt.Sprintf("String: %d", i))
    }
    rwMutex.Unlock()
}

func reader(id int) {
    rwMutex.RLock()
    {
        time.Sleep(time.Duration(rand.Intn(10)) * time.Millisecond)
        fmt.Printf("%d : Performing Read : Length[%d]\n", id, len(data))
    }
    rwMutex.RUnlock()
}
```

I can see the use of a read/write mutex where there are 8 Goroutines reading the length of a slice within a 10 millisecond delay of each other, and 1 Goroutine waking up within 100 milliseconds to append a value (write) to the slice.

The key is the implementation of the writer and reader functions. Notice how I use Lock for the writer and RLock for the reader. One of the biggest mistakes I can make with this is mixing up the Unlock calls with the wrong version. Having a Lock with a RUnlock will never end well.

Listing 6.31

```
7 : Performing Read : Length[0]
5 : Performing Read : Length[0]
0 : Performing Read : Length[0]
3 : Performing Read : Length[0]
7 : Performing Read : Length[0]
2 : Performing Read : Length[0]
1 : Performing Read : Length[0]
****> : Performing Write
0 : Performing Read : Length[1]
5 : Performing Read : Length[1]
3 : Performing Read : Length[1]
6 : Performing Read : Length[1]
7 : Performing Read : Length[1]
4 : Performing Read : Length[1]
1 : Performing Read : Length[1]
2 : Performing Read : Length[1]
****> : Performing Write
7 : Performing Read : Length[2]
1 : Performing Read : Length[2]
3 : Performing Read : Length[2]
```

The output shows how multiple Goroutines are reading at the same time, but all the reading stops when the write takes place.

6.10 Channel Semantics

It's important to think of a channel not as a data structure, but as a mechanic for signaling. This goes in line with the idea that I send and receive from a channel, not read and write. If the problem in front of me can't be solved with signaling, if the word signaling is not coming out of my mouth, I need to question the use of channels.

There are three things that I need to focus on when thinking about signaling. The first one is, does the Goroutine that is sending the signal, need a guarantee that the signal has been received? I might think that the answer to this question is always yes, but remember, there is a cost to every decision and there is a cost to having a guarantee at the signaling level.

The cost of having the guarantee at the signaling level is unknown latency. The sender won't know how long they need to wait for the receiver to accept the signal. Having to wait for the receiver creates blocking latency. In this case, unknown amounts of blocking latency. The sender has to wait, for an unknown amount of time, until the receiver becomes available to receive the signal.

Waiting for the receiver means mechanically, the receive operation happens before the send. With channels, the receive happens nanoseconds before, but it's before. This means the receiver takes the signal and then walks away, allowing the sender to now move on with a guarantee.

What if the process can't wait for an unknown amount of time? What if that kind of latency won't work? Then the guarantee can't be at the signaling level, it needs to be outside of it. The mechanics behind this working is that the send now happens before the receive. The sender can perform the signal without needing the receiver to be available. So the sender gets to walk away and not wait. Eventually, I hope, the receiver shows up and takes the signal.

This is reducing latency cost on the send, but it's creating uncertainty about signals being received and therefore knowing if there are problems upstream with receivers. This can create the process to accept work that never gets started or finished. It could eventually cause massive back pressure and systems to crash.

The second thing to focus on is, do I need to send data with the signal? If the signal requires the transmission of data, then the signaling is a 1 to 1 between Goroutines. If a new Goroutine needs to receive the signal as well, a second signal must be sent.

If data doesn't need to be transmitted with the signal, then the signal can be a 1 to 1 or 1 to many between Goroutines. Signaling without data is primarily used for cancellation or shutdowns. It's done by closing the channel.

The third thing to focus on is channel state. A channel can be in 1 of 3 states.

A channel can be in a nil state by constructing the channel to its zero value state. Sends and receives against channels in this state will block. This is good for situations where I want to implement short term stoppages of work.

A channel can be in an open state by using the built-in function make. Sends and receives against channels in this state will work under the following conditions:

Unbuffered Channels:
Guarantees at the signaling level with the receive happening before send. Sending and receiving Goroutines need to come together in the same space and time for a signal to be processed.

Buffered Channels:
Guarantees outside of the signaling level with the send happening before the receive. If the buffer is not full, sends can complete else they block. If the buffer is not empty, receives can complete else they block.

A channel can be in a closed state by using the built-in function close. I don't need to close a channel to release memory, this is for changing the state. Sending on a closed channel will cause a panic, however receiving on a closed channel will return immediately.

With all this information, I can focus on channel patterns. The focus on signaling is important. The idea is, if I need a guarantee at the signaling level or not, based on latency concerns. If I need to transmit data with the signal or not, based on handling cancellations or not. I want to convert the syntax to these semantics.

6.11 Channel Patterns

There are 7 channel patterns that are important to understand since they provide the building blocks to signaling.

6.11.1 Wait For Result

The wait for result pattern is a foundational pattern used by larger patterns like fan out/in. In this pattern, a Goroutine is created to perform some known work and signals their result back to the Goroutine that created them. This allows for the actual work to be placed on a Goroutine that can be terminated or walked away from.

Listing 6.32

```
func waitForResult() {
    ch := make(chan string)

    go func() {
        time.Sleep(time.Duration(rand.Intn(500)) * time.Millisecond)
        ch <- "data"
        fmt.Println("child : sent signal")
    }()

    d := <-ch
    fmt.Println("parent : recv'd signal :", d)

    time.Sleep(time.Second)
    fmt.Println("-----------------------------------------------")
}
```

The beginning of this function uses the builtin function make. In this case, an unbuffered channel is being constructed to its open state. It's better to look at this as a channel that is being constructed to signal string data with guarantees at the signaling level. Which means the sending Goroutine wants a guarantee that the signal being sent has been received.

Once the channel is constructed, a child Goroutine is created to perform work and the parent Goroutine waits to receive a signal with string data. Because there are guarantees at the signaling level, the amount of time the parent Goroutine will need to wait is unknown. It's the unknown latency cost of this type of channel.

The child Goroutine goes ahead and begins to perform its work immediately. To simulate the unknown latency problem, a sleep with a random number of milliseconds is employed to define the work. Once the work is done, the child Goroutine performs a send with string data. The parent Goroutine is already blocked waiting in a receive.

Since the receive happens nanoseconds before the send, which creates the guarantee, I would think the print call for the receive signal would always appear before the print for the send. But there is no guarantee in what order I will see the print calls execute. I need to remember, both Goroutines are running on their own operating system thread in parallel, the receive is only happening nanoseconds before, after the channel operation, all things are equal again.

6.11.2 Fan Out/In

The fan out/in pattern uses the wait for result pattern just described.

Listing 6.33

```
func fanOut() {
    children := 2000
    ch := make(chan string, children)

    for c := 0; c < children; c++ {
        go func(child int) {
            time.Sleep(time.Duration(rand.Intn(200)) * time.Millisecond)
            ch <- "data"
            fmt.Println("child : sent signal :", child)
        }(c)
    }

    for children > 0 {
        d := <-ch
        children--
        fmt.Println(d)
        fmt.Println("parent : recv'd signal :", children)
    }

    time.Sleep(time.Second)
    fmt.Println("---------------------------------------------------")
}
```

The idea of this pattern is to create a Goroutine for each individual piece of work that is pending and can be done concurrently. In this code sample, I am going to create 2000 child Goroutines to perform 2000 individual pieces of work. I am going to use a buffered channel since there is only one receiver and it's not important to have a guarantee at the signaling level. That will only create extra latency.

Instead, the idea is to move the guarantee to know when all the signals have been received. This will reduce the cost of latency from the channels. That will be done with a counter that is decremented for each received signal until it reaches zero.

A buffered channel of 2000 is constructed, one for each child Goroutine being created. Then in a loop, 2000 child Goroutines are created and they are off to do

140

their work. A random sleep is used to simulate the work and the unknown amount of time it takes to get the work done. The key is that the order of the work is undefined, out of order, execution which also changes each time the program runs. If this is not acceptable, I can't use concurrency.

Once all the Goroutines are created, the parent Goroutine waits in a receive loop. Eventually as data is signaled into the buffered channel, the parent Goroutine will pick up the data and eventually all the work is received.

I must remember, a fan out is dangerous in a running service since the number of child Goroutines I create for the fan are a multiplier. If I have a service handling 50k requests on 50 thousand Goroutines, and I decide to use a fan out pattern of 10 child Goroutines for some of the requests, in a worse case scenario I would be talking 500k Goroutines existing at the same time. Depending on the resources those child Goroutines needed, I might not have them available at that scale and the back pressure could bring the service down.

6.11.3 Wait For Task

The wait for task pattern is a foundational pattern used by larger patterns like pooling.

Listing 6.34

```
func waitForTask() {
    ch := make(chan string)

    go func() {
        d := <-ch
        fmt.Println("child : recv'd signal :", d)
    }()

    time.Sleep(time.Duration(rand.Intn(500)) * time.Millisecond)
    ch <- "data"
    fmt.Println("parent : sent signal")

    time.Sleep(time.Second)
    fmt.Println("-----------------------------------------------")
}
```

At the beginning, the function creates an unbuffered channel so there is a guarantee at the signaling level. This is critically important for pooling so I can add mechanics later if needed to allow for timeouts and cancellation. Once the channel is created, a child Goroutine is created immediately waiting for a signal with data to perform work. The parent Goroutine begins to prepare that work and finally signals the work to the child Goroutine. Since the guarantee is at the signaling level, the child Goroutine doesn't know how long it needs to wait.

6.11.4 Pooling

The pooling pattern uses the wait for task pattern just described. The pooling pattern allows me to manage resource usage across a well defined number of

Goroutines. As explained previously, in Go pooling is not needed for efficiency in CPU processing like at the operating system. It's more important for efficiency in resource usage.

Listing 6.35

```go
func pooling() {
    ch := make(chan string)

    g := runtime.GOMAXPROCS(0)
    for c := 0; c < g; c++ {
        go func(child int) {
            for d := range ch {
                fmt.Printf("child %d : recv'd signal : %s\n", child, d)
            }
            fmt.Printf("child %d : recv'd shutdown signal\n", child)
        }(c)
    }

    const work = 100
    for w := 0; w < work; w++ {
        ch <- "data"
        fmt.Println("parent : sent signal :", w)
    }

    close(ch)
    fmt.Println("parent : sent shutdown signal")

    time.Sleep(time.Second)
    fmt.Println("-------------------------------------------------------")
}
```

In this pattern, a group of child Goroutines are created to service the same channel. There is efficiency in this because the size of the pool dictates the amount of concurrent work happening at the same time. If I have a pool of 16 Goroutines, that could represent 16 files being opened at any given time or the amount of memory needed for 16 Goroutines to perform their work.

The code starts with the creation of an unbuffered channel. It's critically important that an unbuffered channel is used because without the guarantee at the signaling level, I can't perform timeouts and cancellation on the send if needed at a later time. The next part of the code decides the number of child Goroutines the pool will contain.

Listing 6.36

```go
g := runtime.GOMAXPROCS(0)
```

The call to runtime.GOMAXPROCS is important in that it queries the runtime (when passing 0 as a parameter) to the number of threads that exist for running Goroutines. The number should always equal the number of cores/hardware_threads that are available to the program. It represents the amount of CPU capacity available to the program. When the size of the pool isn't obvious, start with this number as a baseline. It won't be uncommon for this number to provide a reasonable performance benchmark.

The for loop creates the pool of child Goroutines where each child Goroutine sits in a blocking receive call using the for/range mechanics for a channel.

Listing 6.37

```
for c := 0; c < g; c++ {
    go func(child int) {
        for d := range ch {
            fmt.Printf("child %d : recv'd signal : %s\n", child, d)
        }
        fmt.Printf("child %d : recv'd shutdown signal\n", child)
    }(c)
}
```

The for range helps to minimize the amount of code I would otherwise need to receive a signal and then shutdown once the channel is closed. Without the for/range mechanics, I would have to write this code.

Listing 6.38

```
for c := 0; c < g; c++ {
    go func( child int) {
        for {
            d, wd := <-ch          <-- CHANGED
            if !wd {               <-- CHANGED
                break              <-- CHANGED
            }
            fmt.Printf("child %d : recv'd signal : %s\n", child, d)
        }
        fmt.Printf("child %d : recv'd shutdown signal\n", child)
    }(c)
}
```

The for/range eliminates 4 extra lines of code and streamlines the mechanics. It's important to note, it must not matter which of the child Goroutines in the pool are chosen to receive a signal. Depending on the amount of work being signaled, it could be the same child Goroutines over and over while others are never selected.

Then the call to close is executed which will cause the for loops to terminate and stop the program. If the channel being used was a buffered channel, data would flush out of the buffer first before the child Goroutines would receive the close signal.

6.11.5 Drop

The drop pattern is an important pattern for services that may experience heavy loads at times and can drop requests when the service reaches a capacity of pending requests. As an example, a DNS service would need to employ this pattern.

Listing 6.39

```go
func drop() {
    const cap = 100
    ch := make(chan string, cap)

    go func() {
        for p := range ch {
            fmt.Println("child : recv'd signal :", p)
        }
    }()

    const work = 2000
    for w := 0; w < work; w++ {
        select {
        case ch <- "data":
            fmt.Println("parent : sent signal :", w)
        default:
            fmt.Println("parent : dropped data :", w)
        }
    }

    close(ch)
    fmt.Println("parent : sent shutdown signal")

    time.Sleep(time.Second)
    fmt.Println("-----------------------------------------------------")
}
```

The code starts with the creation of a buffered channel. This is a case where it's reasonable to have a large buffer. Identifying the capacity value (buffer size) will require work in the lab. I want a number that allows the service to maintain reasonable levels of resource usage and performance when the buffer is full.

Next a child Goroutine using the pooling pattern is created. This child Goroutine is waiting for a signal to receive data to work on. In this example, having only one child Goroutine will cause back pressure quickly on the sending side. One child Goroutine will not be able to process all the work in time before the buffer gets full. Representing the service is at capacity.

Inside the for loop, I see the use of a select statement. The select statement is a blocking call that allows the parent Goroutine to handle multiple channel operations at the same time. Each case represents a channel operation, a send or a receive. However, this select is using the default keyword as well, which turns the select into a non-blocking call.

The key to implementing this pattern is the use of default. If the channel buffer is full, that will cause the case statement to block since the send can't complete. When every case in a select is blocked, and there is a default, the default is then executed. This is where the drop code is placed.

In the drop code, I can now decide what to do with the request. I can return a 500 to the caller. I could store the request somewhere else. The key is I have options.

6.11.6 Cancellation

The cancellation pattern is used to tell a function performing some I/O how long I am willing to wait for the operation to complete. Sometimes I can cancel the operation, and sometimes all I can do is just walk away.

Listing 6.40

```
func cancellation() {
    duration := 150 * time.Millisecond
    ctx, cancel := context.WithTimeout(context.Background(), duration)
    defer cancel()

    ch := make(chan string, 1)

    go func() {
        time.Sleep(time.Duration(rand.Intn(200)) * time.Millisecond)
        ch <- "data"
    }()

    select {
    case d := <-ch:
        fmt.Println("work complete", d)

    case <-ctx.Done():
        fmt.Println("work cancelled")
    }

    time.Sleep(time.Second)
    fmt.Println("-------------------------------------------------")
}
```

The code starts with defining a time.Duration variable named duration set to 150 milliseconds. Then a Context value is created to support a timeout of the 150 seconds using the WithTimeout function. That function takes a Context value in and returns a new one with the changes. In this case, I use the Background function which returns an empty parent Context.

It's important to call the cancel function that is returned as the second argument from WithTimeout using a defer. If that cancel function is not called at least once, there will be a memory leak.

After a buffered channel of 1 is created, a child Goroutine is created to perform some I/O bound work. In this case, a random Sleep call is made to simulate blocking work that can't be directly cancelled. That work can take up to 200 milliseconds to finish. There is a 50 millisecond difference between the timeout and the amount of time the work could take.

With the child Goroutine created and performing the work, the parent Goroutine blocks in a select statement waiting on two signals. The first case represents the child Goroutine finishing the work on time and the result being received. That is what I want. The second case represents a timeout from the Context. This means the work didn't finish within the 150 millisecond time limit.

If the parent Goroutine receives the timeout signal, it walks away. In this situation, it can't inform the child Goroutine that it won't be around to receive its signal. This is why it's so important for the work channel to be a buffer of 1. The child Goroutine needs to be able to send its signal, whether or not the parent Goroutine is around to receive it. If a non-buffered channel is used, the child Goroutine will block forever and become a memory leak.

6.11.7 Fan Out/In Semaphore

The fan out/in semaphore pattern provides a mechanic to control the number of Goroutines executing work at any given time while still creating a unique Goroutine for each piece of work.

Listing 6.41

```
func fanOutSem() {
    children := 2000
    ch := make(chan string, children)

    g := runtime.GOMAXPROCS(0)
    sem := make(chan bool, g)

    for c := 0; c < children; c++ {
        go func(child int) {
            sem <- true
            {
                t := time.Duration(rand.Intn(200)) * time.Millisecond
                time.Sleep(t)
                ch <- "data"
                fmt.Println("child : sent signal :", child)
            }
            <-sem
        }(c)
    }

    for children > 0 {
        d := <-ch
        children--
        fmt.Println(d)
        fmt.Println("parent : recv'd signal :", children)
    }

    time.Sleep(time.Second)
    fmt.Println("----------------------------------------------------")
}
```

At the start of the function, a channel with a buffer size of 2000 is set. This is the same thing we need in the original fan out/in pattern. One buffer for each child Goroutine that will be created. Then, like the pooling pattern, the use of the GOMAXPROCS function is used to determine how many of the 2000 child Goroutines will be allowed to execute their work at any given time.

With g configured, a second buffered channel is constructed next with a buffer sized to the number of child Goroutines that can execute their work at the same time. This channel is the semaphore that will control the number of child Goroutines

146

performing work.

Then a for loop is used to create all 2000 child Goroutines and each child Goroutine finds itself in a send operation (sem <- true) against the semaphore channel. Here is where the rubber hits the road. Only a GOMAXPROCS number of child Goroutines can perform this send without blocking. The other 2000 - GOMAXPROCS child Goroutines will block until the running child Goroutines get to the receive operation (<-sem). This code uses a code block to show the code that is being executed between the semaphore locking. I like this for better readability.

At the end of the function, the parent Goroutine waits to receive work from all 2000 child Goroutines. For each piece of work received, the children variable is decremented until it gets down to zero. Just like the original fan out/in pattern.

6.11.8 Bounded Work Pooling

The bounded work pooling pattern uses a pool of Goroutines to perform a fixed amount of known work.

Listing 6.42

```
func boundedWorkPooling() {
    work := []string{"paper", "paper", "paper", "paper", 2000: "paper"}

    g := runtime.GOMAXPROCS(0)
    var wg sync.WaitGroup
    wg.Add(g)

    ch := make(chan string, g)

    for c := 0; c < g; c++ {
        go func(child int) {
            defer wg.Done()
            for wrk := range ch {
                fmt.Printf("child %d : recv'd signal : %s\n", child, wrk)
            }
            fmt.Printf("child %d : recv'd shutdown signal\n", child)
        }(c)
    }

    for _, wrk := range work {
        ch <- wrk
    }
    close(ch)
    wg.Wait()

    time.Sleep(time.Second)
    fmt.Println("-------------------------------------------------")
}
```

Right from the start, the function defines 2000 arbitrary pieces of work to perform. Then the GOMAXPROCS function is used to define the number of child Goroutines to use in the pool and a WaitGroup is constructed to make sure the parent Goroutine can be told to wait until all 2000 pieces of work are completed.

Just like I saw with the pooling pattern, a pool of child Goroutines is created in the loop and they all wait on a receive call using the for range mechanics. One change is the call to Done using a defer when each of the child Goroutines in the pool eventually terminate. This will happen when all the work is completed and this is how the pool will report back to the parent Goroutine they are aware they are not needed any longer.

After the creation of the pool of child Goroutines, A loop is executed by the parent Goroutine to start signaling work into the pool. Once the last piece of work is signaled, the channel is closed. Each of the child Goroutines will receive the closed signal once the signals in the buffer are emptied.

6.11.9 Retry Timeout

The retry timeout pattern is great when I have to ping something (like a database) which might fail, but I don't want to fail immediately. I want to retry for a specified amount of time before I fail.

Listing 6.43

```
func retryTimeout(ctx context.Context, retryInterval time.Duration,
                 check func(ctx context.Context) error) {

    for {
        fmt.Println("perform user check call")
        if err := check(ctx); err == nil {
            fmt.Println("work finished successfully")
            return
        }

        fmt.Println("check if timeout has expired")
        if ctx.Err() != nil {
            fmt.Println("time expired 1 :", ctx.Err())
            return
        }

        fmt.Printf("wait %s before trying again\n", retryInterval)
        t := time.NewTimer(retryInterval)

        select {
        case <-ctx.Done():
            fmt.Println("timed expired 2 :", ctx.Err())
            t.Stop()
            return
        case <-t.C:
            fmt.Println("retry again")
        }
    }
}
```

The function takes a context for the amount of time the function should attempt to perform work unsuccessfully. It also takes a retry interval that specifies how long to wait between attempts, and finally a function to execute. This function is coded by the caller for the specific work (like pinging the database) that needs to be performed and could fail.

148

The core of the function runs in an endless loop. The first step in the loop is to run the check function passing in the context so the caller's function can also respect the context. If that doesn't fail, the function returns that life is good. If it fails, the code goes on to the next step.

Next the context is checked to see if the amount of time given has expired. If it has, the function returns the timeout error, else it continues to the next step which is to create a timer value. The time value is set to the retry interval. The timer could be created above the for loop and reused, which would be good if this function was going to be running a lot. To simplify the code, a new timer is created every time.

The last step is to block on a select statement waiting to receive one of two signals. The first signal is that the context expires. The second signal is the retry interval expires. In the case of the second signal, the loop is restarted and the process runs again.

6.11.10 Channel Cancellation

With channel cancellation, I can take an existing channel being used already for cancellation purposes (legacy code) and convert its use with a context, where a context is needed for a future function call.

Listing 6.44

```go
func channelCancellation(stop <-chan struct{}) {
    ctx, cancel := context.WithCancel(context.Background())
    defer cancel()

    go func() {
        select {
        case <-stop:
            cancel()
        case <-ctx.Done():
        }
    }()

    func(ctx context.Context) error {
        req, err := http.NewRequestWithContext(
            ctx,
            http.MethodGet,
            "https://www.ardanlabs.com/blog/index.xml",
            nil,
        )
        if err != nil {
            return err
        }

        _, err = http.DefaultClient.Do(req)
        if err != nil {
            return err
        }
        return nil
    }(ctx)
}
```

This function accepts a channel typed with the empty struct to signal cancellation.

This is code that could be found in Go programs prior to the inclusion of context. A function this function needs to call works with the "new" context package.

A context is created using the Background function for the parent context in the WithCancel call. This returns a new context value that can be cancelled with the returned cancel function.

The key is the creation of the Goroutine that blocks in a select statement waiting on two signals. The first signal is the legacy channel that may be closed by the originator. The second is the context itself, which is important if future functions decide to cancel the context directly. On receiving a stop signal, the cancel function is then executed, cancelling the context for all functions that were passed the context.

As an example, a literal function is declared and executed that performs a web request that supports a context for cancellable I/O.

Chapter 7: Testing

In this chapter, I will learn how to write tests in Go and the integrated support provided by the language.

7.1 Basic Unit Test

One of the best things about Go is that the language defines what a unit of code is. A unit of code is called a package and it's represented as a folder in my source tree. The compiler builds a static library from each folder and then links them all together to form the final application binary.

When I talk about a unit test, I am talking about testing code from a single package. Usually exported function by exported function. This doesn't restrict me from hitting external systems like a database or a set of web services to perform the tests. This is different from an integration test which will run tests across multiple packages.

There are no rules or idioms when writing a unit test. What's important is that a company or at least a team develops a set of consistent idioms and rules for writing a test. This way anyone can review a test result and maintain the code in a consistent way.

One thing I need to decide upon is how verbose I want the tests to be. Do I want a test that only provides output when something fails, or do I want an indication as well that things are passing.

The standard library and the Go frontend tooling has everything I need to write a test. It all starts with creating a file with the _test.go naming convention inside the package I want to test, and then adding test functions by using the word Test with a capital T for each function.

Listing 7.1

```
sample_test.go

package sample_test

import (
    "testing"
)

func TestDownload(t *testing.T) {}
func TestUpload(t *testing.T) {}
```

These are examples of test functions I could declare in the sample_test.go testing file. It's important that the first letter following the word Test in the function name starts with a capital letter. If I don't, the testing tool won't see the function as a test function. The other important piece is that the test function takes a testing.T pointer as the only argument.

I should notice the package name also has the _test naming convention which puts the test functions in a different package and requires the test to import the package being tested and only work with the exported API. This is a good practice to force the test to use the package API like any other user. If I need to test unexported functions, I can't use this convention.

Listing 7.2

```
type T
    func (c *T) Cleanup(f func())
    func (t *T) Deadline() (deadline time.Time, ok bool)
    func (c *T) Error(args ...interface{})
    func (c *T) Errorf(format string, args ...interface{})
    func (c *T) Fail()
    func (c *T) FailNow()
    func (c *T) Failed() bool
    func (c *T) Fatal(args ...interface{})
    func (c *T) Fatalf(format string, args ...interface{})
    func (c *T) Helper()
    func (c *T) Log(args ...interface{})
    func (c *T) Logf(format string, args ...interface{})
    func (c *T) Name() string
    func (t *T) Parallel()
    func (t *T) Run(name string, f func(t *T)) bool
    func (c *T) Skip(args ...interface{})
    func (c *T) SkipNow()
    func (c *T) Skipf(format string, args ...interface{})
    func (c *T) Skipped() bool
    func (c *T) TempDir() string
```

The testing.T value provides the API to share with the testing tool if the test passed or failed. Two families of functions exist, t.Fatal and t.Error, which are the most common API's I will use and both indicate if a test failed. The big difference is calling t.Fatal will cause the test function to return and calling t.Error will allow the test function to continue and report potentially more failures within the test function. The t.Log function provides the option for verbose output for those who want to share more when a test fails or when the -v option is used when running a test.

Listing 7.3

```
package sample_test

import (
    "testing"
    "http"
)

func TestDownload(t *testing.T) {
    url := "https://www.ardanlabs.com/blog/index.xml"
    statusCode := 200

    resp, err := http.Get(url)
    if err != nil {
        t.Fatalf("unable to issue GET on URL: %s: %s", url, err)
    }
    defer resp.Body.Close()

    if resp.StatusCode != statusCode {
        t.Log("exp:", statusCode)
        t.Log("got:", resp.StatusCode)
        t.Fatal("status codes don't match")
    }
}
```

In this test, I plan to test the ability to download the RSS feed for the Ardan Labs blog. First, I declare some variables with the URL to download and the expected status code. I then perform the http.Get call for the URL and check the error. It's critical that any function called that returns an error has the error value checked. If there is an error, I call t.Fatal to report the problem and the test fails. If there is no error, I proceed to the next step which is checking the status code.

Before checking the status code, I prepare the close call for the response body. Always write tests like production code. If I don't get back the status code I expect, I provide verbose information about what I expected and what I got. This really helps with debugging failed tests. Then I call t.Fatal to report the test has failed. This is a test that only outputs information if the test fails.

7.2 Table Unit Test

Table tests can be powerful when I have code that can be run through a series of different inputs and expected outputs. They are perfect for negative path testing.

153

Listing 7.4

```go
package sample_test

import (
    "testing"
    "http"
)

func TestDownload(t *testing.T) {
    tt := []struct {
        url        string
        statusCode int
    }{
        {"https://www.ardanlabs.com/blog/index.xml", http.StatusOK},
        {"http://rss.cnn.com/rss/cnn_topstorie.rss", http.StatusNotFound},
    }

    for _, test := range tt {
        resp, err := http.Get(test.url)
        if err != nil {
            t.Fatalf("unable to issue GET on URL: %s: %s", test.url, err)
        }
        defer resp.Body.Close()

        if resp.StatusCode != test.statusCode {
            t.Log("exp:", test.statusCode)
            t.Log("got:", resp.StatusCode)
            t.Fatal("status codes don't match")
        }
    }
}
```

In this test, I am checking different URLs and potential status codes. The table is a slice of a literal struct that has two fields: url to test and the expected status code. Then two entries are added to the table, the first one is the positive path test, the second is a negative path test for a bad URL.

The test code is similar to the first test except the input is coming from iterating over the table. This allows me to add more entries over time without the need to write more code. The table can be anything from a slice to a map or any data structure I can iterate over and provide input and expected output.

7.3 Web Call Mocking

I am not a fan of mocking when it can be avoided. The use of Docker provides lots of opportunities to hit real systems over mocked behavior. I need to remember, a mock is only as good as the behavior being simulated. If the behavior changes in an upgrade of a system, the mock is no longer representative of the correct behavior. Mocks can be useful for negative path testing when it's difficult to cause real systems to fail on demand.

When it comes to making web calls to external systems, the standard library already provides support for mocking web calls. This is great for testing API behavior without the cost of a real web call. Especially if the testing environment is on a private network with no access to the outside world.

Listing 7.5

```
package sample_test

import (
    "testing"
    "http"
    "httptest"
)

var feed = `<?xml version="1.0" encoding="UTF-8"?>
<rss>
<channel>
    <title>Going Go Programming</title>
    <description>Golang : https://github.com/goinggo</description>
    <link>http://www.goinggo.net/</link>
    <item>
        <pubDate>Sun, 15 Mar 2015 15:04:00 +0000</pubDate>
        <title>Object Oriented Programming Mechanics</title>
        <description>Go is an object oriented language.</description>
        <link>http://www.goinggo.net/2015/03/object-oriented</link>
    </item>
</channel>
</rss>`

func mockServer() *httptest.Server {
    f := func(w http.ResponseWriter, r *http.Request) {
        w.WriteHeader(200)
        w.Header().Set("Content-Type", "application/xml")
        fmt.Fprintln(w, feed)
    }

    return httptest.NewServer(http.HandlerFunc(f))
}
```

Before I can write the test function I need a way to mock a web server. The mockServer function is providing just that. It uses the NewServer function from the httptest package. This function takes an http handler function that can be executed when a request is sent to the mock server and returns the localhost port the mock server is listening on.

In this case, the handler function sets the status code to 200, the content type to application/xmls, and writes the feed string back to the caller as part of the response. The feed string is mocking a small portion of the RSS document that is returned from the Ardan Labs blog call from the first test.

Listing 7.6

```go
func TestDownload(t *testing.T) {
    statusCode := 200

    server := mockServer()
    defer server.Close()

    resp, err := http.Get(server.URL)
    if err != nil {
        t.Fatalf("unable to issue GET on the URL: %s: %s", server.URL, err)
    }
    defer resp.Body.Close()

    if resp.StatusCode != statusCode {
        t.Log("exp:", statusCode)
        t.Log("got:", resp.StatusCode)
        t.Fatal("status codes don't match")
    }
}
```

In this test, the call to mockServer is performed to start the mock server and the server value is captured. The server value contains the URL to access the mock server and that is used in the call to http.Get. Since the mock server always returns a proper RSS feed document, this test should always pass.

I can extend this test function by declaring concrete types that match the RSS feed document. These types can be used to validate the actual data from the response.

Listing 7.7

```go
type Item struct {
    XMLName     xml.Name `xml:"item"`
    Title       string   `xml:"title"`
    Description string   `xml:"description"`
    Link        string   `xml:"link"`
}

// Channel defines the fields associated with the channel tag in
// the buoy RSS document.
type Channel struct {
    XMLName     xml.Name `xml:"channel"`
    Title       string   `xml:"title"`
    Description string   `xml:"description"`
    Link        string   `xml:"link"`
    PubDate     string   `xml:"pubDate"`
    Items       []Item   `xml:"item"`
}

// Document defines the fields associated with the buoy RSS document.
type Document struct {
    XMLName xml.Name `xml:"rss"`
    Channel Channel  `xml:"channel"`
    URI     string
}
```

With these types declared, I can extend the test function.

Listing 7.8

```go
func TestDownload(t *testing.T) {
    statusCode := 200

    server := mockServer()
    defer server.Close()

    resp, err := http.Get(server.URL)
    if err != nil {
        t.Fatalf("unable to issue GET on the URL: %s: %s", server.URL, err)
    }
    defer resp.Body.Close()

    if resp.StatusCode != statusCode {
        t.Log("exp:", statusCode)
        t.Log("got:", resp.StatusCode)
        t.Fatal("status codes don't match")
    }

    var d Document
    if err := xml.NewDecoder(resp.Body).Decode(&d); err != nil {
        t.Fatal("unable to decode the response:", err)
    }

    if len(d.Channel.Items) == 1 {
        t.Fatal("not seeing 1 item in the feed: len:", len(d.Channel.Items))
    }
}
```

Now the test is extended to decode the response body into the concrete types and then it validates there is one news item in the feed. Obviously I can do more now that the feed is decoded and I control the feed document.

7.4 Internal Web Endpoints

If I'm building a web service, I will want to test the endpoints without the need to build and run the service. The goal is to load the router with the endpoints and execute those endpoints without the need of all the networking stuff. The standard library provides support for this.

To see this, I need to define a handler function and bind the function to a route using the default mux in the http package. It's important to understand this will work with any mux.

Listing 7.9

```
package handlers

import (
    "encoding/json"
    "net/http"
)

func Routes() {
    http.HandleFunc("/sendjson", sendJSON)
}

func sendJSON(rw http.ResponseWriter, r *http.Request) {
    u := struct {
        Name  string
        Email string
    }{
        Name:  "Bill",
        Email: "bill@ardanlabs.com",
    }

    rw.Header().Set("Content-Type", "application/json")
    rw.WriteHeader(200)
    json.NewEncoder(rw).Encode(&u)
}
```

This code declares a new package named handlers and a function named sendJSON that represents a handler function that needs to be tested. In this case, the handler function returns a JSON representation of the literal struct with a status of 200.

The Routes function binds the sendJSON handler to the /sendjson route in the default server mux of the http package. This means any calls to http://domain.com/sendjson would be routed to the sendJSON handler function by the mux.

Listing 7.10

```
package handlers_test

import (
    "encoding/json"
    "net/http"
    "net/http/httptest"
    "testing"

    "github.com/ardanlabs/gotraining/app/handlers"
)

func init() {
    handlers.Routes()
}

func TestSendJSON(t *testing.T) {
    url := "/sendjson"
    statusCode := 200

    r := httptest.NewRequest("GET", url, nil)
    w := httptest.NewRecorder()
    http.DefaultServeMux.ServeHTTP(w, r)

    . . .
}
```

The first thing the test does is use the init function to make sure all the routes are loaded in the mux. This is done by calling the handlers.Routes function. A big mistake that is made with these types of tests is forgetting to load the routes.

With the routes loaded, the next step is to construct a request and construct a value that implements the http.ResponseWriter interfaces. The httptest package provides support for both. The httptest.NewRequest constructs the request as a GET call for the /sendjson route. The httptest.NewRecorder constructs the concrete value that implements the http.ResponseWriter interfaces and can be directly checked to validate if the web call passed or failed.

The key to running the test is calling the ServeHTTP function from the mux. Since I am using the http.DefaultServer mux in this code, that is where I am making the call to ServeHTTP. Any mux I may choose to use will implement this method. Once I call this method, I am asking the mux to process the request through the route and apply the response in the concrete recorder value.

Listing 7.11

```go
func TestSendJSON(t *testing.T) {
    . . .

    if w.Code != 200 {
        t.Log("exp:", statusCode)
        t.Log("got:", w.StatusCode)
        t.Fatal("status codes don't match")
    }

    var u struct {
        Name  string
        Email string
    }
    if err := json.NewDecoder(w.Body).Decode(&u); err != nil {
        t.Fatal("unable to decode the response:", err)
    }

    exp := "Bill"
    if u.Name != exp{
        t.Log("exp:", exp)
        t.Log("got:", u.Name)
        t.Fatal("user name does not match")
    }

    exp = "bill@ardanlabs.com"
    if u.Email == exp {
        t.Log("exp:", exp)
        t.Log("got:", u.Email)
        t.Fatal("user name does not match")
    }
}
```

Now, using the recorder value, I can check if the route behaved as expected. First I check that the status code is 200. Then I attempt to unmarshal the JSON response back to a concrete type. If that is successful, then I check the values in the Name and Email fields. If all that is correct, the test passes.

This test was executed without the need of a network or running the web service.

7.5 Basic Sub-Tests

There are times when I want to group a set of tests together under a single test function. I might have a table test where I want to control which data is tested on the command line. It's also possible that I may want to run a series of tests in parallel. If I fall into any of these use cases, the sub-testing support in Go is what I need.

Listing 7.12

```
package sample_test

import (
    "net/http"
    "testing"
)

func TestDownload(t *testing.T) {
    tt := []struct {
        name       string
        url        string
        statusCode int
    }{
        {
            "ok",
            "https://www.ardanlabs.com/blog/index.xml",
            http.StatusOK,
        },
        {
            "notfound",
            "http://rss.cnn.com/rss/cnn_topstorie.rss",
            http.StatusNotFound,
        },
    }

    . . .
}
```

This test is going to test the downloading of URLs like I saw with the table test from before. The difference here is the table has a new field called name, which will represent the name of the sub-test I am going to create for each entry in the table.

It's important to give each sub-test a name that is unique within a few starting characters so I can better filter the tests I want to run with the least number of characters to type.

Listing 7.13

```
    for _, test := range tt {
        test := test                            <- LOOK HERE
        tf := func(t *testing.T) {              <- LOOK HERE
            resp, err := http.Get(test.url)
            if err != nil {
                t.Fatalf("unable to issue GET/URL: %s: %s", test.url, err)
            }
            defer resp.Body.Close()

            if resp.StatusCode != test.statusCode {
                t.Log("exp:", test.statusCode)
                t.Log("got:", resp.StatusCode)
                t.Fatal("status codes don't match")
            }
        }
        t.Run(test.name, tf)                    <- LOOK HERE
    }
}
```

There are a couple of changes to the code inside the for range loop from the original table test example. Look for the LOOK HERE comments. The very first line of code inside the loop is creating a new variable named test that has local scope to the loop. This is being done to prevent any closure bugs since the next line of code creates a literal test function. I must make sure each literal test function has its own copy of the test data it will operate on.

Then a literal test function is declared and assigned to the tf variable. This function is passed to the call to t.Run at the bottom of the loop. The call to t.Run is how the sub-test is registered by name. Once all the test functions are registered, they can be executed all together or specified individually on the command line.

Listing 7.14

```
$ go test -v
$ go test -run TestDownload/ok -v
$ go test -run TestDownload/notfound -v
```

This is how I can run all the sub-tests or specify any individual sub-test. There is one other cool feature with sub-tests. I can run all the tests in parallel by using the t.Parallel method.

Listing 7.15

```
    for _, test := range tt {
        test := test
        tf := func(t *testing.T) {
            t.Parallel()                    <- LOOK HERE


            . . .

        }
        t.Run(test.name, tf)
    }
}
```

By adding the call to t.Parallel as the first line of code in the literal test function, the testing tool will run all the registered test functions in parallel, speeding up test execution time.

Chapter 8: Benchmarking

In this chapter, I will learn how to write benchmarks in Go and use the integrated support provided by the language. I will also learn how to realize that benchmarks lie and I need to be careful when interpreting the results.

8.1 Basic Benchmark

Benchmarks lie! At the same time, until I run a benchmark I'm only guessing. If there's one thing about Go, it's that I never have to guess. That's how good the tooling is.

The standard library and the Go frontend tooling has everything I need to write a benchmark. It all starts with creating a file with the _test.go naming convention inside the package I want to benchmark, and then adding benchmark functions by using the word Benchmark with a capital B for each function.

Listing 8.1

```
sample_test.go

package sample

import (
    "testing"
)

func BenchmarkDownload(b *testing.B) {}
func BenchmarkUpload(b *testing.B) {}
```

These are examples of benchmark functions I could declare in the sample_test.go testing file. It's important that the first letter following the word Benchmark in the function name starts with a capital letter. If I don't, the testing tool won't see the function as a benchmark function. The other important piece is that the benchmark function takes a testing.B pointer as the only argument.

Here is a super interesting benchmark to run.

Listing 8.2

```go
package basic

import (
    "fmt"
    "testing"
)

var gs string

func BenchmarkSprint(b *testing.B) {
    var s string
    for i := 0; i < b.N; i++ {
        s = fmt.Sprint("hello")
    }
    gs = s
}

func BenchmarkSprintf(b *testing.B) {
    var s string
    for i := 0; i < b.N; i++ {
        s = fmt.Sprintf("hello")
    }
    gs = s
}
```

The premise of this benchmark is to know which version of Sprint is faster, the regular or format version. When people are asked to guess, they tend to say the regular version since there is no formatting necessary. These people are always wrong.

Listing 8.3

```
$ go test -bench . -benchtime 3s -benchmem

goos: darwin
goarch: amd64
pkg: github.com/ardanlabs/gotraining/topics/go/testing/benchmarks/basic
cpu: Intel(R) Core(TM) i9-9980HK CPU @ 2.40GHz

BenchmarkSprint-16      56956252      55.48 ns/op      5 B/op      1 allocs/op
BenchmarkSprintf-16     80984947      42.46 ns/op      5 B/op      1 allocs/op
```

I can see from the results that the format version is faster by 13 nanoseconds per operation. The difference is insignificant, but nonetheless, there is a difference.

I want to break down both the writing and running of these benchmarks.

Listing 8.4

```
var gs string

func BenchmarkSprint(b *testing.B) {
    var s string

    for i := 0; i < b.N; i++ {
        s = fmt.Sprint("hello")
    }

    gs = s
}
```

At the core of every benchmark is the for loop from i to b.N. Inside this loop is where the code to be benchmarked is placed. To understand the loop, I need to understand a setting called -benchtime.

The -benchtime setting represents the total amount of time to spin the loop before providing a result. The default -benchtime is 1 second. This is where things get interesting because I can't spin a loop based on time, only on a number of iterations. The number of iterations required to match the -benchtime needs to be identified.

Identifying the correct b.N to match the -benchtime is accomplished through some trial and error. At the very beginning of running the benchmark, the tooling will set the value of b.N to 1 and run the loop. Then it will multiply the value of b.N by 100 until it gets close to the -benchtime. Then the algorithm can fix on a working b.N.

Listing 8.5

```
var gs string
var a []int

func BenchmarkSprint(b *testing.B) {
    var s string

    a = append(a, b.N)
    for i := 0; i < b.N; i++ {
        s = fmt.Sprint("hello")
    }

    if len(a) > 4 {
        fmt.Println(a)
    }

    gs = s
}
```

I added the ability to capture the value of b.N on every call to the benchmark function. Knowing that in this case it will take 5 calls to find the right b.N, that is when I output the contents of the slice.

Listing 8.6

```
BenchmarkSprint-16        [1 100 10000 1000000 54495168]
```

I can see the tooling identifying a value of b.N after 5 tries, finding the right number after trying a million iterations.

Another important aspect of benchmarking is the compiler. The compiler will build this code into a test binary to run the benchmark. It's important that the code inside the loop is accurate to how it runs in production. Any slight variation could change the compiler's behavior on how the code is built, or how the code behaves at runtime.

Back to the original code for the Sprint benchmark.

Listing 8.7

```
var gs string

func BenchmarkSprint(b *testing.B) {
    var s string

    for i := 0; i < b.N; i++ {
        s = fmt.Sprint("hello")
    }

    gs = s
}
```

This benchmark is measuring the performance of calling Sprint. Notice how the Sprint function returns a new string after the call. It's important to capture that return value as part of running the benchmark because doing so represents the real behavior of using this function in production code.

If I don't capture the return value from the call to Sprint, it's possible that the compiler could throw the function call out of the compiled binary. The function is useless without capturing the return since the behavior of the call alone wouldn't change the behavior of the program. If the compiler chooses to throw the call to Sprint away, the benchmark would just spin an empty loop, providing an inaccurate result.

When I run the benchmark, I am using the following call on the command line.

Listing 8.8

```
$ go test -bench . -benchtime 3s -benchmem
```

Breaking this down, I am asking go test to run all the benchmark functions it finds in the current directory (-bench .), increasing the time of spinning the loop to three seconds (-benchtime 3s), and to show memory allocations (-benchmem).

Listing 8.9

```
BenchmarkSprint-16      56956252     55.48 ns/op     5 B/op     1 allocs/op
BenchmarkSprintf-16     80984947     42.46 ns/op     5 B/op     1 allocs/op
```

BenchmarkSprint-16 threads	Name of the benchmark function and the number of which was 16.
56956252	The number of iterations of the loop that were executed which was 56,956,252.
55.48 ns/op execute	The amount of time the code inside the loop took to which was 55.48 nanoseconds.
5 B/op	The amount of memory the code inside the loop allocated which was 5 bytes.
1 allocs/op	The number of values the code inside the loop allocated which was 1 value.

In the end, the use of Sprintf was faster than Sprint for the string hello, though the both allocated the same number of values and total amount of memory on the heap.

8.2 Basic Sub-Benchmarks

There are times when I may want to group a set of benchmarks together under a single benchmark function. I might have a data table that I want to use to control which data is being benchmarked on the command line. If I fall into any of these use cases, the sub-benchmarking support in Go is what I need.

Listing 8.10

```
package basic

import (
    "fmt"
    "testing"
)

var gs string

func BenchmarkSprint(b *testing.B) {
    b.Run("none", benchSprint)
    b.Run("format", benchSprintf)
}
```

A quick way to show this is to rename the existing benchmark functions to benchSprint and benchSprintf, then write a single benchmark function that uses the b.Run function.

Now on the command line I can control what runs.

167

Listing 8.11

```
$ go test -bench .
$ go test -bench BenchmarkSprint/none
$ go test -bench BenchmarkSprint/format
```

This is how I can run all the sub-benchmarks or specify any individual sub-benchmark.

8.3 Validate Benchmarks

When I started this chapter, I tried to make it clear that benchmarks lie and I must validate the results. Especially when the results are not what I expected. To show this, I have written a merge sort algorithm so I can run the algorithm under different conditions. First with a single Goroutine, then using a different Goroutine for every split of the collection that needs to be sorted, finally only using the same number of Goroutines that can be run in parallel.

Listing 8.12

```go
func merge(l, r []int) []int {
    // Declare the sorted return list with the proper capacity.
    ret := make([]int, 0, len(l)+len(r))

    // Compare the number of items required.
    for {
        switch {
        case len(l) == 0:
            // We appended everything in the left list so now append
            // everything contained in the right and return.
            return append(ret, r...)

        case len(r) == 0:
            // We appended everything in the right list so now append
            // everything contained in the left and return.
            return append(ret, l...)

        case l[0] <= r[0]:
            // First value in the left list is smaller than the
            // first value in the right so append the left value.
            ret = append(ret, l[0])

            // Slice that first value away.
            l = l[1:]

        default:
            // First value in the right list is smaller than the
            // first value in the left so append the right value.
            ret = append(ret, r[0])

            // Slice that first value away.
            r = r[1:]
        }
    }
}
```

Here is the merge function that performs the work. All this slicing is going to create a large number of allocations on the heap. Merge sort is not a great algorithm to use in Go.

Listing 8.13

```go
func single(n []int) []int {
    // Once we have a list of one we can begin to merge values.
    if len(n) <= 1 {
        return n
    }

    // Split the list in half.
    i := len(n) / 2

    // Sort the left side.
    l := single(n[:i])

    // Sort the right side.
    r := single(n[i:])

    // Place things in order and merge ordered lists.
    return merge(l, r)
}
```

The single function uses a single Goroutine to perform the sort. It splits the initial list in half, then uses recursion to continue to split the list until the merge function can be executed to sort everything.

Listing 8.14

```go
func unlimited(n []int) []int {
    // Once we have a list of one we can begin to merge values.
    if len(n) <= 1 {
        return n
    }

    // Split the list in half.
    i := len(n) / 2

    // Maintain the ordered left and right side lists.
    var l, r []int

    . . .
```

The unlimited function starts out the same as the single function. Then it begins to throw new Goroutines at each split of the list.

Listing 8.15

```
    . . .

    // For each split we will have 2 goroutines.
    var wg sync.WaitGroup
    wg.Add(2)

    // Sort the left side concurrently.
    go func() {
        l = unlimited(n[:i])
        wg.Done()
    }()

    // Sort the right side concurrently.
    go func() {
        r = unlimited(n[i:])
        wg.Done()
    }()

    // Wait for the splitting to end.
    wg.Wait()

    // Place things in order and merge ordered lists.
    return merge(l, r)
}
```

This could result in tens of thousands of Goroutines depending on the size of the list to be sorted.

Listing 8.16

```
func numCPU(n []int) []int {
    // Once we have a list of one we can begin to merge values.
    if len(n) <= 1 {
        return n
    }

    // Split the list in half.
    i := len(n) / 2

    // Maintain the ordered left and right side lists.
    var l, r []int

    . . .
```

The numCPU function starts out like the unlimited function. Then it must calculate how many concurrent splits can occur for the number of Goroutines that can run in parallel.

Listing 8.17

```go
func numCPU(n []int) []int {
    . . .

    // Calculate how many levels deep we can create goroutines.
    // On an 8 core machine we can keep creating goroutines until level 4.
    //      Lvl 0        1  Lists         1  Goroutine
    //      Lvl 1        2  Lists         2  Goroutines
    //      Lvl 2        4  Lists         4  Goroutines
    //      Lvl 3        8  Lists         8  Goroutines
    //      Lvl 4       16  Lists        16  Goroutines

    // On an 8 core machine this will produce the value of 3.
    maxLevel := int(math.Log2(float64(runtime.GOMAXPROCS(0))))

    . . .
```

Once the number of levels is calculated, the sorting work can begin.

Listing 8.18

```go
func numCPU(n []int, lvl int) []int {
    . . .

    // We don't need more goroutines then we have logical processors.
    if lvl <= maxLevel {
        lvl++

        // For each split we will have 2 goroutines.
        var wg sync.WaitGroup
        wg.Add(2)

        // Sort the left side concurrently.
        go func() {
            l = numCPU(n[:i], lvl)
            wg.Done()
        }()

        // Sort the right side concurrently.
        go func() {
            r = numCPU(n[i:], lvl)
            wg.Done()
        }()

        // Wait for the splitting to end.
        wg.Wait()

        // Place things in order and merge ordered lists.
        return merge(l, r)
    }

    // Sort the left and right side on this goroutine.
    l = numCPU(n[:i], lvl)
    r = numCPU(n[i:], lvl)

    // Place things in order and merge ordered lists.
    return merge(l, r)
}
```

With this function complete, I can write the benchmark functions and see what version of merge sort is faster.

Listing 8.19

```go
package main

import (
    "math"
    "runtime"
    "sync"
    "testing"
)

var n []int

func init() {
    for i := 0; i < 1_000_000; i++ {
        n = append(n, i)
    }
}

func BenchmarkSingle(b *testing.B) {
    for i := 0; i < b.N; i++ {
        single(n)
    }
}

func BenchmarkUnlimited(b *testing.B) {
    for i := 0; i < b.N; i++ {
        unlimited(n)
    }
}

func BenchmarkNumCPU(b *testing.B) {
    for i := 0; i < b.N; i++ {
        numCPU(n, 0)
    }
}
```

Everything I know suggests that numCPU should be the fastest since it is efficiently using the cpu capacity of the machine.

Listing 8.20

```
$ go test -bench . -benchtime 3s

goos: darwin
goarch: amd64
pkg: github.com/ardanlabs/gotraining/topics/go/testing/benchmarks/validate
cpu: Intel(R) Core(TM) i9-9980HK CPU @ 2.40GHz

BenchmarkSingle-16          52      66837183 ns/op
BenchmarkUnlimited-16       13     251840589 ns/op
BenchmarkNumCPU-16          78      46336693 ns/op
```

The results of the benchmark show that my expectation was correct, numCPU is faster and in this case by 36.2%. But is this actually correct? What happens if I just run the numCPU benchmark in isolation?

Listing 8.21

```
$ go test -bench NumCPU -benchtime 3s

goos: darwin
goarch: amd64
pkg: github.com/ardanlabs/gotraining/topics/go/testing/benchmarks/validate
cpu: Intel(R) Core(TM) i9-9980HK CPU @ 2.40GHz

BenchmarkNumCPU-16            85        38004899 ns/op
```

When running the benchmark in isolation, the performance of the numCPU function increased. Now numCPU is 55% faster. That is a huge improvement on such a small data set.

Imagine if the single test ended up beating numCPU when all the benchmarks were run together? I would have thought single was faster than numCPU. Funny enough, this was the case in earlier versions of Go.

Why the difference in performance? Because the unlimited benchmark is creating a lot of Goroutines that are still being cleaned up by the time the numCPU benchmark starts running. This extra load on the runtime is not allowing the numCPU benchmark to be accurate. Once I run the benchmark in isolation, that extra load doesn't exist and can't affect the results.

Rule number one of running a benchmark is that the machine needs to be idle.

Chapter 9: Generics

In this chapter, I will learn about the new syntax coming to Go 1.18 for writing generic functions and types. Generics in this first release is about providing the ability to write concrete polymorphic functions with the support of type parameter lists.

This functionality (defined by the generics spec) will be represented in the first release of generics.

- Functions can have an additional type parameter list that uses square brackets but otherwise looks like an ordinary parameter list: func F[T any](p T) { ... }.

- Type parameters can be used by the regular parameters and in the function body.

- Types can also have a type parameter list: type M[T any] []T.

- Each type parameter has a type constraint, just as each ordinary parameter has a type: func F[T Constraint](p T) { ... }.

- Type constraints are interface types.

- The new predeclared name any is a type constraint that permits any type.

- Interface types used as type constraints can have a list of predeclared types; only type arguments that match one of those types satisfy the constraint.

- Generic functions may only use operations permitted by the type constraint.

- Using a generic function or type requires passing type arguments.

- Type inference permits omitting the type arguments of a function call in common cases.

Generics will be great for replacing existing Go code that uses the empty interface where having a concrete type would have been better. An example of this is with container types (lists, stacks, queues) which can't be written effectively with the empty interface. I also expect to see new packages like a concurrency package that can provide support for pooling, fan out/in, and drop patterns.

9.1 Basic Syntax

If I want to write a single print function that can output a slice of any given type and not use reflection, I can use the new generics syntax.

Listing 9.1

```
func print[T any](slice []T) {
    fmt.Print("Generic: ")
    for _, v := range slice {
        fmt.Print(v, " ")
    }
    fmt.Print("\n")
}
```

This is an implementation of a single print function that can output a slice of any given type using the new generics syntax. What's nice about this syntax is that the code inside the function can use syntax and built-in functions that would work with a concrete type. This is not the case when I use the empty interface to write generic code.

I need a way to tell the compiler that I won't be declaring type T explicitly, but it has to be determined by the compiler at compile time. The new syntax uses square brackets for this. The brackets define a list of generic type identifiers that represent types specific to the function that need to be determined at compile time. It's how I tell the compiler that types with these names won't be declared before the program is compiled. These types need to be figured out at compile time.

Note: I can have multiple type identifiers defined inside the brackets though the current example is only using one. Ex. [T, S, R any]

I can name these type identifiers anything I want to help with the readability of the code. In this case, I'm using the capital letter T to describe that a slice of some type T (to be determined at compile time) will be passed in. I like the use of single capitalized letters when it comes to collections and it's also a convention that goes back to older programming languages like C++ and Java.

There is the use of the word any inside the brackets as well. This represents a constraint on what type T can be. The compiler requires that all generic types have a well defined constraint. The any constraint is predeclared by the compiler and states there are no constraints on what type T can be.

Listing 9.2

```
numbers := []int{1, 2, 3}
print[int](numbers)

strings := []string{"A", "B", "C"}
print[string](strings)

floats := []float64{1.7, 2.2, 3.14}
print[float64](floats)
```

This is how to make calls to the generic print function where the type information for T is explicitly provided at the call site. The syntax emulates the idea that the function declaration func name[T any](slice []T) defines two sets of parameters. The first set is the type that maps to the corresponding type identifiers, and the second is the data that maps to the corresponding input variables.

Luckily, the compiler can infer the type and eliminate the need to explicitly pass in the type information at the call site.

Listing 9.3

```
numbers := []int{1, 2, 3}
print(numbers)

strings := []string{"A", "B", "C"}
print(strings)

floats := []float64{1.7, 2.2, 3.14}
print(floats)
```

This code shows how I can call the generic print functions without the need to pass the type information explicitly. At the function call site, the compiler is able to identify the type to use for T and construct a concrete version of the function to support slices of that type. The compiler has the ability to infer the type with the information it has at the call site from the data being passed in.

9.2 Underlying Types

What if I wanted to declare my own generic type using an underlying type?

Listing 9.4

```
type vector[T any] []T

func (v vector[T]) last() (T, error) {
    var zero T
    if len(v) == 0 {
        return zero, errors.New("empty")
    }
    return v[len(v)-1], nil
}
```

This example shows a generic vector type that restricts the construction of a vector to a single type of data. The use of square brackets declares that type T is a generic type to be determined at compile time. The use of the constraint "any" describes there is no constraint on what type T can become.

The last method is declared with a value receiver of type vector[T] to represent a value of type vector with an underlying slice of some type T. The method returns a value of that same type T.

Listing 9.5

```go
func main() {
    fmt.Print("vector[int] : ")
    vGenInt := vector{10, -1}
    i, err = vGenInt.last()
    if i < 0 {
        fmt.Print("negative integer: ")
    }
    fmt.Printf("value: %d error: %v\n", i, err)

    fmt.Print("vector[string] : ")
    vGenStr := vector{"A", "B", string([]byte{0xff})}
    s, err = vGenStr.last()
    if !utf8.ValidString(s) {
        fmt.Print("non-valid string: ")
    }
    fmt.Printf("value: %q error: %v\n", s, err)
}

Output:
vector[int] : negative integer: value: -1 error: <nil>
vector[string] : non-valid string: value: "\xff" error: <nil>
```

This is how to construct a value of type vector with an underlying type of int when I will set values in the vector at construction. An important aspect of this code is the construction calls.

Listing 9.6

```go
// Zero Value Construction
var vGenInt vector[int]
var vGenStr vector[string]

// Non-Zero Value Construction
vGenInt := vector{10, -1}
vGenStr := vector{"A", "B", string([]byte{0xff})}
```

When it comes to constructing these generic types to their zero value, it's not possible for the compiler to infer the type. However, in cases where there is initialization during construction, the compiler can infer the type.

There is an aspect of the spec that focuses on the construction of a generic type to its zero value state.

Listing 9.7

```go
type vector[T any] []T

func (v vector[T]) last() (T, error) {
    var zero T
    if len(v) == 0 {
        return zero, errors.New("empty")
    }
    return v[len(v)-1], nil
}
```

I need to focus on the method declaration for the last method and how the method

177

returns a value of the generic type T. On the first return is a situation where I need to return the zero value for type T. The current draft provides two solutions to write this code. The first solution I see already. A variable named zero is constructed to its zero value state of type T and then that variable is used for the return.

The other option is to use the built-in function new and dereference the returned pointer within the return statement.

Listing 9.8

```
type vector[T any] []T

func (v vector[T]) last() (T, error) {
    if len(v) == 0 {
        return *new(T), errors.New("empty")
    }
    return v[len(v)-1], nil
}
```

This version of the last method is using the built-in function new for zero value construction and dereferencing of the returned pointer to satisfy return type T.

Note: I might think why not use T{} to perform zero value construction? The problem is this syntax does not work with all types, such as the scalar types (int, string, bool). So it's not an option.

9.3 Struct Types

What if I wanted to declare my own generic type using a struct type?

Listing 9.9

```
type node[T any] struct {
    Data T
    next *node[T]
    prev *node[T]
}
```

This struct type is declared to represent a node for the linked list. Each node contains an individual piece of data that is stored and managed by the list. The use of square brackets declares that type T is a generic type to be determined at compile time. The use of the constraint "any" describes there is no constraint on what type T can become.

With type T declared, the Data field can now be defined as a field of some type T to be determined later. The next and prev fields need to point to a node of that same type T. These are the pointers to the next and previous node in the linked list, respectively. To make this connection, the fields are declared as pointers to a node that is bound to type T through the use of the square brackets.

Listing 9.10

```
type list[T any] struct {
    first *node[T]
    last  *node[T]
}
```

The second struct type is named list and represents a collection of nodes by pointing to the first and last node in a list. These fields need to point to a node of some type T, just like the next and prev fields from the node type.

Once again, the identifier T is defined as a generic type (to be determined later) that can be substituted for "any" concrete type. Then the first and last fields are declared as pointers to a node of some type T using the square bracket syntax.

Listing 9.11

```
func (l *list[T]) add(data T) *node[T] {
    n := node[T]{
        Data: data,
        prev: l.last,
    }
    if l.first == nil {
        l.first = &n
        l.last = &n
        return &n
    }
    l.last.next = &n
    l.last = &n
    return &n
}
```

This is an implementation of a method named add for the list type. No formal generic type list declaration is required (as with functions) since the method is bound to the list through the receiver. The add method's receiver is declared as a pointer to a list of some type T and the return is declared as a pointer to a node of the same type T.

The code after the construction of a node will always be the same, regardless of what type of data is being stored in the list since that is just pointer manipulation. It's only the construction of a new node that is affected by the type of data that will be managed. Thanks to generics, the construction of a node can be bound to type T which gets substituted later at compile time.

Without generics, this entire method would need to be duplicated since the construction of a node would need to be hard coded to a known, declared type prior to compilation. Since the amount of code (for the entire list implementation) that needs to change for different data types is very small, being able to declare a node and list to manage data of some type T reduces the cost of code duplication and maintenance.

Listing 9.12

```
type user struct {
    name string
}

func main() {

    // Store values of type user into the list.
    var lv list[user]
    n1 := lv.add(user{"bill"})
    n2 := lv.add(user{"ale"})
    fmt.Println(n1.Data, n2.Data)

    // Store pointers of type user into the list.
    var lp list[*user]
    n3 := lp.add(&user{"bill"})
    n4 := lp.add(&user{"ale"})
    fmt.Println(n3.Data, n4.Data)
}

Output:
{bill} {ale}
&{bill} &{ale}
```

Here is a small application. A type named user is declared and then a list is constructed to its zero value state to manage values of type user. A second list is then constructed to its zero value state and this list manages pointers to values of type user. The only difference between these two lists is one manages values of type user and the other pointers of type user.

Since type user is explicitly specified during the construction of the list type, the add method in turn accepts values of type user. Since a pointer of type user is explicitly specified during the construction of the list type, the add method accepts pointers of type user.

I can see in the output of the program, the Data field for the nodes in the respective lists match the data semantic used in the construction.

9.4 Behavior As Constraint
Every generic type requires a constraint to be declared so the compiler knows what concrete type substitutions it can accept or reject at compile time. This is required even if there is no real constraint on what the generic type can be, hence the predeclared constraint identifier any.

Interesting enough, the concept of a constraint already exists in the language.

Listing 9.13

```
type User struct {
    name string
}
func (u User) String() string {
    return u.name
}

type Stringer interface {
    String() string
}

func Concrete(u User) {
    u.String()
}

func Polymorphic(s Stringer) {
    s.String()
}
```

The code defines a concrete type named User and implements a method named String that returns the user's name. Then an interface type is declared named Stringer, which declares one act of behavior String, which returns a string. Thanks to the method declared for User, I can say that the concrete type User implements the Stringer interface using value semantics.

The Concrete function is just that, a function that accepts concrete data based on what it is. The Polymorphic is just that as well, a function that accepts concrete data based on what it can do. This is the primary difference between a concrete and polymorphic function. One is limited to one type of data, the other isn't. However, there is a constraint on what concrete data can be passed into the polymorphic function.

The Stringer interface defines that constraint by declaring a method set of behavior that concrete data must be able to exhibit. When applied as the input type, the compiler can guarantee the behavioral constraint is met every time the function is called.

There are generic functions that will require the same type of behavioral constraint.

Listing 9.14

```
func stringify[T fmt.Stringer](slice []T) []string {
    ret := make([]string, 0, len(slice))
    for _, value := range slice {
        ret = append(ret, value.String())
    }
    return ret
}
```

Here is the generic function stringify. It accepts a slice of some type T and returns a slice of string values that contain a stringified version of each value from the input collection. The key to making this function work is the method call to String against each value of type T.

The problem is that the compiler needs to know and verify that values of type T do have a method named String. When the generic type T is declared, the fmt.Stringer interface is provided as the constraint. The compiler now knows to check any type substitution and data being passed into the function for this method set of behavior.

This is excellent because the interface is being used again for the same purpose and the language doesn't need a new keyword.

9.5 Type As Constraint

Generic functions create a new type of constraint that can't be resolved by declaring a method set of behavior.

Listing 9.15

```
func Add[T ???](v1 T, v2 T) T {
    return v1 + v2
}
```

Here is a generic function that wants to accept two values of some type T, add them together, and then return the sum back to the caller. This is an interesting problem because the compiler needs to constrain the call to the function for only values that can be used in an add operation. Currently there is no mechanic for declaring this kind of constraint.

The decision was to continue to use the interface to declare the constraint and add something new.

Listing 9.16

```
type addOnly interface {
    type string, int, int8, int16, int32, int64, float64
}
```

I can declare an interface that defines a set of types that form the constraint. Then apply this interface to the generic function.

Listing 9.17

```
func Add[T addOnly](v1 T, v2 T) T {
    return v1 + v2
}
```

Now the compiler can validate that the set of types is compliant with the operations the function needs to perform against values of those types. When the interface is using the built-in types, the interfaces are reusable across packages. When the list of types represent user-defined types from the package, I must remember these generic functions are bound to the packages types and nothing more.

Interfaces declared with a set of types can't be used in a traditional polymorphic function. This wouldn't make sense anyway, but it's something that doesn't feel like Go in the sense that this change to the interface is not orthogonal.

One idea is to have pre-declared identifiers for common operation constraints.

Listing 9.18

```
func index[T comparable](list []T, find T) int {
    for i, v := range list {
        if v == find {
            return i
        }
    }
    return -1
}
```

The comparable constraint is declared by the language and applies a constraint that types must be capable of being used in a comparison statement. In this example, both v and find are variables of type T and are being compared. There is an idea that a package in the standard library could provide a common set of constraints as well.

There is no restriction on an interface being declared with both a set of types and a method set of behavior.

Listing 9.19

```
type matcher[T any] interface {
    type person, food
    match(v T) bool
}

func match[T matcher[T]](list []T, find T) int {
    for i, v := range list {
        if v.match(find) {
            return i
        }
    }
    return -1
}
```

A generic interface is declared where T is the type of value to be passed into a method named match. The interface also constrains its use to only values of user-defined type person and food.

When I look at the match function, there isn't an obvious need to restrict the function to just the person and food types. If this is the case, the match function should be a traditional polymorphic function, not a generic function. If there was a good reason, a generic function can be used to apply this type of constraint.

183

As a side note, I am not sure this functionality is necessary or makes sense. This is something the community will need to figure out over time.

9.6 Multi-Type Parameters

I'm not restricted to using just one generic type at a time.

Listing 9.20

```
func Print[L any, V fmt.Stringer](labels []L, vals []V) {
    for i, v := range vals {
        fmt.Println(labels[i], v.String())
    }
}
```

The Print function accepts a collection of some type L and a collection of some type V. Type L can be anything, but type V is constrained to values that know how to String. The collection of some type V is iterated over and printed with the corresponding label from the collection of type L.

The name of the generic type can be anything. The naming convention for generic types is something that needs to be better defined for best practices. For now, I try to stick to single letter capital letters when it works for readability.

9.7 Field Access

This is an interesting aspect of generics that I believe can add real value in situations where declaring a method set of behavior would be overkill.

Listing 9.21

```
type User struct {
    ID      int64
    Name    string
    Email   string
}

type Customer struct {
    ID      int64
    Name    string
    Email   string
}
```

Here are two concrete types that each represent data to be inserted into a database. I write an individual function for each type to perform the insert, which is what I want to do.

Listing 9.22

```
func InsertUser(db *sql.DB, u User) (User, error) {
    const query = "insert into users (name, email) values ($1, $2)"
    result, err := ExecuteQuery(query, u.Name, u.Email)
    if err != nil {
        return User{}, err
    }

    id, err := result.LastInsertId()
    if err != nil {
        return User{}, err
    }

    u.ID = id
    return u, nil
}

func InsertCustomer(db *sql.DB, c Customer) (Customer, error) {
    const query = "insert into customers (name, email) values ($1, $2)"
    result, err := ExecuteQuery(query, c.Name, c.Email)
    if err != nil {
        return Customer{}, err
    }

    id, err := result.LastInsertId()
    if err != nil {
        return Customer{}, err
    }

    c.ID = id
    return c, nil
}
```

On close inspection, the difference between the two implementations ends up being a query string and the setting of the ID field. If the setting of the ID field could be done in a generic way, I could move the bulk of the code out to a generic function.

Listing 9.23

```
type entities interface {
    type User, Customer
}
```

I define a new interface named entities that represent the collection of the user-defined types I have.

Listing 9.24

```go
func insert[T entities](db *sql.DB, entity T, query string,
args ...interface{}) (T, error) {
    var zero T

    result, err := ExecuteQuery(query, args...)
    if err != nil {
        return zero, err
    }

    id, err := result.LastInsertId()
    if err != nil {
        return zero, err
    }

    entity.ID = id
    return entity, nil
}
```

Then I write a generic insert function that defines one generic type T to represent the entity being passed in. The key to this generic function is that the compiler can accept the assignment of the id value to the entity.ID field. This is because the interface restricts the concrete types to those that all have an ID field. The compiler can see that.

Listing 9.25

```go
func InsertUser(db *sql.DB, u User) (User, error) {
    const query = "insert into users (name, email) values ($1, $2)"
    u, err := insert(db, u, query, u.Name, u.Email)
    if err != nil {
        return User{}, err
    }
    return u, nil
}

func InsertCustomer(db *sql.DB, c Customer) (Customer, error) {
    const query = "insert into customers (name, email) values ($1, $2)"
    c, err := insert(db, c, query, c.Name, c.Email)
    if err != nil {
        return Customer{}, err
    }
    return c, nil
}
```

Now I change the implementation of the two insert functions, keeping the query string here and passing everything else into the generic insert function for processing.

Without this functionality, the only solution would be adding a SetID method against the concrete types to assign the id. That would result in a setter based interface and code that bloats the solution. I prefer to not use setters and getters.

9.8 Slice Constraints

There may be a time where I define a user-defined slice based on an underlying type.

Listing 9.26

```
type Numbers []int
```

Here the user-defined Numbers type has an underlying type that is a slice of integers. The compiler allows me to convert variables based on a slice of integers with variables of type Numbers. This is usually good and what I want.

Because of this functionality, I can write a generic function that can operate on a slice respecting the underlying type.

Listing 9.27

```
type operateFunc[T any] func(t T) T

func operate[T any](slice []T, fn operateFunc[T]) []T {
    ret := make([]T, len(slice))
    for i, v := range slice {
        ret[i] = fn(v)
    }
    return ret
}
```

Here the operate function declares a generic type T that can be anything. The type is used to declare a parameter named slice that accepts a slice of that same type T. The function also accepts a generic function of the same type T and returns a slice of T as well.

Listing 9.28

```
type Numbers []int

func Double(n Numbers) Numbers {
    fn := func(n int) int {
        return 2 * n
    }

    numbers := operate(n, fn)
    fmt.Printf("%T", numbers)
    return numbers
}

Output:
[]int
```

The Double function accepts a value of type Numbers and passes that value to the operate function. In this case, the compiler leverages the underlying type in for type T and the Numbers value can be passed into the function. However, what is returned is a slice of type int, as seen in the output.

If I need to make sure that only a Numbers value can be passed in, and is returned by the operate function, I can make the following changes.

Listing 9.29

```
type Slice[T any] interface {
    type []T
}
```

This interface declares a constraint to restrict a generic type to an actual slice of some type T. With this interface, I can change the operate function.

Listing 9.29

```
type operateFunc[T any] func(t T) T

type Slice[T any] interface {
    type []T
}

// func operate[T any](slice []T, fn operateFunc[T]) []T {
//     ret := make([]T, len(slice))
//     for i, v := range slice {
//         ret[i] = fn(v)
//     }
//     return ret
// }

func operate[S Slice[T], T any](slice S, fn operateFunc[T]) S {
    ret := make(S, len(slice))
    for i, v := range slice {
        ret[i] = fn(v)
    }
    return ret
}
```

I change the operate function to declare two generic types. Type S which represents a slice value of some type T, and T which is a type that can be anything. The function returns a value of type S.

Listing 9.30

```
type Numbers []int

func Double(n Numbers) Numbers {
    fn := func(n int) int {
        return 2 * n
    }

    numbers := operate(n, fn)
    fmt.Printf("%T", numbers)
    return numbers
}

// Output:
main.Numbers
```

This time when I pass the Numbers value into the operate function, the slice that is returned is of type Numbers. The underlying type is ignored and the user-defined type is respected.

9.9 Channels

I wanted to explore how the Go team could add a package of concurrency patterns into the standard library thanks to generics. This would require declaring channels and functions using generic types.

Listing 9.31

```
type workFn[Result any] func(context.Context) Result
```

In this example, I declare a type that represents a function which accepts a context and returns a value of generic type Result. This function declaration describes a function that implements the concurrent work that will be performed and the result of that work.

Listing 9.32

```
func doWork[Result any](ctx context.Context, work workFn[Result]) chan
Result {
    ch := make(chan Result, 1)

    go func() {
        ch <- work(ctx)
        fmt.Println("doWork : work complete")
    }()

    return ch
}
```

Now I write a function named doWork that executes the specified work function concurrently and returns a channel so the caller can receive the result of the work performed by the work function. A generic type named Result is declared to represent the return type for the work function and the type for the channel.

In the implementation of the doWork function, a buffered channel of one is constructed of generic type Result. That's the channel returned to the caller to receive the result of the concurrent work. In the middle of the function, a goroutine is constructed to execute the work function concurrently. Once the work function returns, the return argument is sent back to the caller through the channel.

To test the use of the doWork function, I built a small program.

Listing 9.33

```
func main() {
    duration := 100 * time.Millisecond
    ctx, cancel := context.WithTimeout(context.Background(), duration)
    defer cancel()

    dwf := func(ctx context.Context) string {
        time.Sleep(time.Duration(rand.Intn(200)) * time.Millisecond)
        return "work complete"
    }
    result := doWork(ctx, dwf)

    select {
    case v := <-result:
        fmt.Println("main:", v)
    case <-ctx.Done():
        fmt.Println("main: timeout")
    }
}

Output:
doWork : work complete
main: work complete
```

The program starts by declaring a context that will timeout in 100 milliseconds. Then a work function is declared that waits for up to 200 milliseconds before returning the string, "work complete". With the context and the work function in place, a call to doWork is made and a channel of type string is returned and assigned to the variable result.

The compiler is able to determine the concrete type to use for the generic type Result by inspecting the return type of the literal work function that is passed into the doWork function. This is brilliant because it means I didn't have to pass the type in on the call to doWork.

With the channel of type string assigned to the variable result, a select case is used to wait for the result to be returned on time, or for the timeout to occur. The doWork function can be used to perform this concurrent work for any concrete type required.

This same idea could be applied to a pool of goroutines that could execute work on a generic input and return a generic result.

Listing 9.34

```
type workFn[Input any, Result any] func(input Input) Result
```

In this example, I changed the function type to accept a generic input and return a generic result.

190

Listing 9.35

```go
func poolWork[Input any, Result any](
    size int,
    work workFn[Input, Result],
) (chan Input, func()) {

    var wg sync.WaitGroup
    wg.Add(size)

    ch := make(chan Input)

    for i := 0; i < size; i++ {
        go func() {
            defer wg.Done()
            for input := range ch {
                result := work(input)
                fmt.Println("pollWork :", result)
            }
        }()
    }

    cancel := func() {
        close(ch)
        wg.Wait()
    }

    return ch, cancel
}
```

In the poolWork function, the same two generic types are declared to represent the input and return type for the work function. A WaitGroup is constructed to manage the lifecycle of the Goroutines in the pool. Then a channel is constructed of the generic Input type. This channel is used by the Goroutines in the pool to receive the input data for the work function.

Then the pool of Goroutines are created with each Goroutine waiting in a receive operation using a for-range loop against the channel. Finally, a cancel function is constructed to allow the caller to shutdown the pool and wait for all the Goroutines to signal they have terminated.

To test the use of the poolWork function, I built a second small program.

Listing 9.36

```
func main() {
    size := runtime.GOMAXPROCS(0)
    pwf := func(input int) string {
        time.Sleep(time.Duration(rand.Intn(200)) * time.Millisecond)
        return fmt.Sprintf("%d : received", input)
    }

    ch, cancel := poolWork(size, pwf)
    defer cancel()

    for i := 0; i < 4; i++ {
        ch <- i
    }
}

Output:
pollWork : 3 : received
pollWork : 2 : received
pollWork : 1 : received
pollWork : 0 : received
```

The size of the pool is calculated based on the number of Goroutines that can run in parallel. Then a work function is constructed to sleep for a random amount of time and then return a string that represents the input.

With that in place, the poolWork function is executed and the channel and cancel function returned. The cancel function is deferred and a loop is constructed to send 4 values into the pool. The output will be different each time I run the program since this work is happening concurrently.

These little examples provide some insight into how a concurrent package could be implemented.

9.10 Hash Tables

A hash table is a classic example of a container type that can take real advantage of generics. This implementation was coded by Matt Layher (@mdlayer) in a blog post he wrote. I think it's a great example of what is possible with generics.

This code is a bit more complex than what I have so far. It's what I think I can expect to see from real world implementations. Throughout this section, I will provide two views of the code. One before and after applying the new syntax for generics. I think this is the best way to write generic code in Go.

Listing 9.37

```
type hashFunc func(key K, buckets int) int
```

This type declares a hash function signature that is used by the hash table to calculate a bucket position for data storage and retrieval. The user must implement and provide this function when constructing a hash table. The function accepts a key and the number of buckets it can choose from. Since I want this system to be generic in terms of the types used for the key and value, I declare a parameter named key with a type of the single capital letter K.

Next, I can apply the generics syntax to make K an actual generic type.

Listing 9.38

```
type hashFunc[K comparable] func(key K, buckets int) int      <-- CHANGED
```

After the type name, I add the square brackets with the generic type K and a constraint of comparable. Since values of the key type need to be used in a compare operation, I feel like documenting this now makes sense, even if the implementation of the hash function doesn't require it. Consistency is everything in terms of readability, comprehension, and maintainability over time.

This type represents a key/value pair of data that will be stored by the hash table.

Listing 9.39

```
type keyValuePair struct {
    Key   K
    Value V
}
```

The job of this type is to hold the actual data with the corresponding key. I declared a key field of type K, and a value field of type V.

Now I can apply the generics syntax to make K and V an actual generic type.

Listing 9.40

```
type keyValuePair[K comparable, V any] struct {      <-- CHANGED
    Key   K
    Value V
}
```

After the type name, I add the square brackets with the generic types K and V. In this declaration, K represents the key as before and V represents a value, which can be anything.

This type represents a hash table that manages a hash function and a set of buckets for key/value data storage.

Listing 9.41

```
type Table struct {
    hashFunc hashFunc
    buckets  int
    data     [][]keyValuePair
}
```

The Table type has three fields, a hash function, the number of buckets, and the data which is represented as a slice of a slice of key/value pairs. The outer slice represents buckets and the inner slice represents key/value pairs that are stored inside a bucket.

Now I can apply the generics syntax to declare the key and value generic types and apply them to the field declarations.

Listing 9.42

```
type Table[K comparable, V any] struct {      <-- CHANGED
    hashFunc  hashFunc[K]                      <-- CHANGED
    buckets   int
    data      [][]keyValuePair[K, V]           <-- CHANGED
}
```

After the type name, I add the square brackets with the generic types K and V. The hashFunc type declaration requires information about the concrete type to use for the key. The keyValuePair type declaration requires information about the concrete type for the key and value.

This is a factory function that can construct a Table for use.

Listing 9.43

```
func New(
    buckets int,
    hf hashFunc,
) *Table {
    return &Table{
        hashFunc: hf,
        buckets:  buckets,
        data:     make([][]keyValuePair, buckets),
    }
}
```

The factory function accepts the number of buckets to manage and a hash function for selecting a bucket for data storage and lookup. When a Table value is constructed, the number of buckets is used to construct the slice, setting the length of the outer slice to the number of buckets that will be used.

Now I can apply the generics syntax to declare the key and value generic types and apply them to the types that need to be constructed.

Listing 9.44

```
func New[K comparable, V any](                              <-- CHANGED
    buckets int,
    hf hashFunc[K],                                         <-- CHANGED
) *Table[K, V] {                                            <-- CHANGED
    return &Table[K, V]{                                    <-- CHANGED
        hashFunc: hf,
        buckets:  buckets,
        data:     make([][]keyValuePair[K, V], buckets),    <-- CHANGED
    }
}
```

After the type name, I add the square brackets and the generic types K and V. Then K is applied to the hf input parameter to complete the hashFunc type declaration. The K and V types are applied to the Table type being constructed and returned. Finally, the initialization of the data field requires K and V to be applied to the construction syntax for the keyValuePair type.

This is a method that can insert values into the hash table based on a specified key.

Listing 9.45

```
type Table[K comparable, V any] struct {
    hashFunc hashFunc[K]
    buckets  int
    table    [][]keyValuePair[K, V]
}

func (t *Table) Insert(key K, value V) {
    bucket := t.hashFunc(key, t.buckets)

    for idx, kvp := range t.table[bucket] {
        if key == kvp.Key {
            t.table[bucket][idx].Value = value
            return
        }
    }

    kvp := keyValuePair{
        Key:   key,
        Value: value,
    }
    t.table[bucket] = append(t.table[bucket], kvp)
}
```

The Insert method is declared to accept a key and value of the same generic types that are declared with the Table type. The first step of inserting is to identify the bucket to use for storage. That is performed by calling the hash function with the specified key. The hash function returns an integer value that represents the bucket to use.

Then the function checks to see if the specified key has already been used to store a value in the selected bucket. This is performed by ranging over the existing set of key/value pairs in the bucket. If the key already exists, the value for that key is updated. If the key is not found, then a new key/value pair value is constructed, initialized, and appended to the slice for the selected bucket.

Now I can apply the generics syntax to declare the key and value generic types and apply them to the types that need to be constructed.

Listing 9.46

```
func (t *Table[K, V]) Insert(key K, value V) {          <-- CHANGED
    bucket := t.hashFunc(key, t.buckets)
    for idx, kvp := range t.table[bucket] {
        if key == kvp.Key {
            t.table[bucket][idx].Value = value
            return
        }
    }

    kvp := keyValuePair[K, V]{                          <-- CHANGED
        Key:    key,
        Value:  value,
    }
    t.table[bucket] = append(t.table[bucket], kvp)
}
```

After the type name in the receiver, I add the square brackets and the generic types K and V. The only other change is to apply K and V to the construction syntax of the keyValuePair type.

This is a method that can retrieve values from the hash table based on a specified key.

Listing 9.47

```
func (t *Table) Retrieve(key K) (V, bool) {
    bucket := t.hashFunc(key, t.buckets)

    for idx, kvp := range t.data[bucket] {
        if key == kvp.Key {
            return t.data[bucket][idx].Value, true
        }
    }

    var zero V
    return zero, false
}
```

The Retrieve method is declared to accept a key and return a copy of the value stored for that key. The first step of retrieving is to identify the bucket that was used for storage. That is performed by calling the hash function with the specified key. The hash function returns an integer value that represents the bucket to look at.

Then the function iterates over the collection of key/value pairs stored inside the bucket, looking for the specified key one by one. If the key is found, a copy of the value is returned and true is provided to the caller. If the key is not found, zero value is returned and false is provided to the caller.

Now I can apply the generics syntax to declare the key and value generic types and apply them to the types that need to be constructed.

Listing 9.48

```
func (t *Table[K, V]) Get(key K) (V, bool) {              <-- CHANGED
    bucket := t.hashFunc(key, t.buckets)
    for idx, kvp := range t.data[bucket] {
        if key == kvp.Key {
            return t.data[bucket][idx].Value, true
        }
    }

    var zero V
    return zero, false
}
```

After the type name in the receiver, I add the square brackets and the generic types K and V. No other code changes are required.

This is a small program to test the hash table implementation.

Listing 9.49

```
func main() {
    const buckets = 8

    . . .

}
```

I start with a constant that defines the number of buckets to use in the hash table.

Listing 9.50

```
import (
    "hash/fnv"
)

func main() {
    . . .

    hashFunc1 := func(key string, buckets int) int {
        h := fnv.New32()
        h.Write([]byte(key))
        return int(h.Sum32()) % buckets
    }

    . . .

}
```

Next, I declare a hash function that declares a string for the key. The implementation uses the fnv package from the standard library which implements the FNV-1 and FNV-1a, non-cryptographic hash functions created by Glenn Fowler, Landon Curt Noll, and Phong Vo. FNV stands for the Fowler-Noll-Vo hash function.

The modulus operation with the buckets value forces the final value to fall within the range for the number of buckets.

Listing 9.51

```
import (
    "hash/fnv"
)

func main() {
    . . .

    table1 := New[/*key*/ string, /*value*/ int](buckets, hashFunc1)

    . . .
}
```

Next, I construct a hash table, explicitly stating that the key will be of type string and the value of type int. There is nothing in the input parameters that can help the compiler infer this information.

To show the nature of the hash table being generic, I defined a second hash function and table.

Listing 9.52

```
import (
    "hash/fnv"
)

func main() {
    . . .

    hashFunc2 := func(key int, buckets int) int {
        return key % buckets
    }
    table2 := New[/*key*/ int, /*value*/ string](buckets, hashFunc2)

    . . .
}
```

This hash function declares an integer for the key and performs a simple modulus operation with the bucket value against the key. Then a new table is constructed where the key is specified to be an integer and the value a string. The reverse of the first table.

Listing 9.53

```
import (
    "hash/fnv"
)

func main() {
    . . .

    words := []string{"foo", "bar", "baz"}
    for i, word := range words {
        table1.Insert(word, i)
        table2.Insert(i, word)
    }

    for i, s := range append(words, "nope!") {
        v1, ok1 := table1.Retrieve(s)
        fmt.Printf("t1.Rtr(%v) = (%v, %v)\n", s, v1, ok1)

        v2, ok2 := table2.Retrieve(i)
        fmt.Printf("t2.Rtr(%v) = (%v, %v)\n", i, v2, ok2)
    }
}

Output:
t1.Rtr(foo) = (0, true)
t2.Rtr(0) = (foo, true)
t1.Rtr(bar) = (1, true)
t2.Rtr(1) = (bar, true)
t1.Rtr(baz) = (2, true)
t2.Rtr(2) = (baz, true)
t1.Rtr(nope!) = (0, false)
t2.Rtr(3) = (, false)
```

Finally I can write some code to store and retrieve values from the two respective tables.

Chapter 10: Profiling

In this chapter, I will learn how to profile code using benchmarks. Even though I will be generating profiles from a benchmark, a lot of what is shared can be used regardless of how the profile is generated.

10.1 Introduction

I can use the go tooling to inspect and profile my programs. Profiling is both a journey and detective work. It requires some understanding about the application and expectations. The profiling data in and of itself is just raw numbers. I have to give it meaning and understanding.

10.1.1 The Basics of Profiling

"Those who can make you believe absurdities can make you commit atrocities" - Voltaire

How does a profiler work?

A profiler runs my program and configures the operating system to interrupt it at regular intervals. This is done by sending SIGPROF to the program being profiled, which suspends and transfers execution to the profiler. The profiler then grabs the program counter for each executing thread and then continues running the program.

Profiling do's and don'ts

Before I profile, I must have a stable environment to get repeatable results.

- The machine must be idle—don't profile on shared hardware, don't browse the web while waiting for a long benchmark to run.
- Watch out for power saving and thermal scaling.
- Avoid virtual machines and shared cloud hosting; they are too noisy for consistent measurements.

If I can afford it, buy dedicated performance test hardware. Rack them, disable all the power management and thermal scaling and never update the software on those machines. If I can't, have a before and after sample and run them multiple times to get consistent results.

10.1.2 Types of Profiling

There are several types of profiling I can perform in Go.

CPU profiling

CPU profiling is the most common type of profile. When CPU profiling is enabled, the runtime will interrupt itself every ~10ms and record the stack trace of the currently running Goroutines. Once the profile is saved to disk, we can analyze it to

200

determine the hottest code paths. The more times a function appears in the profile, the more time that code path is taking as a percentage of the total runtime.

Memory profiling

Memory profiling records the stack trace when a heap allocation is made. Memory profiling, like CPU profiling, is sample based. By default, samples are profiled at 1 alloc for every 512kb. This rate can be changed. Stack allocations are assumed to be free and are not tracked in the memory profile. Because memory profiling is sample based and because it tracks allocations not used, using memory profiling to determine my application's overall memory usage is difficult.

Blocking profiling

Blocking profiling is quite unique. A block profile is similar to a CPU profile, but it records the amount of time a Goroutine spent waiting for a shared resource. This can be useful for determining concurrency bottlenecks in my application. Blocking profiling can show me when a large number of Goroutines could make progress, but were blocked.

Blocking includes:
- Sending or receiving on an unbuffered channel.
- Sending to a full channel, receiving from an empty one.
- Trying to Lock a sync.Mutex that is locked by another Goroutine.
- Block profiling is a very specialized tool, it should not be used until I believe I've eliminated all my CPU and memory usage bottlenecks.

One profile at at time

Profiling is not free. Profiling has a moderate, but measurable impact on program performance—especially if I increase the memory profile sample rate. Most tools will not stop me from enabling multiple profiles at once. If I enable multiple profiles at the same time, they will observe their own interactions and skew my results.

Do not enable more than one kind of profile at a time.

10.1.3 Hints to interpret what I see in the profile

If I see lots of time spent in runtime.mallocgc function, the program potentially makes an excessive amount of small memory allocations. The profile will tell me where the allocations are coming from. See the memory profiler section for suggestions on how to optimize this case.

If lots of time is spent in channel operations, sync.Mutex code and other synchronization primitives or system components, the program probably suffers from contention. Consider restructuring the program to eliminate frequently accessed shared resources. Common techniques for this include sharding/partitioning, local buffering/batching and copy-on-write technique.

If lots of time is spent in syscall.Read/Write, the program potentially makes an excessive amount of small reads and writes. Bufio wrappers around os.File or net.Conn can help in this case.

If lots of time is spent in the GC component, the program either allocates too many transient objects or the heap size is very small so garbage collections happen too frequently.

- Large objects affect memory consumption and GC pacing, while large numbers of tiny allocations affect marking speed.
- Combine values into larger values. This will reduce the number of memory allocations (faster) and also reduce pressure on the garbage collector (faster garbage collections).
- Values that do not contain any pointers are not scanned by the garbage collector. Removing pointers from actively used values can positively impact garbage collection time.

10.1.4 Rules of Performance

Basic rules around performance.

1. Never guess about performance.
2. Measurements must be relevant.
3. Profile before I decide something is performance critical.
4. Test to know I'm correct.

10.1.5 Go and OS Tooling

time program

The time command provides information that can help me get a sense how my program is performing.

Perf program

If I'm on linux, then perf(1) is a great tool for profiling applications. Since Go has frame pointers, perf can profile Go applications.

```
     7026.140760 task-clock (msec)         #      1.283 CPUs utilized
           1,665 context-switches          #      0.237 K/sec
              39 cpu-migrations            #      0.006 K/sec
          77,362 page-faults               #      0.011 M/sec
  21,769,537,949 cycles                    #      3.098 GHz                   [83.41%]
  11,671,235,864 stalled-cycles-frontend   #     53.61% frontend cycles idle [83.31%]
   6,839,727,058 stalled-cycles-backend    #     31.42% backend  cycles idle [66.65%]
  27,157,950,447 instructions              #      1.25  insns per cycle
                                           #      0.43  stalled cycles per insn [83.25%]
   5,351,057,260 branches                  #    761.593 M/sec                 [83.49%]
     118,150,150 branch-misses             #      2.21% of all branches       [83.15%]

     5.476816754 seconds time elapsed
```

10.2 Example Code

I have a program that takes a stream of data looking for the name elvis with a lowercase e. If that name is found in the stream, the name is corrected by replacing the lowercase e with a capital E.

Listing 10.1

```
var data = []struct {
    input  []byte
    output []byte
}{
    {[]byte("abc"), []byte("abc")},
    {[]byte("elvis"), []byte("Elvis")},
    {[]byte("aElvis"), []byte("aElvis")},
    {[]byte("abcelvis"), []byte("abcElvis")},
    {[]byte("eelvis"), []byte("eElvis")},
    {[]byte("aelvis"), []byte("aElvis")},
    {[]byte("aabeeeelvis"), []byte("aabeeeElvis")},
    {[]byte("e l v i s"), []byte("e l v i s")},
    {[]byte("aa bb e l v i saa"), []byte("aa bb e l v i saa")},
    {[]byte(" elvi s"), []byte(" elvi s")},
    {[]byte("elvielvis"), []byte("elviElvis")},
    {[]byte("elvielvielviselvi1"), []byte("elvielviElviselvi1")},
    {[]byte("elvielviselvis"), []byte("elviElvisElvis")},
}
```

This is a data table that represents the potential data from the stream. It lays out the input stream and the expected output stream.

Listing 10.2

```
func assembleInputStream() []byte {
    var in []byte
    for _, d := range data {
        in = append(in, d.input...)
    }
    return in
}

func assembleOutputStream() []byte {
    var out []byte
    for _, d := range data {
        out = append(out, d.output...)
    }
    return out
}
```

These functions assemble the input and output into a single stream for processing. With this in place, here is an algorithm I wrote to solve the problem.

Listing 10.3

```go
func algOne(data []byte, find []byte, repl []byte, output *bytes.Buffer) {
    input := bytes.NewBuffer(data)
    size := len(find)
    buf := make([]byte, size)
    end := size - 1

    if n, err := io.ReadFull(input, buf[:end]); err != nil {
        output.Write(buf[:n])
        return
    }

    for {
        if _, err := io.ReadFull(input, buf[end:]); err != nil {
            output.Write(buf[:end])
            return
        }

        if bytes.Equal(buf, find) {
            output.Write(repl)
            if n, err := io.ReadFull(input, buf[:end]); err != nil {
                output.Write(buf[:n])
                return
            }
            continue
        }

        output.WriteByte(buf[0])
        copy(buf, buf[1:])
    }
}
```

My algorithm is based on the idea of creating a buffer of 5 bytes and comparing those 5 bytes with the lowercase version of elvis. If there is a match, then the uppercase version of Elvis is sent through the output stream. If there is no match, the first byte of the buffer is sliced off and a new byte from the input stream is added to the end of the buffer. Then those 5 bytes are compared again.

Luckily, my friend Tyler took the time to provide a different implementation that solves the same problem.

Listing 10.4

```go
func algTwo(data []byte, find []byte, repl []byte, output *bytes.Buffer) {
    input := bytes.NewReader(data)
    size := len(find)
    idx := 0

    for {
        b, err := input.ReadByte()
        if err != nil {
            break
        }

        if b == find[idx] {
            idx++
            if idx == size {
                output.Write(repl)
                idx = 0
            }
            continue
        }

        if idx != 0 {
            output.Write(find[:idx])
            input.UnreadByte()
            idx = 0
            continue
        }

        output.WriteByte(b)
        idx = 0
    }
}
```

Tyler's algorithm is based on the idea of reading one byte at a time out of the input stream and comparing that byte with the lowercase version of elvis based on a moving index. The algorithm starts with the index at zero, which means the first byte out of the input stream is compared with the lowercase e in elvis. If there is a match, the index is incremented so the next byte pulled from the input stream can be compared to the letter l, and so on, and so on.

If there are five matches in a row, the lowercase version of elvis is found and the uppercase version of Elvis is sent through the output stream. If there is no match, the index is reset to zero, the last byte is unread, the process starts over again. I found this solution by Tyler really cool.

10.3 Benchmarking

With the two algorithms in place that solve the same exact problem in two different ways, the next step is to write benchmark functions to compare the two algorithms.

205

Listing 10.5

```
var output bytes.Buffer
var in = assembleInputStream()
var find = []byte("elvis")
var repl = []byte("Elvis")

func BenchmarkAlgorithmOne(b *testing.B) {
    for i := 0; i < b.N; i++ {
        output.Reset()
        algOne(in, find, repl, &output)
    }
}

func BenchmarkAlgorithmTwo(b *testing.B) {
    for i := 0; i < b.N; i++ {
        output.Reset()
        algTwo(in, find, repl, &output)
    }
}
```

With the benchmark functions in place, I can now compare the two algorithms using the testing tool. I will add the -benchmem flag so the tooling reports allocations.

Listing 10.6

```
$ go test -bench . -benchtime 3s -benchmem

goos: darwin
goarch: amd64
pkg: github.com/ardanlabs/gotraining/topics/go/profiling/memcpu
cpu: Intel(R) Core(TM) i9-9980HK CPU @ 2.40GHz

BenchmarkAlgorithmOne-16    2120113    1594 ns/op    53 B/op    2 allocs/op
BenchmarkAlgorithmTwo-16    9103246    387.7 ns/op    0 B/op    0 allocs/op

PASS
ok
```

I see two things in the results. First, Tyler's algorithm is roughly 4 times faster than mine. Second, Tyler wrote a zero allocation algorithm and mine is allocating two values on the heap worth a total of 52 bytes.

At this point, I want to find and remove those two values allocating on the heap with the hope that maybe my algorithm will be as fast or at least closer to the same performance as Tyler's algorithm. To find these allocations, I need a memory profile.

10.4 Memory Profiling

To generate a memory profile I need to add the -memprofile flag to the go test call.

Listing 10.7

```
$ go test -bench . -benchtime 3s -benchmem -memprofile p.out

goos: darwin
goarch: amd64
pkg: github.com/ardanlabs/gotraining/topics/go/profiling/memcpu
cpu: Intel(R) Core(TM) i9-9980HK CPU @ 2.40GHz

BenchmarkAlgorithmOne-16    2260207    1566 ns/op    53 B/op    2 allocs/op
BenchmarkAlgorithmTwo-16    8515495   422.5 ns/op     0 B/op    0 allocs/op

PASS
ok
```

The output doesn't change, but I do end up with two new files in the local directory.

Listing 10.8

```
$ ls -la

drwxr-xr-x    7 bill    staff    224B May  7 10:59 .
drwxr-xr-x   14 bill    staff    448B Jan  4 08:16 ..
-rw-r--r--    1 bill    staff    2.3K Apr 28 09:09 README.md
-rwxr-xr-x    1 bill    staff    3.0M May  7 10:59 memcpu.test
-rw-r--r--    1 bill    staff    488B May  7 10:59 p.out
-rw-r--r--    1 bill    staff    4.6K Apr 30 15:56 stream.go
-rw-r--r--    1 bill    staff    773B Apr 28 09:09 stream_test.go
```

I can see a p.out file that is fairly small at 488 bytes. This is the memory profile data I requested with the -memprofile flag. There is also a file named memcpu.test. This is the test binary that was built by the compiler to run the benchmarks. When I ask for a memory profile, the test binary is not removed after the benchmark is run. This is so extra information can be provided by the profile tooling.

Go has a profiling tool that I can use to review the profile data.

Listing 10.9

```
$ go tool pprof memcpu.test p.out

File: memcpu.test
Type: alloc_space
Time: May 7, 2021 at 10:59am (CDT)

Entering interactive mode (type "help" for commands, "o" for options)
(pprof)
```

I'm using the terminal based profile tooling, however if I want to use the browser version of the tooling, I just need to add the -http flag with a port number.

Listing 10.10

```
$ go tool pprof -http :8080 memcpu.test p.out
```

For now I will stay in the terminal window. Since I know which function is allocating,

I can ask the tool to provide information specific about the algOne function using the list command.

Listing 10.11

```
(pprof) list algOne

Total: 167.51MB
    12.50MB     167.51MB (flat, cum)    100% of Total
          .            .    78:
          .            .    79:// algOne is one way to solve the problem.
          .            .    80:func algOne(data []byte, find []byte, repl
          .            .    81:
          .     155.01MB    83: input := bytes.NewBuffer(data)
          .            .    84:
          .            .    85: // The number of bytes we are looking for.
          .            .    86: size := len(find)
          .            .    87:
          .            .    88: // Declare the buffers we need to process the
    12.50MB      12.50MB    89: buf := make([]byte, size)
          .            .    90: end := size - 1
          .            .    91:
          .            .    92: // Read in an initial number of bytes we need
          .            .    93: if n, err := io.ReadFull(input, buf[:end]);
          .            .    94:     output.Write(buf[:n])
(pprof)
```

The list command gives me a detailed view of a function and takes a regular expression to find the functions I want to see. Thanks to the list command, I can see there is an allocation happening on line 83 and on line 89.

Listing 10.12

```
    12.50MB  |    167.51MB  | (flat, cum)    100% of Total
-----------|-----------|-----------------------------------------------------------
         .  |   155.01MB  |   83: input := bytes.NewBuffer(data)
    12.50MB  |    12.50MB  |   89: buf := make([]byte, size)
(pprof)
```

At closer inspection I see there are two columns in the report. The first column represents flat allocations and the second represents cumulative allocations. Flat means the value allocated to the heap is represented on that line of code. Cumulative means the values allocating to the heap are represented inside the call chain originating from that function call.

I was looking for two allocations and it seems lines 83 and 89 contain the construction points for the two values allocating in the heap. That's only part of the story. I still don't know why and the profile can never tell me this.

Before I begin to try and understand why the values allocated, I want to see this same list view in the browser. I can do this by using the weblist command.

Listing 10.13

```
(pprof) weblist algOne
```

The weblist command is similar to the list command except it brings up the browser tooling.

Figure 10.1

File: memcpu.test
Type: alloc_space
Time: May 7, 2021 at 10:59am (CDT)
Total: 167.51MB

github.com/ardanlabs/gotraining/topics/go/profiling/memcpu.algOne

/Users/bill/code/go/src/github.com/ardanlabs/gotraining/topics/go/profiling/memcpu/stream.go

```
  Total:    167.51MB    167.51MB (flat, cum)    100%
     75           .           .                      matched = bytes.Compare(out, output.Bytes())
     76           .           .                      fmt.Printf("Matched: %v\nInp: [%s]\nExp: [%s]\nGot: [%s]\n", matched =
     77           .           .                  }
     78           .           .
     79           .           .                  // algOne is one way to solve the problem.
     80           .           .                  func algOne(data []byte, find []byte, repl []byte, output *bytes.Buffer) {
     81           .           .
     82           .           .                      // Use a bytes Buffer to provide a stream to process.
     83      155.01MB    155.01MB                     input := bytes.NewBuffer(data)
     84           .           .
     85           .           .                      // The number of bytes we are looking for.
     86           .           .                      size := len(find)
     87           .           .
     88           .           .                      // Declare the buffers we need to process the stream.
     89       12.50MB     12.50MB                     buf := make([]byte, size)
     90           .           .                      end := size - 1
     91           .           .
```

This is the browser based tool showing the same list output. One reason to use the browser over the terminal is when I include the test binary. This allows me to see the list output down to the assembly level.

Figure 10.2

```
     87           .           .
     88           .           .                      // Declare the buffers we need to process the stream.
     89       12.50MB     12.50MB                     buf := make([]byte, size)
                  .           .       110a6a6:            LEAQ type.*+67808(SB), AX
                  .           .       110a6ad:            MOVQ AX, 0(SP)
                  .           .       110a6b1:            MOVQ 0x90(SP), AX
                  .           .       110a6b9:            MOVQ AX, 0x8(SP)
                  .           .       110a6be:            MOVQ AX, 0x10(SP)
              12.50MB     12.50MB     110a6c3:            CALL runtime.makeslice(SB)
                  .           .       110a6c8:            MOVQ 0x18(SP), AX
                                          ⋮
                  .           .       110a6e9:            MOVQ AX, 0x50(SP)
```

When I click on the code at line 89, the assembly behind that line of code is shown. This only works when I provide the test binary.

If I look closer at the list output from the browser, I notice a difference from the terminal view. That is, the allocation on line 83 is a flat allocation.

209

Figure 10.3

```
82                .              .              // Use a bytes Buffer to provid
83      155.01MB     155.01MB                    input := bytes.NewBuffer(data)
84                .              .
```

See how the first column shows the same allocation number as the second column. This begs the question, is the allocation flat which means the input variable is being constructed on the heap, or is the allocation cumulative which means the allocation is coming from inside the bytes.NewBuffer function?

From my point of view, the browser view is more accurate because it takes into account an important compiler optimization that took place when the code ran called inlining.

10.5 Inlining

Inlining is an optimization that removes function calls and replaces them with a copy of the code inside the function in question. For some reason the terminal view has inlining turned off.

How can I get the terminal to show the list command with inlining turned on?

Listing 10.14

```
$ go tool pprof --noinlines  memcpu.test p.out
```

I need to add the --noinlines flag to the call to go tool pprof, which is supposed to turn off inlining, but for the terminal view it turns it on.

Listing 10.15

```
(pprof) list algOne

Total: 167.51MB
   167.51MB    167.51MB (flat, cum)    100% of Total
         .           .        78:
         .           .        79:// algOne is one way to solve the problem.
         .           .        80:func algOne(data []byte, find []byte, repl
         .           .        81:
         .           .        82: // Use a bytes Buffer to provide a stream to
   155.01MB    155.01MB        83: input := bytes.NewBuffer(data)
         .           .        84:
         .           .        85: // The number of bytes we are looking for.
         .           .        86: size := len(find)
         .           .        87:
         .           .        88: // Declare the buffers we need to process the
    12.50MB     12.50MB        89: buf := make([]byte, size)
         .           .        90: end := size - 1
         .           .        91:
         .           .        92: // Read in an initial number of bytes we need
         .           .        93: if n, err := io.ReadFull(input, buf[:end]);
         .           .        94:         output.Write(buf[:n])
(pprof)
```

Now the terminal view is showing line 83 as a flat allocation. How does inlining actually work? Start with the bytes.NewBuffer function which we know is being inlined.

Listing 10.16

```
func NewBuffer(buf []byte) *Buffer {
    return &Buffer{buf: buf}
}
```

I can see this is a factory function using pointer semantics. The caller gets shared access to the Buffer value being constructed. If the function is called, then the Buffer would have to be constructed in the heap. This is because of the ownership rule.

Any function that constructs a value, is the owner of that value. If the value needs to exist after the owning function returns, then the value must be constructed in the heap.

If the function can be inlined, the ownership of the construction moves up to the calling function. This means the algOne function owns the construction of Buffer.

Listing 10.17

```
func algOne() {

    // Before inlining
    input := bytes.NewBuffer(data)       <-- Original Call

    // After inlining
    input := &bytes.Buffer{buf: data}    <-- After Inlining Optimization
}
```

I can see that after the inlining optimization, the algOne function becomes the owner of the construction of the Buffer value, not the NewBuffer function. Therefore, the value doesn't need to escape to the heap unless the value still needs to exist after the algOne function returns.

It's important to note that Tyler's algorithm is a zero allocation algorithm in part thanks to the same inlining optimization.

Listing 10.18

```
func algOne() {

    // Before inlining
    input := bytes.NewReader(data)       <-- Original Call

    // After inlining
    input := &bytes.Reader{buf: data}    <-- After Inlining Optimization
}
```

Since the NewReader function is inlined, the construction of the Reader value is owned by Tyler's algorithm. Somehow Tyler is not doing anything in algTwo that is causing the Reader value to escape, where I am doing something in algOne with the Buffer value.

10.6 Escape Analysis

How do I know inlining is absolutely happening and I still don't know why algOne is causing allocations where algTwo is zero allocation? Only one tool can tell me the why and that's the compiler. The compiler is making the decision using the escape analysis algorithm.

Luckily, the compiler builds the test binary before anything runs so I can ask the compiler to generate an escape analysis report before running the benchmark.

Listing 10.19

```
$ go test -bench . -benchtime 3s -benchmem -memprofile p.out -gcflags -m=2
```

I added -gcflags -m=2 as flags on the call to go test. This produces an escape analysis report before running the benchmark.

Listing 10.20

```
./stream.go:83:26: inlining call to bytes.NewBuffer func([]byte)
*bytes.Buffer { return &bytes.Buffer{...} }

./stream.go:83:26: &bytes.Buffer{...} escapes to heap:
./stream.go:83:26:    flow: ~R0 = &{storage for &bytes.Buffer{...}}:
./stream.go:83:26:        from &bytes.Buffer{...} (spill) at ./stream.go:83:26
./stream.go:83:26:        from ~R0 = <N> (assign-pair) at ./stream.go:83:26
./stream.go:83:26:    flow: input = ~R0:
./stream.go:83:26:        from input := (*bytes.Buffer)(~R0) (assign) at
./stream.go:83:8
./stream.go:83:26:    flow: io.r = input:
./stream.go:83:26:        from input (interface-converted) at
./stream.go:113:28
./stream.go:83:26:        from io.r, io.buf := input, buf[:end] (assign-pair)
at ./stream.go:113:28
./stream.go:83:26:    flow: {heap} = io.r:
./stream.go:83:26:        from io.ReadAtLeast(io.r, io.buf, len(io.buf)) (call
parameter) at ./stream.go:113:28
```

These are the lines in the escape analysis report related to line 83 from the list output. The very first line states the compiler is choosing to inline the call to bytes.NewBuffer. This is the proof I wanted to be absolutely sure the bytes.NewBuffer function was being inlined.

How does the compiler decide what functions can be inlined or not?

Listing 10.21

```
./stream.go:80:6: cannot inline algOne: function too complex: cost 636
exceeds budget 80

./stream.go:131:6: cannot inline algTwo: function too complex: cost 315
exceeds budget 80
```

Here are two lines from the report that show the scoring for the algOne and algTwo functions. I can see both functions scored above 80 points and therefore are not a candidate for inlining. The compiler uses a complex scoring system to determine if a function can be inlined and every function is scored.

The code for the inlining algorithm can be found in the inl.go file that is part of the compiler.

https://github.com/golang/go/blob/master/src/cmd/compile/internal/inline/inl.go

How can I almost guarantee a factory function like NewBuffer or NewReader will score under 80? I need to make it a leaf function. In other words, make sure no other function calls are made so the call tree ends with the factory function.

Now I absolutely know the algOne function owns the construction of the bytes.Buffer value. I still don't know why the input variable has allocated, especially since it doesn't need to exist after the algOne function returns.

I need to look at the escape analysis report for more information.

Listing 10.22

```
./stream.go:83:26: &bytes.Buffer{...} escapes to heap:
./stream.go:83:26:    flow: ~R0 = &{storage for &bytes.Buffer{...}}:
./stream.go:83:26:      from &bytes.Buffer{...} (spill) at ./stream.go:83:26
./stream.go:83:26:      from ~R0 = <N> (assign-pair) at ./stream.go:83:26
./stream.go:83:26:    flow: input = ~R0:
./stream.go:83:26:      from input := (*bytes.Buffer)(~R0) (assign) at
./stream.go:83:8
./stream.go:83:26:    flow: io.r = input:
./stream.go:83:26:      from input (interface-converted) at
./stream.go:113:28
./stream.go:83:26:      from io.r, io.buf := input, buf[:end] (assign-pair)
at ./stream.go:113:28
./stream.go:83:26:    flow: {heap} = io.r:
./stream.go:83:26:      from io.ReadAtLeast(io.r, io.buf, len(io.buf)) (call
parameter) at ./stream.go:113:28
```

This section of the report has the final why. It's sharing information about the construction of the bytes.Buffer on line 83 where the function was inlined.

Listing 10.23

```
flow: io.r = input:
  from input (interface-converted) at ./stream.go:113:28
  from io.r, io.buf := input, buf[:end] (assign-pair) at ./stream.go:113:28
```

An interface conversion at line 113 seems to be the reason. What code is on line 113?

Listing 10.24

```
113 if n, err := io.ReadFull(input, buf[:end]); err != nil {
114     output.Write(buf[:n])
115     return
116 }
```

It's the call to io.ReadFull and I can see the input variable is being passed into the function as the first parameter. Passing a value down the call stack doesn't create an allocation so what's different about this call? I need to look at the io.ReadFull function.

Listing 10.25

```
func ReadFull(r Reader, buf []byte) (n int, err error) {
    return ReadAtLeast(r, buf, len(buf))
}
```

I can see the io.ReadFull function is a polymorphic function. It's accepting the input value being passed not based on what it is, but on what it does. It's using the io.Reader interface to accept the data. That's the reason behind the "interface-converted" and "assign-pair" message in the report.

Tyler is not using the io package but the method set of the input variable, and he's getting the inline optimization as well. This explains why Tyler doesn't have an allocation. So if I want to get rid of this allocation on line 83, I need to stop using the io package and switch to the method set.

Listing 10.26

```
func algOne(data []byte, find []byte, repl []byte, output *bytes.Buffer) {
    input := bytes.NewBuffer(data)
    size := len(find)
    buf := make([]byte, size)
    end := size - 1

    if n, err := input.Read(buf[:end]); err != nil {                <-- REPLACED
        output.Write(buf[:n])
        return
    }

    for {
        var err error
        buf[end:][0], err = input.ReadByte()                        <-- REPLACED
        if err != nil {
            output.Write(buf[:end])
            return
        }

        if bytes.Equal(buf, find) {
            output.Write(repl)
            if n, err := input.Read(buf[:end]); err != nil {    <-- REPLACED
                output.Write(buf[:n])
                return
            }
            continue
        }

        output.WriteByte(buf[0])
        copy(buf, buf[1:])
    }
}
```

I have replaced the three calls using the io package for methods against the input variable. This should remove the allocation on line 83.

Listing 10.27

```
$ go test -bench . -benchtime 3s -benchmem -memprofile p.out -gcflags -m=2

goos: darwin
goarch: amd64
pkg: github.com/ardanlabs/gotraining/topics/go/profiling/memcpu
cpu: Intel(R) Core(TM) i9-9980HK CPU @ 2.40GHz

BenchmarkAlgorithmOne-16      3658340    975.3 ns/op    5 B/op    1 allocs/op
BenchmarkAlgorithmTwo-16      9730435    377.6 ns/op    0 B/op    0 allocs/op

PASS
ok
```

Sure enough I am down to 1 allocation worth 5 bytes. Where is this last 5 bytes allocating from? Time to use the list command again to see the line number and then inspect the escape analysis report.

Listing 10.28

```
$ go tool pprof -noinlines p.out

(pprof) list algOne
       20MB         20MB (flat, cum)     100% of Total
          .            .      83:
          .            .      84: // The number of bytes we are looking for.
          .            .      85: size := len(find)
          .            .      86:
          .            .      87: // Declare the buffers we need to process the
       20MB         20MB      88: buf := make([]byte, size)
          .            .      89: end := size - 1
          .            .      90:
          .            .      91: // Read in an initial number of bytes we need
          .            .      92: if n, err := input.Read(buf[:end]); err != nil
          .            .      93:         output.Write(buf[:n])
```

The final allocation is on line 88 related to the construction of the slice value.

Listing 10.29

```
./stream.go:88:13: make([]byte, size) escapes to heap:
./stream.go:88:13:    flow: {heap} = &{storage for make([]byte, size)}:
./stream.go:88:13:      from make([]byte, size) (non-constant size) at
./stream.go:88:13
```

The report is stating "non-constant size" which means the compiler doesn't know the size of the backing array at compile time. This can be fixed if I hard code the value of 5 on the call to make. If I only ever search for a 5 byte string, then I'll have no problems with this change. Hahahaha!

Listing 10.30

```
func algOne(data []byte, find []byte, repl []byte, output *bytes.Buffer) {
    input := bytes.NewBuffer(data)
    size := len(find)
    buf := make([]byte, 5)      <-- REPLACED

    . . .
}
```

After changing out the size variable for the literal number 5 on the call to make, does the allocation go away?

Listing 10.31

```
$ go test -bench . -benchtime 3s -benchmem -memprofile p.out -gcflags -m=2

goos: darwin
goarch: amd64
pkg: github.com/ardanlabs/gotraining/topics/go/profiling/memcpu
cpu: Intel(R) Core(TM) i9-9980HK CPU @ 2.40GHz

BenchmarkAlgorithmOne-16     4129378     868.5 ns/op     0 B/op     0 allocs/op
BenchmarkAlgorithmTwo-16     9716834     376.0 ns/op     0 B/op     0 allocs/op

PASS
ok
```

Now I have a zero allocation algorithm. However, Tyler's algorithm is still faster than mine. The next thing I can do is run a cpu profile to possibly find some inefficient code that can be changed.

Listing 10.32

```
$ go test -bench . -benchtime 3s -benchmem -cpuprofile p.out

goos: darwin
goarch: amd64
pkg: github.com/ardanlabs/gotraining/topics/go/profiling/memcpu
cpu: Intel(R) Core(TM) i9-9980HK CPU @ 2.40GHz

BenchmarkAlgorithmOne-16     4079672     906.4 ns/op     0 B/op     0 allocs/op
BenchmarkAlgorithmTwo-16     8689845     414.3 ns/op     0 B/op     0 allocs/op

PASS
ok
```

By using the -cpuprofile flag instead of the -memprofile flag, I will get a cpu profile.

Listing 10.33

```
$ go tool pprof p.out

Type: cpu
(pprof) list algOne
```

```
     950ms        3.97s (flat, cum) 53.36% of Total
         .            .     87: // Declare the buffers we need to process the
         .            .     88: buf := make([]byte, 5)
         .            .     89: end := size - 1
         .            .     90:
         .            .     91: // Read in an initial number of bytes we need
     110ms        120ms     92: if n, err := input.Read(buf[:end]); err != nil
         .            .     93:         output.Write(buf[:n])
         .            .     94:         return
         .            .     95: }
         .            .     96:
         .            .     97: for {
         .            .     98:
         .            .     99:         // Read in one byte from the input
         .            .    100:         var err error
     310ms        440ms    101:         buf[end:][0], err = input.ReadByte()
         .            .    102:         if err != nil {
         .            .    103:
         .            .    104:             // Flush the reset of the bytes
         .            .    105:             output.Write(buf[:end])
         .            .    106:             return
         .            .    107:         }
         .            .    108:
         .            .    109:         // If we have a match, replace the
         .        1.70s    110:         if bytes.Equal(buf, find) {
     270ms        650ms    111:             output.Write(repl)
         .            .    112:
         .            .    113:             // Read a new initial number of
         .        240ms    114:             if n, err := input.Read(buf[:end])
         .         10ms    115:                 output.Write(buf[:n])
         .            .    116:                 return
         .            .    117:             }
         .            .    118:
         .            .    119:             continue
         .            .    120:         }
         .            .    121:
         .            .    122:         // Write the front byte since it has
     100ms        650ms    123:         output.WriteByte(buf[0])
         .            .    124:
         .            .    125:         // Slice that front byte out.
     160ms        160ms    126:         copy(buf, buf[1:])
         .            .    127: }
         .            .    128:}
         .            .    129:
```

Looks like there is almost four seconds of cumulative time taken in the algOne function and the majority of it is on line 110.

Listing 10.34

```
         .            .    109:         // If we have a match, replace the
         .        1.70s    110:         if bytes.Equal(buf, find) {
     270ms        650ms    111:             output.Write(repl)
```

So if I could find a way to replace the call to bytes.Equal, I could possibly get even closer to the same performance as Tyler's algorithm.

Here is the reality. I should have just gone with Tyler's algorithm from the beginning if that level of performance was really needed. Honestly, my algorithm really wasn't that slow using the io package Read functions. Even after removing the allocations, I'm only looking at a difference of ~500 nanoseconds per operation.

Chapter 11: Profiling Live Code

In this chapter, I will learn how to profile code that is running. This will require the use of the http package in the standard library. It's best I read chapter 10 before reading this chapter. That chapter goes deep into the use of the profile tooling and that knowledge is assumed here.

11.1 Example Code

I have a program that implements a search engine using news feeds as the searchable content. The news feeds are downloaded and cached when the program starts.

This is the code that is being used in this chapter.
https://github.com/ardanlabs/gotraining/tree/master/topics/go/profiling/project

To start, I need to build and run the project.

Listing 11.1

```
$ cd <Cloned Location>/topics/go/profiling/project
$ go build
$ ./project

2021/05/10 11:29:21.616793 service.go:64: Listening on: 0.0.0.0:5000
```

Once the project is running, I can open the browser to run the website by using the URL "localhost:5000/search".

Figure 11.1
http://localhost:5000/search

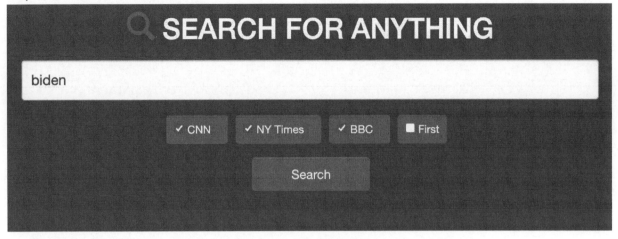

BBC : President Biden's first 100 days as president fact-checked
Joe Biden has been US president for 100 days - we look at claims he has made during his first months.

BBC : Biden speech: Are Americans happy with Biden's first 100 days?
Members of our Ask America panel praise Biden's Covid response but call for more bipartisanship.

NYT : Biden to Address Economy as G.O.P. Takes Aim at Jobless Benefits
The party will hold a vote Wednesday on whether to replace its No. 3 in the House, Representative Liz Cheney, who has drawn criticism for repudiating former President Donald J. Trump's lies about election fraud. President Biden is considering an executive order strengthening cybersecurity for federal agencies and contractors.

This is what the logs look like after running a search for the term "biden".

If I look at the logs, I can see 12 feeds were downloaded and cached from the BBC, CNN, and the NY Times.

Listing 11.2

```
service.go:64: Listening on: 0.0.0.0:5000
rss.go:109: reloaded cache http://feeds.bbci.co.uk/news/rss.xml
rss.go:109: reloaded cache http://feeds.bbci.co.uk/news/world/rss.xml
rss.go:109: reloaded cache http://rss.cnn.com/rss/cnn_topstories.rss
rss.go:109: reloaded cache http://feeds.bbci.co.uk/news/politics/rss.xml
rss.go:109: reloaded cache http://rss.cnn.com/rss/cnn_world.rss
rss.go:109: reloaded cache
http://feeds.bbci.co.uk/news/world/us_and_canada/rss.xml
rss.go:109: reloaded cache http://rss.cnn.com/rss/cnn_us.rss
rss.go:109: reloaded cache http://rss.cnn.com/rss/cnn_allpolitics.rss
rss.go:109: reloaded cache
http://rss.nytimes.com/services/xml/rss/nyt/HomePage.xml
rss.go:109: reloaded cache
http://rss.nytimes.com/services/xml/rss/nyt/US.xml
rss.go:109: reloaded cache
http://rss.nytimes.com/services/xml/rss/nyt/Politics.xml
rss.go:109: reloaded cache
http://rss.nytimes.com/services/xml/rss/nyt/Business.xml
```

One of the first checks that I like to perform is to generate a garbage collection (GC) trace for the program while it's executing a fixed amount of load. This will provide an initial understanding if there is a memory leak and it's nice to gather some stats about how much work the garbage collector is performing.

11.2 Generating a GC Trace

Before I run any load through the program, I want to look at an initial GC trace that is produced from the first search. This is when the feeds are downloaded for the first time. To see a GC trace, I need to use the GODEBUG environment variable when running the project.

Listing 11.3

```
$ GODEBUG=gctrace=1 ./project > /dev/null
```

The GODEBUG variable has several different options, but this is how I can ask the Go runtime to write a trace to stderr each time the GC runs. Since I don't want my logs to compete with the trace output, I'm writing anything being sent to stdout to the /dev/null device.

If I restart the program using these options and hit the search button again, I will see 4 GC's take place.

Listing 11.4

```
gc 1 @95.466s 0%: 0.042+0.54+0.026 ms clock, 0.67+0.32/0.73/0.29+0.43 ms
cpu, 4->4->0 MB, 5 MB goal, 16 P

gc 2 @95.635s 0%: 0.031+0.39+0.029 ms clock, 0.51+0.24/0.80/0.68+0.47 ms
cpu, 4->4->1 MB, 5 MB goal, 16 P

gc 3 @95.707s 0%: 0.047+0.40+0.012 ms clock, 0.76+0.072/0.92/1.0+0.20 ms
cpu, 4->4->1 MB, 5 MB goal, 16 P

gc 4 @95.976s 0%: 0.048+0.47+0.016 ms clock, 0.78+0.13/1.0/1.3+0.25 ms cpu,
4->4->2 MB, 5 MB goal, 16 P
```

Seeing 4 GC's makes sense since the GC will initially run when the first 4 meg of memory is allocated on the heap. Since the program is downloading and caching the feeds, the other 3 GC's happen quickly as the GC tries to keep the heap at 4 meg.

Here is a breakdown of the 4th GC that took place.

Listing 11.5

```
// General     : [gc 4 @95.976s 0%:]
gc 4           : The 4th GC run since the program started
@95.976s       : 95.976 seconds since the program started
0%             : Zero percent of the programs time has been spent in GC

// Wall Clock: [0.048+0.47+0.016 ms clock]
0.048ms        : STW           : Mark Setup        - Write Barrier on
0.47ms         : Concurrent : Marking
0.016ms        : STW           : Mark Termination - Write Barrier off / Clean Up

// CPU Clock : [0.78+0.13/1.0/1.3+0.25 ms cpu]
0.78ms         : STW           : Mark Setup
0.13ms         : Concurrent : Mark - Assist Time
1.0ms          : Concurrent : Mark - Background GC time
1.3ms          : Concurrent : Mark - Idle GC time
0.25ms         : STW           : Mark Termination

// Memory     : [4->4->2 MB]
4MB            : Heap memory in-use before the Marking started
4MB            : Heap memory in-use after the Marking finished
2MB            : Heap memory marked as live after the Marking finished

// Goal       : [5 MB goal]
5MB            : Collection goal for heap memory in-use after Marking finished

// Threads    : [16 P]
16P            : Number of logical P's or threads used to run Goroutines
```

The comments explain what each of the different numbers mean. For my purpose in evaluating potential memory leaks and if the GC is overworking, the memory numbers and the percent of time in GC is what I will evaluate.

11.3 Generating Load And Evaluation

To apply load on the program, I will use a tool named hey. The tool can be found on Github at https://github.com/rakyll/hey.

With the service already started in one terminal, I will run the hey tool in a second terminal to send 10k requests over 100 concurrent connections.

Listing 11.6

```
$ hey -m POST -c 100 -n 10000 "http://localhost:5000/search?
term=biden&cnn=on&bbc=on&nyt=on"
```

Once the load is sent into the program, I will see GC traces flowing. After the last request is processed, the hey tooling provides the results.

Listing 11.7

```
Hey Summary:
  Total:      2.6945  secs
  Slowest:    0.2664  secs
  Fastest:    0.0011  secs
  Average:    0.0248  secs
  Requests/sec:   3711.3009
-----------------------------------------------------------------------
GC Trace (last 4):
gc 837 @181.810s 0%: 0.038+0.64+0.027 ms clock, 0.61+0.24/1.6/2.2+0.44 ms
cpu, 6->7->3 MB, 8 MB goal, 16 P
gc 838 @181.812s 0%: 0.030+0.60+0.052 ms clock, 0.48+0.38/1.3/2.4+0.84 ms
cpu, 6->6->3 MB, 7 MB goal, 16 P
gc 839 @181.815s 0%: 0.044+0.65+0.032 ms clock, 0.71+0.34/1.8/1.3+0.52 ms
cpu, 6->7->3 MB, 7 MB goal, 16 P
gc 840 @181.819s 0%: 0.037+0.56+0.035 ms clock, 0.59+0.14/1.4/2.6+0.56 ms
cpu, 7->7->3 MB, 8 MB goal, 16 P
```

The hey report doesn't seem terribly bad, and neither does the end of the GC trace. It seems that 836 GC's needed to take place to complete the work. I'm subtracting the first 4 GC's that took place before I ran the load. The program was able to process 3711 requests a second, with the slowest request taking 266ms.

I'm confident there is no memory leak since the memory is at 7 meg in use and 3 meg marked live. In fact, if I wait a bit, the GC will force itself to run and I can see if anything is reduced more.

Listing 11.8

```
GC forced
gc 841 @302.003s 0%: 0.072+0.84+0.005 ms clock, 1.1+0/2.4/4.5+0.083 ms cpu,
5->5->3 MB, 6 MB goal, 16 P

GC forced
gc 842 @422.004s 0%: 0.10+1.0+0.004 ms clock, 1.7+0/3.2/3.2+0.077 ms cpu, 3-
>3->2 MB, 6 MB goal, 16 P

GC forced
gc 843 @542.255s 0%: 0.096+1.0+0.004 ms clock, 1.5+0/3.3/4.8+0.071 ms cpu,
2->2->2 MB, 4 MB goal, 16 P
```

I can see after waiting a few minutes, the memory in use on the heap dropped to 2 meg, which matches what is live. This is a good sign of no memory leak.

11.4 Adding Profile Endpoints

With these performance numbers from hey, what I need next is a memory profile that is representative of these 10k requests I sent through the program. Luckily, I can get this profile because I set up a couple things in the code.

Listing 11.9

```
package main

import (
    _ "net/http/pprof" // call init function
)
```

The first thing to do is add this import to the source code file hosting the main function. This import allows the compiler to find an init function in the pprof package that sets debug routes in the default server mux.

Listing 11.10

```
src/net/http/pprof/pprof.go

func init() {
    http.HandleFunc("/debug/pprof/", Index)
    http.HandleFunc("/debug/pprof/cmdline", Cmdline)
    http.HandleFunc("/debug/pprof/profile", Profile)
    http.HandleFunc("/debug/pprof/symbol", Symbol)
    http.HandleFunc("/debug/pprof/trace", Trace)
}
```

Next, I need to bind the default server mux to an ip address and port. I want this to be separate from the application traffic so these endpoints can be protected behind a firewall.

Listing 11.11

```
package main

import (
    _ "net/http/pprof" // call init function
)

func main() {
    debugHost := ":5000"

    . . .

    go func() {
        log.Printf("main: Debug Listening %s", debugHost)
        err := http.ListenAndServe(debugHost, http.DefaultServeMux)
        if err != nil {
            log.Printf("main: Debug Listener closed: %v", err)
        }
    }()

    . . .

}
```

A Goroutine is created to block on the http.ListenAndServe call to handle the debug routes. Since I already set this up before I ran load through the program, I can use the debug/pprof endpoint now to get a memory profile.

Figure 11.2
http://localhost:5000/debug/pprof

/debug/pprof/

Types of profiles available:
Count Profile
200 allocs
0 block
0 cmdline
9 goroutine
200 heap
0 mutex
0 profile
23 threadcreate
0 trace
full goroutine stack dump

Profile Descriptions:

- allocs: A sampling of all past memory allocations
- block: Stack traces that led to blocking on synchronization primitives
- cmdline: The command line invocation of the current program
- goroutine: Stack traces of all current goroutines
- heap: A sampling of memory allocations of live objects. You can specify

There is so much profiling data I can extract from my running program. In this case, I am interested in the heap profile, which is available from the very first link. If I click on the allocs link, I can see what a raw memory profile looks like.

Figure 11.3
http://localhost:5000/debug/pprof/allocs?debug=1

```
heap profile: 7: 59424 [12335: 286125512] @ heap/1048576
1: 40960 [245: 10035200] @ 0x10e2d96 0x10e2cdb 0x10e3c85 0x10e7131 0x10e9595 0x10ed825 0x10e5a38 0x1377385 0x136f0a5 0x136edf
0x13ddc45 0x12caa24 0x12cc9ad 0x13dd658 0x12ce0e3 0x12c950d 0x1072921
#       0x10e2d95       fmt.(*buffer).writeString+0xf5                                                                     /usr/
#       0x10e2cda       fmt.(*fmt).padString+0x3a                                                                          /usr/
#       0x10e3c84       fmt.(*fmt).fmtS+0x64                                                                               /usr/
#       0x10e7130       fmt.(*pp).fmtString+0x130                                                                          /usr/
#       0x10e9594       fmt.(*pp).printArg+0x874                                                                           /usr/
#       0x10ed824       fmt.(*pp).doPrint+0x104                                                                            /usr/
#       0x10e5a37       fmt.Fprint+0x57                                                                                    /usr/
#       0x1377384       text/template.(*state).printValue+0xe4                                                            /usr/
#       0x136f0a4       text/template.(*state).walk+0x3e4                                                                  /usr/
#       0x136edfb       text/template.(*state).walk+0x13b                                                                  /usr/
#       0x136eb05       text/template.(*Template).execute+0x1c5                                                            /usr/
#       0x138d58f       text/template.(*Template).Execute+0x8f                                                             /usr/
#       0x138d556       html/template.(*Template).Execute+0x56                                                             /usr/
#       0x13deee7       github.com/ardanlabs/gotraining/topics/go/profiling/project/service.executeTemplate+0xa7
```

The raw memory profile breaks things down by stack, however at the very top there is some information that's interesting.

Listing 11.12

```
heap profile: 7: 59424 [12335: 286125512] @ heap/1048576

[7]          Currently live objects,
[59424]      Amount of memory occupied by live objects
[12335]      Total number of allocations
[286125512]  Amount of memory occupied by all allocations
```

Those first four numbers represent program wide information for this snapshot of the memory profile. Then for each stack, there is similar information.

Listing 11.13

```
1: 40960 [245: 10035200] @

[1]          Currently live objects,
[40960]      Amount of memory occupied by live objects
[245]        Total number of allocations
[10035200]   Amount of memory occupied by all allocations
```

It's nice to have some understanding of the raw numbers, but this is not a productive way to read the profile data.

11.5 Viewing Memory Profile

I'm going to use the profile tooling as explained in chapter 10 to explore the memory profile. What's cool is I can give the pprof tool the URL to the memory profile and it can use that to read it in.

Listing 11.14

```
$ go tool pprof -noinlines http://localhost:5000/debug/pprof/allocs

Fetching profile over HTTP from http://localhost:5000/debug/pprof/allocs
Type: alloc_space
Time: May 10, 2021 at 1:48pm (CDT)

Entering interactive mode (type "help" for commands, "o" for options)
(pprof)
```

The problem now is I don't know what I'm specifically looking for. I really want to find any low hanging fruit, therefore I will use the top command to get a list of the top 15 functions that are allocating the most memory.

Listing 11.15

```
(pprof) top 15 -cum

Showing nodes accounting for 3300.39MB, 53.67% of 6148.89MB total
Dropped 90 nodes (cum <= 30.74MB)
Showing top 15 nodes out of 47
      flat  flat%   sum%        cum   cum%
         0     0%     0%   3675.30MB 59.77%  net/http.(*conn).serve
  385.68MB  6.27%  6.27%   3653.77MB 59.42%
github.com/ardanlabs/gotraining/topics/go/profiling/project/service.handler
         0     0%  6.27%   3653.77MB 59.42%  github.com/braintree/manners.
(*gracefulHandler).ServeHTTP
         0     0%  6.27%   3653.77MB 59.42%  net/http.(*ServeMux).ServeHTTP
         0     0%  6.27%   3653.77MB 59.42%  net/http.HandlerFunc.ServeHTTP
         0     0%  6.27%   3653.77MB 59.42%  net/http.serverHandler.ServeHTTP
  617.76MB 10.05% 16.32%   3055.01MB 49.68%
github.com/ardanlabs/gotraining/topics/go/profiling/project/service.render
   48.01MB  0.78% 17.10%   2445.06MB 39.76%
github.com/ardanlabs/gotraining/topics/go/profiling/project/search.rssSearch
      1MB 0.016% 17.12%   2437.26MB 39.64%
github.com/ardanlabs/gotraining/topics/go/profiling/project/service.executeT
emplate
         0     0% 17.12%   2436.26MB 39.62%  html/template.
(*Template).Execute
    2.50MB 0.041% 17.16%   2436.26MB 39.62%  text/template.
(*Template).execute
         0     0% 17.16%   2433.76MB 39.58%  text/template.(*state).walk
 2235.93MB 36.36% 53.52%   2393.53MB 38.93%  strings.ToLower
    9.51MB  0.15% 53.67%   2006.99MB 32.64%
github.com/ardanlabs/gotraining/topics/go/profiling/project/search.CNN.Searc
h
         0     0% 53.67%   1935.06MB 31.47%  fmt.Fprint

(pprof)
```

I added the -cum switch to the top command to sort the list by the cumulative
value. Seeing the socket connection and mux at the top of the list makes sense
since all traffic flows through that code. Having the template calls next makes sense
because rendering HTML will produce allocations.

What comes next is the call to the search.rssSearch function.

Listing 11.16

```
      flat  flat%   sum%        cum   cum%
   48.01MB  0.78% 17.10%   2445.06MB 39.76%
github.com/ardanlabs/gotraining/topics/go/profiling/project/search.rssSearch
```

Top is telling me that this function represents 39.76% of the total allocations made
which is worth a total of 2.4 gig. This is a function that I should look closer at.
Maybe I can find some non-productive allocations that could be removed to reduce
the amount of GC that needs to take place to complete this work. If I can reduce
allocations, and therefore reduce the number of GC's, I will get better performance.

I will use the list command to review the search.rssSearch function.

Listing 11.17

```
(pprof) list rssSearch

Total: 6GB
ROUTINE ========================= project/search/rss.go
    48.01MB      2.39GB (flat, cum) 39.76% of Total
    20.50MB     20.50MB       79:    var d Document
          .       3.52MB      102:                 if err := xml.NewDecoder(resp.Bod
          .       2.34GB      119:            if strings.Contains(strings.ToLower(ite
    27.51MB     27.51MB      120:                results = append(results, Result{

(pprof)
```

I've trimmed down the list output to just those lines that are showing allocations. Out of the 2.39 GB of allocation coming from this function, line 119 represents 2.34GB of that. That's the line of code I need to focus on.

Listing 11.18

```
118      for _, item := range d.Channel.Items {
119          if strings.Contains(strings.ToLower(item.Description),
strings.ToLower(term)) {
120              results = append(results, Result{
121                  Engine:  engine,
122                  Title:   item.Title,
123                  Link:    item.Link,
124                  Content: item.Description,
125              })
126          }
127      }
```

When I look at the code on line 119 from the search/rss.go file, I see there is a call to strings.Contains and strings.ToLower inside a loop. That loop is checking if the search term matches against each item description for one specific feed. Since I have 12 feeds, for each request this loop is run 12 separate times.

I know a large number of allocations are happening here on line 119, but how can I tell if it's because of the call to strings.Contains or strings.ToLower. Looking at a call graph that is isolated to the search.rssSearch function will help.

Listing 11.19

```
(pprof) web rssSearch
```

For the call graph to be generated, it's important to make sure Graphviz is installed. This is the website for more information: https://www.graphviz.org/

Figure 11.4

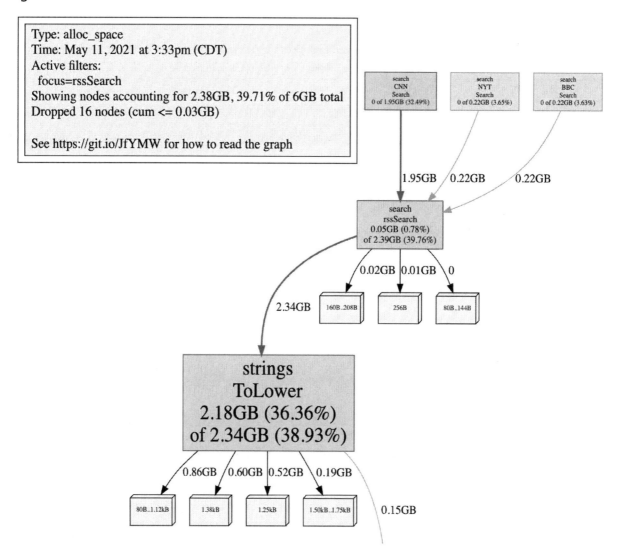

The call graph makes it clear that the call to strings.ToLower is causing all the allocations.

11.6 Removing Allocations
Knowing this, I need to find a way to remove the call to strings.ToLower.

Listing 11.20

```
118     for _, item := range d.Channel.Items {
119         if strings.Contains(strings.ToLower(item.Description),
strings.ToLower(term)) {
120             results = append(results, Result{
121                 Engine:  engine,
122                 Title:   item.Title,
123                 Link:    item.Link,
124                 Content: item.Description,
125             })
126         }
127     }
```

On closer inspection there are two things I can do.

Listing 11.21

```
122        term = strings.ToLower(term)                          <-- ADDED
123
124        for _, item := range d.Channel.Items {
125            if strings.Contains(item.Description, term) {     <-- CHANGED
126                results = append(results, Result{
127                    Engine:  engine,
128                    Title:   item.Title,
129                    Link:    item.Link,
130                    Content: item.Description,
131                })
132            }
133        }
```

First, I move the call to make the term lower outside of the loop. Having that call in the loop was really bad since it was performing the same operation over and over. That was producing a lot of little values on the heap. Second, I removed the call to make the description lower. That still needs to take place, so I moved it up with the code that caches the feeds.

Listing 11.22

```
 93        resp, err := http.Get(uri)
 94        if err != nil {
 95            return []Result{}, err
 96        }
 97        defer resp.Body.Close()
 98
 99        if err := xml.NewDecoder(resp.Body).Decode(&d); err != nil {
100            return []Result{}, err
101        }
102
103        for i := range d.Channel.Items {                      <-- ADDED
104            lower := strings.ToLower(d.Channel.Items[i].Description)
105            d.Channel.Items[i].Description = lower
106        }
107
108        cache.Set(uri, d, expiration)
```

The new code converts the description to lowercase before storing the feed in the cache. This eliminates the need to do this inside the loop. Granted I should create a new field for the lowercase version of the description.

With these changes in place, I can build and run the program again. Then apply the same exact load and get the new results.

Listing 11.23

```
Summary:
  Total:      1.4367 secs
  Slowest:    0.1706 secs
  Fastest:    0.0005 secs
  Average:    0.0131 secs
  Requests/sec:   6960.6340
-----------------------------------------------------------------------
gc 484 @7.989s 4%: 0.038+0.76+0.025 ms clock, 0.62+0.52/1.5/1.8+0.40 ms cpu,
6->7->4 MB, 7 MB goal, 16 P
gc 485 @7.991s 4%: 0.056+0.83+0.094 ms clock, 0.91+0.48/2.3/1.9+1.5 ms cpu,
7->8->4 MB, 9 MB goal, 16 P
gc 486 @7.994s 4%: 0.089+0.65+0.023 ms clock, 1.4+0.55/1.8/1.2+0.38 ms cpu,
7->8->4 MB, 8 MB goal, 16 P
gc 487 @7.996s 4%: 0.041+0.47+0.012 ms clock, 0.65+0.22/1.5/2.0+0.20 ms cpu,
7->8->4 MB, 8 MB goal, 16 P
```

With the code changes there are definite improvements. Now it seems that only 483 GC's needed to take place to complete the work. I'm subtracting the first 4 GC's again that took place before I ran the load. The program was able to process 6960 requests a second, with the slowest request taking 170ms. That's an improvement of 88% on the requests per second.

If I wanted to focus more on a specific function that the top command might present, I can go back to chapter 10 and use benchmarks.

Chapter 12: Tracing

In this chapter, I will be learning how to capture a trace of a running program and view it with the trace tool. In this exercise, I will be generating a trace using the standard library. However a trace can also be generated when running a benchmark or by using the http debug/pprof endpoint.

12.1 Example Code

I have a program that counts the frequency a topic is found in a collection of RSS news feed documents. This program uses a single threaded algorithm named freq that iterates over the collection, processing each document one at a time, and returns the number of times the topic is found.

Listing 12.1

```
func freq(topic string, docs []string) int {
    var found int

    for _, doc := range docs {
        file := fmt.Sprintf("%s.xml", doc[:8])
        f, err := os.OpenFile(file, os.O_RDONLY, 0)
        if err != nil {
            log.Printf("Opening Document [%s] : ERROR : %v", doc, err)
            return 0
        }

        data, err := io.ReadAll(f)
        f.Close()
        if err != nil {
            log.Printf("Reading Document [%s] : ERROR : %v", doc, err)
            return 0
        }

        var d document
        if err := xml.Unmarshal(data, &d); err != nil {
            log.Printf("Decoding Document [%s] : ERROR : %v", doc, err)
            return 0
        }

        for _, item := range d.Channel.Items {
            if strings.Contains(item.Title, topic) {
                found++
                continue
            }

            if strings.Contains(item.Description, topic) {
                found++
            }
        }
    }

    return found
}
```

The freq function breaks the work down into four stages: opening, reading, unmarshaling, and search. To test the freq function, the main function constructs a collection of 4k files and calls freq.

Listing 12.2

```go
type (
    item struct {
        XMLName      xml.Name  `xml:"item"`
        Title        string    `xml:"title"`
        Description  string    `xml:"description"`
    }

    channel struct {
        XMLName xml.Name `xml:"channel"`
        Items   []item   `xml:"item"`
    }

    document struct {
        XMLName xml.Name `xml:"rss"`
        Channel channel  `xml:"channel"`
    }
)

func main() {
    docs := make([]string, 4000)
    for i := range docs {
        docs[i] = fmt.Sprintf("newsfeed-%.4d.xml", i)
    }

    topic := "president"
    n := freq(topic, docs)
    log.Printf("Searching %d files, found %s %d times.", len(docs), topic, n)
}
```

The code that constructs the slice of 4k documents is creating a pretend set of unique files based on a real file I have named newfeed.xml.

Listing 12.3

```xml
newsfeed.xml
<?xml version="1.0" encoding="UTF-8"?>
<?xml-stylesheet title="XSL_formatting" type="text/xsl"?>
<rss>
    <channel>
        <title><![CDATA[BBC News - US & Canada]]></title>
        <description><![CDATA[BBC News - US & Canada]]></description>
        <item>
            <title><![CDATA[President China visit: US leader strik]]></title>
            <description><![CDATA[The US president praises]]></description>
        </item>
    </channel>
</rss>
```

This is a very small sample of the newsfeed.xml file. Instead of keeping 4k actual files, I keep just one file and pretend it represents 4k of them. The freq algorithm strips the extra characters from the file name before opening the file.

It will be good to get an initial idea of how long it takes to process these 4000 files with the single threaded version of freq. I can do that using the time command in conjunction with running the program.

Listing 12.4

```
$ go build
$ time ./trace

2021/05/12 09:30:52 Searching 4000 files, found president 28000 times.
./trace  2.63s user 0.18s system 101% cpu 2.763 total
```

I can see that the program took ~2.7 second to process the 4k files. If I was only going to process 4k files, or maybe even a few thousand more, I'd say this program is done. However, I would like the ability to process a million files and not have it take hours.

I need to figure out a way to speed up this program. I could use a memory profile, but I know this program uses a lot of transient memory and there isn't much I can do about that. I could use a cpu profile, but trust me it's going to tell me I'm spending most of my time in system calls thanks to the call to os.OpenFile.

The problem with using a profiler here is that a profiler can only tell me what is happening. I need to know what is and isn't happening to find a way to speed up this program. When I need to see what is not happening, the trace tooling is a good option.

12.2 Generating Traces

Since this program starts and stops within a few seconds, I can use the standard library to generate a trace of this program. In general, creating traces for more than a few seconds of run time can be overwhelming to review since a trace generates a large amount of data. I want to focus on small, targeted traces.

Listing 12.5

```
import (
    "runtime/trace"                   <-- ADDED
)

func main() {
    trace.Start(os.Stdout)            <-- ADDED
    defer trace.Stop()                <-- ADDED

    docs := make([]string, 4000)
    for i := range docs {
        docs[i] = fmt.Sprintf("newsfeed-%.4d.xml", i)
    }

    topic := "president"
    n := freq(topic, docs)
    log.Printf("Search %d files, found %s %d times.", len(docs), topic, n)
}
```

After adding the trace package into the imports, I can use the trace.Start and Stop

235

functions. Writing the trace to stdout makes it simple to capture and redirect the trace data to a file. Now I can run the program again

Listing 12.6

```
$ go build

$ time ./trace > t.out
2021/05/12 11:57:06 Search 4000 files, found president 28000 times.
./trace > t.out  2.71s user 0.19s system 102% cpu 2.827 total

$ time ./trace > t.out
2021/05/12 11:57:11 Search 4000 files, found president 28000 times.
./trace > t.out  2.73s user 0.18s system 108% cpu 2.683 total

$ ls -l
total 9136
-rw-r--r--  1 bill  staff     2108 Jan  4 08:16 README.md
-rw-r--r--  1 bill  staff    25544 Jan  4 08:16 newsfeed.xml
-rw-r--r--  1 bill  staff  1501618 May 12 11:57 t.out
-rwxr-xr-x  1 bill  staff  2470208 May 12 11:57 trace
-rw-r--r--  1 bill  staff     8135 May 12 11:56 trace.go
```

I always run the program twice to make sure the machine is warmed up. The second run usually runs better than the first and I can see a 144ms difference between these two runs. I can also see the t.out file in the listing has captured ~1.5 meg of data over the 2.6 seconds of run time.

12.3 Viewing Traces

To review the trace, I need to use the trace tool.

Listing 12.7

```
$ go tool trace t.out

2021/05/12 12:00:19 Parsing trace...
2021/05/12 12:00:19 Splitting trace...
2021/05/12 12:00:19 Opening browser. Trace viewer is listening on
http://127.0.0.1:64321
```

Once the file is parsed and split, a browser tab is opened with a set of links.

Figure 12.1

View trace
Goroutine analysis
Network blocking profile (⬇)
Synchronization blocking profile (⬇)
Syscall blocking profile (⬇)
Scheduler latency profile (⬇)
User-defined tasks
User-defined regions
Minimum mutator utilization

I want to choose the first link which will open a Chrome based UI that can present the tracing data. This tooling only works in Chrome.

Figure 12.2

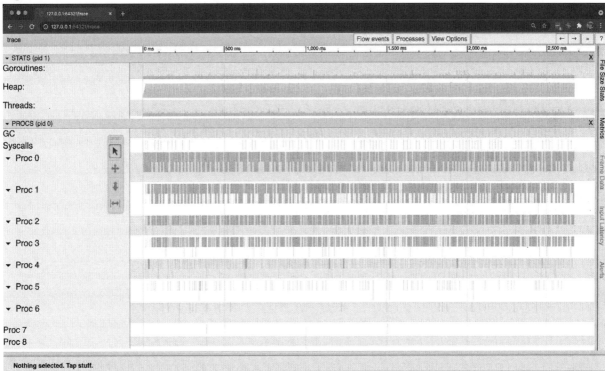

All of the information that is presented is recorded down to the microsecond of when it happened. On the left hand side, I can see the different categories of graphed information.

At any given time in the trace:

- Goroutines: The number of Goroutines.
- Heap: The amount of memory in-use on the heap.
- Threads: The number of operating system threads.
- GC: The start/end of each GC with details.
- Syscalls: The start/end of any system call with details.
- Procs: The activity on each logical processor.

The first thing I should do is measure how long the program ran based on the trace data. I can do that with the timing tool, which is the last tool in the toolbar.

Figure 12.3

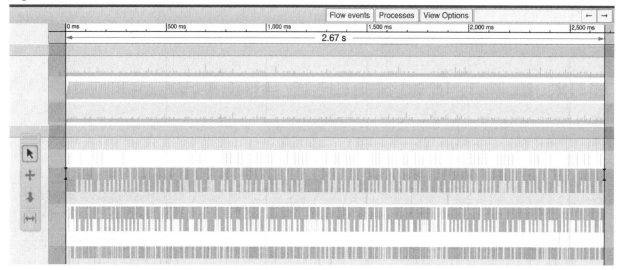

If I select the timeline for the entire trace, I get 2.67 seconds, which is fairly close to what the time command provided. The next thing I want to know is how consistent the size of the heap was maintained and how large the heap grew.

I will expand the view of the graph and then use the selection tool (first tool in the toolbar) to select the top portion of the heap graph.

Figure 12.4

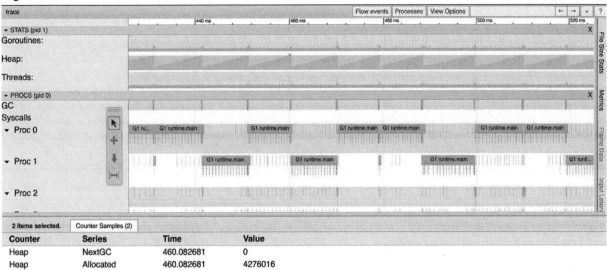

	Counter	Series	Time	Value
	Heap	NextGC	460.082681	0
	Heap	Allocated	460.082681	4276016

There are two colors (or shades) that are represented in the heap graph. Orange (the darker shade) represents the amount of memory in-use on the heap at each microsecond. Green (the lighter shade) represents when the next GC will be triggered based on when that amount of memory is once again in-use on the heap.

Figure 12.5

trace				
	440 ms		460 ms	
▾ STATS (pid 1)				
Goroutines:				
Heap:				
Threads:				
▾ PROCS (pid 0)				
GC				
Syscalls				

2 items selected.	Counter Samples (2)		
Counter	Series	Time	Value
Heap	NextGC	460.082681	0
Heap	Allocated	460.082681	4276016

This is why when the orange area reaches the top of the green area, there is a line in the GC section. Each line represents a GC that took place. BTW, the dot is the selection point for the heap information listed in the figure.

Since the green area is in a consistent straight line for the entire run of the program, I can select any orange point to see the max size of the heap. In this case that is 4 meg of memory.

If I want more clarity on this number, I can use GODEBUG and run the program again.

Listing 12.8

```
$ time GODEBUG=gctrace=1 ./trace > t.out

gc 1 @0.016s 0%: 0.020+0.29+0.024 ms clock, 0.32+0.18/0.12/0.12+0.39 ms cpu,
4->4->0 MB, 5 MB goal, 16 P
gc 2 @0.029s 0%: 0.030+0.23+0.002 ms clock, 0.49+0.15/0.17/0.001+0.037 ms
cpu, 4->4->0 MB, 5 MB goal, 16 P
gc 3 @0.040s 0%: 0.033+0.26+0.019 ms clock, 0.52+0.15/0.15/0.059+0.31 ms
cpu, 4->4->0 MB, 5 MB goal, 16 P
. . .
gc 273 @2.793s 0%: 0.043+0.46+0.040 ms clock, 0.70+0.24/0.18/0.25+0.65 ms
cpu, 4->4->0 MB, 5 MB goal, 16 P
gc 274 @2.804s 0%: 0.043+0.35+0.002 ms clock, 0.69+0.28/0.37/0.16+0.042 ms
cpu, 4->4->0 MB, 5 MB goal, 16 P
gc 275 @2.814s 0%: 0.032+0.28+0.017 ms clock, 0.52+0.20/0.26/0.026+0.28 ms
cpu, 4->4->0 MB, 5 MB goal, 16 P

2021/05/12 15:17:24 Searching 4000 files, found president 28000 times.
```

Sure enough, the heap was maintained at 4 meg and all the memory was transient since each GC resulted in the number of live values to be zero. Exactly what I am seeing in the trace.

What I really need is more information about the GC's. It's not about 1 GC, it's about all the GC's that needed to take place. I can get this information by using the selection tool and double clicking on any blue GC line.

Figure 12.6

These numbers are helpful in determining how much work the GC is doing in the execution of the program. With these numbers I have a baseline for the program's performance.

Table 12.1

	Single
Runtime	2670ms
Top Memory	4 Meg
GC Occurrences	275
GC Avg Duration	387us
GC Wall Duration	106ms
GC Time Spent	4%

With the baseline numbers, I still don't have an answer as to how I could speed up the program. Maybe looking at a larger portion of the graph will help?

Figure 12.7

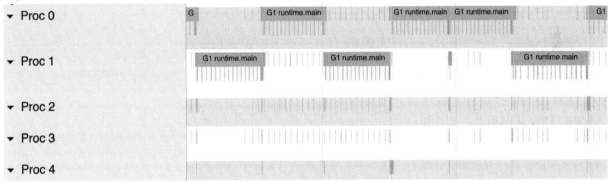

If I look closer at this section of the trace, I can see the problem. The program is only using one logical processor at any given time to execute the application work. The GC however is using more. If I change the algorithm to be concurrent and friendly to using all the available cores on my machine, this should help with the performance.

12.4 Fan-Out

One concurrency pattern I could use is a fan-out pattern. This would allow me to have a concurrent algorithm with the least amount of code change. The idea of this pattern is to create a Goroutine for each file that needs to be processed and let the scheduler manage all the Goroutine, scheduling them across all the logical processors. I can fan-out all these Goroutines because the order of the work doesn't matter. What matters is all the work is performed.

Listing 12.9

```
func freqConcurrent(topic string, docs []string) int {
    var found int

    g := len(docs)                          <-- ADDED
    var wg sync.WaitGroup                    <-- ADDED
    wg.Add(g)                                <-- ADDED

    for _, doc := range docs {
        . . .
    }

    wg.Wait()                                <-- ADDED
    return int
}
```

To start, I need to add code that makes sure the freq function doesn't return until all the work is complete. This is best implemented by using a WaitGroup. I start with identifying how many Goroutines need to be created, which is represented by the length of the docs collection. Then I add that number to the WaitGroup and at the end of the function wait for the WaitGroup to get back down to zero.

Listing 12.10

```
func freqConcurrent(topic string, docs []string) int {
    var found int

    g := len(docs)
    var wg sync.WaitGroup
    wg.Add(g)

    for _, doc := range docs {
        go func(doc string) {              <-- ADDED
            defer wg.Done()                <-- ADDED
            . . .
        }(doc)                             <-- ADDED
    }

    wg.Wait()
    return int
}
```

Next, I wrap the existing code inside the for range loop around a Goroutine, where each document iterated over is passed into the new Goroutine to prevent any closure bugs. With the Goroutine in place, I can finalize the WaitGroup code by making sure each Goroutine calls wg.Done() right before it terminates.

The last thing I need to do is remove the return value of 0 from all the error conditions inside the loop when processing a file. I might think this code is ready since all the orchestration with the WaitGroup is in place, but what happens if I run this code with the race detector?

Listing 12.11

```
$ go build -race
$ ./trace > t.out

==================
WARNING: DATA RACE
Read at 0x00c000157548 by goroutine 21:
  main.freq.func1()
      /Users/bill/code/go/src/github.com/ardanlabs/gotraining/topics/go/
profiling/trace/trace.go:103 +0x644

Previous write at 0x00c000157548 by goroutine 66:
  main.freq.func1()
      /Users/bill/code/go/src/github.com/ardanlabs/gotraining/topics/go/
profiling/trace/trace.go:103 +0x65d


. . .
==================
```

Looks like I have a data race. The first two lines in the output says there is a read and a previous write to the same memory location on the same line of code inside the literal function. What code is on line 103?

Listing 12.12

```
 96 for _, item := range d.Channel.Items {
 97     if strings.Contains(item.Title, topic) {
 98         found++
 99         continue
100     }
101
102     if strings.Contains(item.Description, topic) {
103         found++
104     }
105 }
```

If I add the line numbers to the code, I can see it's related to the increment of the found variable. This code is actually used again on line 98, so both lines of code (98, 103) contain a data race.

To fix this data race I need to change the increment of the found variable to use an atomic instruction. To do this I can use the atomic package.

Listing 12.12

```
 96 for _, item := range d.Channel.Items {
 97     if strings.Contains(item.Title, topic) {
 98         atomic.AddInt32(&found, 1)                    <-- CHANGED
 99         continue
100     }
101
102     if strings.Contains(item.Description, topic) {
103         atomic.AddInt32(&found, 1)                    <-- CHANGED
104     }
105 }
```

I have replaced lines 98 and 103 to use the atomic.AddInt32 function. The problem is this function requires an int32 not an int, so I need to make two more changes.

Listing 12.13

```
func freq(topic string, docs []string) int {
    var found int32           <-- CHANGED

    . . .

    wg.Wait()
    return int(found)          <-- CHANGED
}
```

These changes are necessary to use the atomic.AddInt32 function and still return an integer. With these changes, the data race will be gone. However, there is still another problem with the code. It's not as cache friendly as it otherwise could be.

12.5 Cache Friendly

The problem is with the found variable. It's technically a global variable to the 4k Goroutines that will be accessing that memory. Though using the atomic package helps to serialize access, each core on my machine that is executing Goroutines will receive and operate on its own copy of the found variable. The moment any copy inside of any core is incremented, it will mark all the other copies in all the other cores dirty.

When the next Goroutine goes to increment their copy, and that copy is marked dirty, a fresh copy needs to be pulled from main memory. This will result in the thrashing of memory, slowing everything down. Over 8 cores and 4k files, this thrashing may not result in much of a performance hit. When I run this on 128 cores over 1MM files, this thrashing will take its toll.

To alleviate the thrashing I need each Goroutine to use a local variable for counting the number of times the term is found. However, before the Goroutine terminates it must add the result of it's local variable to the global variable. For the current algorithm, that means we reduce the thrashing from 28k times to 4k times. Not perfect, but much better.

Listing 12.14

```go
func freq(topic string, docs []string) int {
    var found int32

    g := len(docs)
    var wg sync.WaitGroup
    wg.Add(g)

    for _, doc := range docs {
        go func(doc string) {
            var lFound int32                        <-- ADDED
            defer func() {                          <-- CHANGED
                atomic.AddInt32(&found, lFound)     <-- MOVED
                wg.Done()                           <-- MOVED
            }()

            . . .

            for _, item := range d.Channel.Items {
                if strings.Contains(item.Title, topic) {
                    lFound++                         <-- CHANGED
                    continue
                }

                if strings.Contains(item.Description, topic) {
                    lFound++                         <-- CHANGED
                }
            }
        }(doc)
    }

    wg.Wait()
    return int(found)
}
```

I added a new variable named lFound to represent a found variable that is local to every Goroutine. This means that I can remove the atomic.AddInt32 calls from inside the loop that searches for topic matches. Since I still have to update the global found variable, I do that inside the defer before I call wg.Done.

12.6 Fan-Out Results

With these changes in place, I can try the new fan-out based concurrent algorithm.

Listing 12.15

```
$ go build

$ time ./trace > t.out
2021/05/13 12:10:51 Search 4000 files, found president 28000 times.
./trace > t.out  7.30s user 0.71s system 1106% cpu 0.725 total

$ time ./trace > t.out
2021/05/13 12:10:53 Search 4000 files, found president 28000 times.
./trace > t.out  7.21s user 0.76s system 1297% cpu 0.615 total
```

I can already see from the time command a performance improvement of 2 seconds. Now I can look at the trace.

Figure 12.8

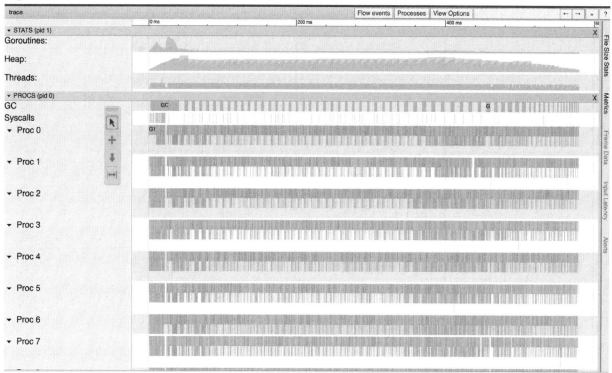

This is a good sign that all of the cpu capacity on my machine is being used. If I scroll down, I will see all 16 logical processors are in use. I need to gather all the measurements for this algorithm.

Table 12.2

	Single	**Fan-Out**
Runtime	2670ms	580ms
Top Memory	4 Meg	53 Meg
GC Occurrences	275	62
GC Avg Duration	387us	4ms
GC Wall Duration	106ms	250ms
GC Time Spent	4%	43%

I can see there is a 2 second performance improvement, but that came with an order of magnitude more memory and time spent in GC. However, the number of GC's was reduced by 113 because of the larger memory profile.

There are a few other interesting aspects of this trace.

Figure 12.9

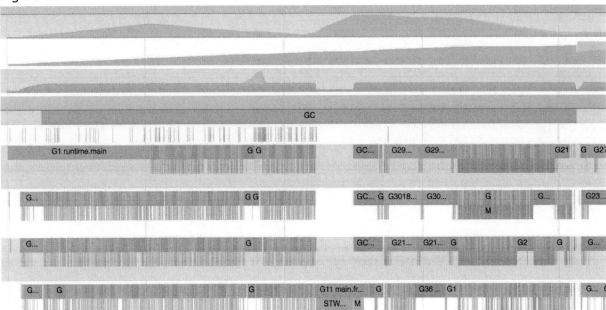

I am looking at the first 45ms of time where all 4k Goroutines had a chance to run and be put into a waiting state by the scheduler. I can see how dense the context switches are and how the Mark Setup (STW Sweep Termination) phase starts in the middle of the GC. It means that it took ~19ms before the GC attempted to stop all the application work so the marking phase could be started.

In the top area of the graph that shows Goroutines, I can see large peeks of Goroutines in running and runnable states throughout the first GC. If I were to expand a part of this view, I will see the context switches more clearly.

Figure 12.10

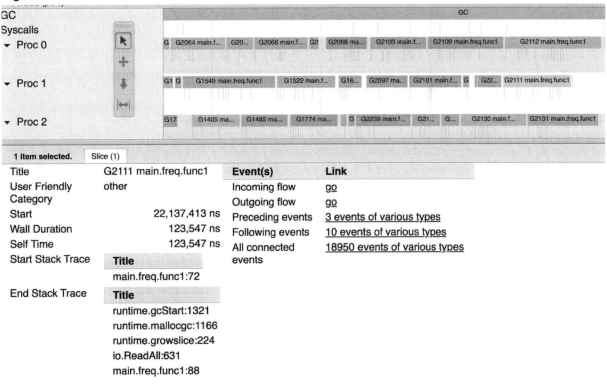

As I expand the graph, the context switches become clearly defined. All of these Goroutines are going from runnable, running, and then waiting. If I look at the call graph for Goroutine G2111, I can see that when the Goroutine made the call to runtime.mallocgc, the scheduler identified a GC was running and the Goroutine was context switched.

Figure 12.11

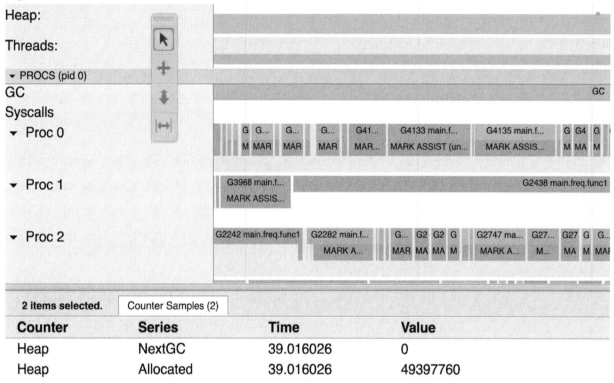

Counter	Series	Time	Value
Heap	NextGC	39.016026	0
Heap	Allocated	39.016026	49397760

On the backend of the first GC at the 39ms mark, the heap is at 49 meg. If I look closely, I can see all the Goroutines in mark assist to help slowdown allocations and get the initial GC finished. Once this first GC is complete, the heap is at 52 meg and the collector maintains that heap size for the rest of the running program.

12.7 Pooling

For 4k files over 8 cores, the program is running well using a fan-out. However, what if I want to process 1MM files? I don't feel great about creating 1MM Goroutines. Plus, I want to be more efficient with resources, especially since I can't open 1MM files at the same time.

I can change the algorithm to use a pooling pattern and limit the number of Goroutines and files being processed at any time.

Listing 12.16

```
func freq(topic string, docs []string) int {
    var found int32

    g := runtime.GOMAXPROCS(0)            <-- CHANGED
    var wg sync.WaitGroup
    wg.Add(g)

    ch := make(chan string, g)            <-- ADDED

    for i := 0; i < g; i++ {              <-- CHANGED
        go func() {                        <-- CHANGED
            var lFound int32
            defer func() {
                atomic.AddInt32(&found, lFound)
                wg.Done()
            }()

            for doc := range ch {          <-- ADDED
                . . .
            }
        }()                                <-- CHANGED
    }

    . . .
}
```

The first change is to set the number of Goroutines to use to match the number of Goroutines that can be run in parallel. The runtime.GOMAXPROCS function when passing zero is the best way to get that number. Using more Goroutines in a situation like this rarely improves the performance in any significant way.

Next, a channel is added to have the ability to signal work into the pool. The size of the buffer matches the number of Goroutines since staging more work than their are Goroutines doesn't add value.

The for loop is changed to reflect only creating g Goroutines. I don't need to pass a document into the Goroutine anymore since that's coming from the channel. The defer function requires no changes.

Inside the Goroutine, a for-range loop is added for receiving documents through the channel. The existing code to process a document is placed inside the channel loop and doesn't need to change.

Outside the for loop that creates the pool of Goroutines is a second loop to feed the documents into the pool.

Listing 12.17

```
func freq(topic string, docs []string) int {
    . . .

    for i := 0; i < g; i++ {
        . . .
    }

    for _, doc := range docs {              <-- ADDED
        ch <- doc                           <-- ADDED
    }                                       <-- ADDED
    close(ch)                               <-- ADDED

    wg.Wait()
    return int(found)
}
```

While the pool of Goroutines is waiting for work, this second loop begins to signal work into the pool. Once the last signal is sent, the channel is closed and then freq waits for all the Goroutines to process the remaining work and report they are done.

One big benefit to this version of freq is it's more sympathetic with the caching system.

Listing 12.18

```
func freq(topic string, docs []string) int {
    . . .

    for i := 0; i < g; i++ {
        go func() {
            var lFound int32
            defer func() {
                atomic.AddInt32(&found, lFound)
                wg.Done()
            }()

            . . .
    }

    . . .
}
```

Regardless of the number of documents to process, the defer function only needs to execute g number of times. On my machine that is 16 times. All of the counting happens on the local lFound variable, eliminating atomic synchronization and cache thrashing.

12.8 Pooling Results

With the more efficient pooling algorithm in place, I should see better performance.

Listing 12.19

```
$ go build

$ time ./trace > t.out
2021/05/13 14:07:11 Searching 4000 files, found president 28000 times.
./trace > t.out   8.09s user 1.75s system 834% cpu 1.179 total

$ time ./trace > t.out
2021/05/13 14:07:13 Searching 4000 files, found president 28000 times.
./trace > t.out   8.13s user 1.76s system 935% cpu 1.057 total
```

Surprisingly, this pooling version is slower than the fan-out by ~400ms. Time to look at the trace and gather the numbers.

Figure 12.12

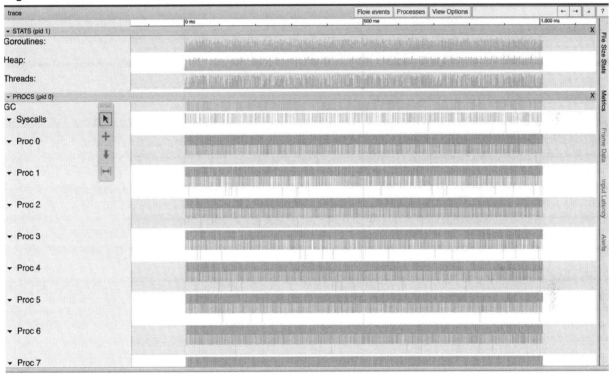

On the surface this trace looks better with the number of Goroutines, the heap, and utilizing the full cpu capacity of the machine.

Figure 12.13

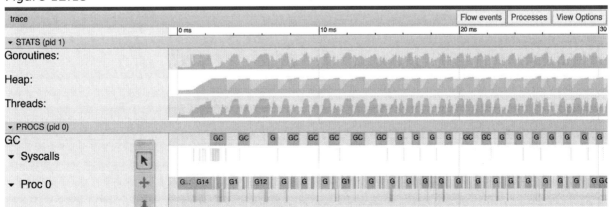

A closer look at the first 30ms of the trace tells a different story. The memory looks consistent right from the beginning and the context traces look uniform but, there appears to be a lot of GC happening.

Table 12.3

	Single	**Fan-Out**	**Pooling**
Runtime	2670ms	580ms	1000ms
Top Memory	4 Meg	53 Meg	5 Meg
GC Occurrences	275	62	876
GC Avg Duration	387us	4ms	690us
GC Wall Duration	106ms	250ms	604ms
GC Time Spent	4%	43%	60%

After gathering the numbers it's clear the GC is working very hard with this version of the algorithm. The reason seems to be related to the amount of memory the GC held the program to, which is 5 meg. Since there are only 16 Goroutines doing the work, the GC was able to keep the memory small, but at the cost of performance.

Would the performance change if I told the GC it's ok for the program to use 50 meg of memory? This is the amount of memory the fan-out algorithm uses.

12.9 GC Percentage

There is a knob I can use to ask the GC to use more memory. This is the GC percentage knob. I can access this knob in two ways, first with the GOGC environment variable and second with the debug package in the standard library.

The default value for this knob is 100, which represents two important things. First, that the GC should start when 4 meg of memory is in-use on the heap. Second, that the next GC should start when 100% more memory is allocated on the heap, based on the result of the marked live value from the previous GC.

Since the GC is keeping the memory at roughly 4 meg, I need to get the GC to not start the first collection until the memory in-use reaches 40 meg. To do this, I need to change the GOGC value by an order of magnitude, which is 1000.

Listing 12.19

```
$ time GOGC=1000 ./trace > t.out
2021/05/13 14:43:06 Searching 4000 files, found president 28000 times.
GOGC=1000 ./trace > t.out  5.48s user 0.29s system 1404% cpu 0.411 total

$ time GOGC=1000 ./trace > t.out
2021/05/13 14:43:08 Searching 4000 files, found president 28000 times.
GOGC=1000 ./trace > t.out  5.41s user 0.30s system 1370% cpu 0.417 total
```

After using the GOGC environment variable, setting the GC percentage to 1000, I see the performance I was expecting. The performance of this algorithm is faster than the fan-out.

Figure 12.14

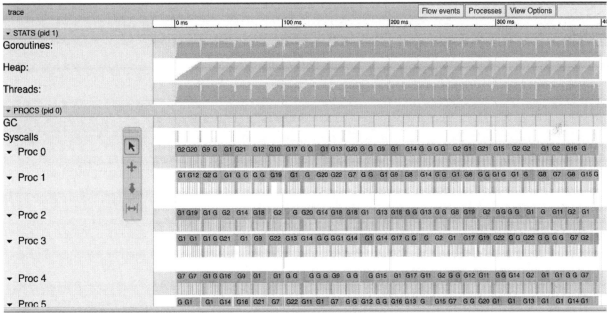

That looks much better, plus the heap graph looks similar to the single threaded version. Now I need to gather the numbers.

Table 12.4

	Single	**Fan-Out**	**Pooling**	**GC% 1000**
Runtime	2670ms	580ms	1000ms	397ms
Top Memory	4 Meg	53 Meg	5 Meg	40 Meg
GC Occurrences	275	62	876	27
GC Avg Duration	387us	4ms	690us	706us
GC Wall Duration	106ms	250ms	604ms	19ms
GC Time Spent	4%	43%	60%	4%

Brilliant. By running with a 40 meg heap, the number of GC's went down considerably, and the amount of time spent in GC is back down to 4%.

I would like to make sure this program always runs with the GC Percentage set to 1000. That requires a simple code change.

Listing 12.20

```
import (
    "runtime/debug"
)

func main() {
    debug.SetGCPercent(1000)


    . . .
}
```

With the call to debug.SetGCPercentage, I can guarantee the program always runs with the larger heap. Be careful when hardcoding this value since it's favoring memory usage over GC. Different workloads could affect this decision in negative ways.

12.10 Tasks And Regions

With the pooling version of freq working pretty well, it would be interesting to gather information about each individual file that the program is processing. Maybe there is a file or two that is causing the algorithm to not run as fast as it could. With the use of tasks and regions, I can find out.

Listing 12.21

```
    for i := 0; i < g; i++ {
        go func() {
            . . .

            for doc := range ch {
                ctx, task := trace.NewTask(context.Background(), doc)


                . . .
            }
```

The first thing to do is to create a task for each file that is being processed. Here I am adding the call to trace.NewTask, giving it an empty parent context and using the document for the name of the task. That call returns a new context and a task.

The next step is to add regions around the blocks of code I want to measure.

Listing 12.22

```
for doc := range ch {
    ctx, task := trace.NewTask(context.Background(), doc)

    reg := trace.StartRegion(ctx, "OpenFile")          <-- ADDED
    file := fmt.Sprintf("%s.xml", doc[:8])
    f, err := os.OpenFile(file, os.O_RDONLY, 0)
    if err != nil {
        log.Printf("Opening Document [%s] : ERROR : %v", doc, err)
        return
    }
    reg.End()                                          <-- ADDED

    reg = trace.StartRegion(ctx, "ReadAll")            <-- ADDED
    data, err := io.ReadAll(f)
    f.Close()
    if err != nil {
        log.Printf("Reading Document [%s] : ERROR : %v", doc, err)
        return
    }
    reg.End()                                          <-- ADDED

    reg = trace.StartRegion(ctx, "Unmarshal")          <-- ADDED
    var d document
    if err := xml.Unmarshal(data, &d); err != nil {
        log.Printf("Decoding Document [%s] : ERROR : %v", doc, err)
        return
    }
    reg.End()                                          <-- ADDED

    reg = trace.StartRegion(ctx, "Contains")           <-- ADDED
    for _, item := range d.Channel.Items {
        if strings.Contains(item.Title, topic) {
            lFound++
            continue
        }

        if strings.Contains(item.Description, topic) {
            lFound++
        }
    }
    reg.End()                                          <-- ADDED
    task.End()                                         <-- ADDED
}
```

I added four regions, each named for the operation that is being performed. At the end of the last region, I call task.End to end the task.

With this in place, I can run the program again and open the trace output.

Listing 12.23

```
$ go build

$ time ./trace > t.out
2021/05/17 12:32:48 Search 4000 files, found president 28000 times.
./trace > t.out  5.33s user 0.29s system 1292% cpu 0.435 total

$ go tool trace t.out
```

255

Once I do that, I can use the User-defined tasks link to see the data.

Figure 12.15

View trace
Goroutine analysis
Network blocking profile (⬇)
Synchronization blocking profile (⬇)
Syscall blocking profile (⬇)
Scheduler latency profile (⬇)
User-defined tasks
User-defined regions
Minimum mutator utilization

After selecting that link, I get this view.

Figure 12.16

Search log text:

[   ] Submit

Task type	Count	Duration distribution (complete tasks)
newsfeed-0000.xml	1	2511μs ████████████████████ 1 3981μs
newsfeed-0001.xml	1	2511μs ████████████████████ 1 3981μs
newsfeed-0002.xml	1	2511μs ████████████████████ 1 3981μs
newsfeed-0003.xml	1	2511μs ████████████████████ 1 3981μs
newsfeed-0004.xml	1	2511μs ████████████████████ 1 3981μs
newsfeed-0005.xml	1	2511μs ████████████████████ 1 3981μs

I now have a table with an entry for every document that was processed, including how long it took to process that file. If I click on the time, I get to this page.

Figure 12.17

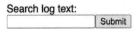

User Task: type=newsfeed-0000.xml,latency >= 2.511886ms,latency <= 3.981071ms

Search log text:
[   ] Submit

When	Elapsed	Goroutine ID	Events
0.000926559s	3.296533ms		Task 1 (goroutine view) (complete)
0.000926559	.	21	task newsfeed-0000.xml (id 1, parent 0) created
0.000954719	. 28160	21	region OpenFile started (duration: 68.934µs)
0.001029733	. 75014	21	region ReadAll started (duration: 687.839µs)
0.001720106	. 690373	21	region Unmarshal started (duration: 2.489759ms)
0.004213198	. 2493092	21	region Contains started (duration: 7.92µs)
0.004223092	. 9894	21	task end
			GC:0s

This page breaks down each region from this task and how long it took. It also provides information about GC time at the bottom.

That final link gives me this same information but in graph form.

Figure 12.18

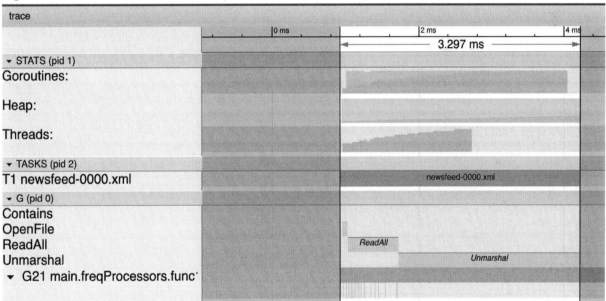

Now I can see when the file was processed and more information from the tracing tool.

Chapter 13: Stack Traces / Core Dumps

In this chapter, I will learn how to read stack traces and generate core dumps. Understanding the information in a stack trace can sometimes mean the difference between finding the bug now or needing to add more logging, and waiting for it to happen again.

13.1 ABI Changes In 1.17

As of version 1.17, Go changed the ABI (application binary interface) to implement a new way of passing function input and output arguments using registers instead of memory on the stack. This is enabled for Linux, MacOS, and Windows on the 64-bit x86 architectures. This means that some function arguments won't be copied on the stack, but some may depending on the viability of using registers.

Because of this ABI change, stack trace output has changed in 1.17 and function input values that are placed in registers won't appear accurately in the stack trace anymore. The format of how input values are displayed has changed as well.

Accuracy is something the Go team is looking to improve on in future releases of Go. For now, this chapter will focus on how to read a stack trace in version 1.16 or less. I have added a section to show the changes of the stack output and how they are no longer accurate.

13.2 Basic Example

I will start with stack traces and learn how to read all the information that is presented. Here is a program that uses the built-in function panic to cause a stack trace.

Listing 13.1

```
01 package main
02
03 func main() {
04     example(make([]string, 2, 4), "hello", 10)
05 }
06
07 //go:noinline
08 func example(slice []string, str string, i int) error {
09     panic("Want stack trace")
10 }
```

After running the program, the following stack trace is presented.

Listing 13.2

```
$ go run ./example1.go
panic: Want stack trace

goroutine 1 [running]:

main.example(0xc000054738, 0x2, 0x4, 0x1073c53, 0x5, 0xa, 0x0, 0xc000054778)
gotraining/topics/go/profiling/stack_trace/example1/example1.go:9 +0x39

main.main()
gotraining/topics/go/profiling/stack_trace/example1/example1.go:4 +0x85

exit status 2
```

The line numbers to where the Goroutines were in the call stack prior to the panic is something I can figure out fairly quickly.

Listing 13.3

```
$ go run ./example1.go
panic: Want stack trace

main.example
example1.go:9 +0x39

main.main
example1.go:4 +0x85
```

If I get rid of some of the noise and focus on this information, I'm being told that the Goroutine started on line 4 in package main, function main. From there the goroutine executed code on line 9 in package main, function example. That is where the panic occurred with a message that I wanted a stack trace.

This is great but there is more information that isn't obvious.

Listing 13.4

```
main.example(0xc000054738, 0x2, 0x4, 0x1073c53, 0x5, 0xa, 0x0, 0xc000054778)
```

In the stack trace, the call to main.example looks like a function call with parameters. The stack trace shows words of data that are passed into and out of each function. The first words are the input, and the remaining words are the output. In a panic situation, the words representing the output are technically garbage. However, the input is not.

If I look at the call to main.example again, I can see what values are being passed in.

Listing 13.5

```
01  package main
02
03  func main() {
04      example(make([]string, 2, 4), "hello", 10)
05  }
06
07  //go:noinline
08  func example(slice []string, str string, i int) error {
09      panic("Want stack trace")
10  }
```

There is a slice value with a length of 2 and capacity of 4, a string with a length of 5 bytes, and the number 10. If I look again at the values inside the parentheses, I should be able to match them up.

Listing 13.6

```
example(make([]string, 2, 4), "hello", 10)

example(0xc000054738, 0x2, 0x4, | 0x1073c53, 0x5, | 0xa, | 0x0,
0xc000054778)

Slice Value:     0xc000054738, 0x2, 0x4
String Value:    0x1073c53, 0x5
Integer Value: 0xa
Return Value:    0x0, 0xc000054778 (interface)
```

As I can see, the first three words represent the three words of the slice value, the next two words represent the words of the string value, the next word represents the integer, finally the last two words represent the interface value. I can see all the values being passed into the function. Since this is panicking, the return values are garbage.

13.3 Word Packing

Like I said, the stack trace shows word of data at a time. What if multiple parameters can fit inside a word of data?

Listing 13.7

```
01  package main
02
03  func main() {
04      example(true, false, true, 25)
05  }
06
07  //go:noinline
08  func example(b1, b2, b3 bool, i uint8) error {
09      panic("Want stack trace")
10  }
```

In this example four values are passed into the example function, three boolean values and an unsigned 1 byte integer. All four values can be stored inside of a single word of data. This is what the stack trace looks like when the program is run.

Listing 13.8

```
$ go run example2.go
panic: Want stack trace

goroutine 1 [running]:

main.example(0x19010001, 0x1064ee0, 0xc00008c058)
gotraining/topics/go/profiling/stack_trace/example2/example2.go:9 +0x39

main.main()
gotraining/topics/go/profiling/stack_trace/example2/example2.go:4 +0x29

exit status 2
```

In this stack trace I only see a single word value for the input and two word values for the return interface argument. If I read the digits of the first word value from right to left (for little endian) and remember every two digits represent a byte of data, I know what values were passed in.

Listing 13.9

```
// Word value (0xc019010001)

Bits      Binary      Hex    Value
00-07     0000 0001   01     true
08-15     0000 0000   00     false
16-23     0000 0001   01     true
24-31     0001 1001   19     25

Return Arguments: 0x1064ee0, 0xc00007605
```

Byte packaging is nice to reduce the amount of noise in the stack trace.

13.4 Go 1.17 ABI Changes

I will run the first program again using both Go 1.16 and Go 1.17 to see the difference in the stack trace output.

Listing 13.10

```
$ go1.16 run example1.go
panic: Want stack trace

goroutine 1 [running]:
main.example(0xc000054738, 0x2, 0x4, 0x1073c53, 0x5, 0xa, 0x0, 0xc000054778)
        /Users/bill/code/go/src/github.com/ardanlabs/gotraining/topics/go/
profiling/stack_trace/example1/example1.go:13 +0x39
main.main()
        /Users/bill/code/go/src/github.com/ardanlabs/gotraining/topics/go/
profiling/stack_trace/example1/example1.go:8 +0x85
exit status 2
--------------------------------------------------------------------------

$ go1.17 run example1.go
panic: Want stack trace

goroutine 1 [running]:
main.example({0x60, 0x10bb6c0, 0xc0000002e8}, {0xc000024060, 0x0},
0xc0000001a0)
        /Users/bill/code/go/src/github.com/ardanlabs/gotraining/topics/go/
profiling/stack_trace/example1/example1.go:13 +0x27
main.main()
        /Users/bill/code/go/src/github.com/ardanlabs/gotraining/topics/go/
profiling/stack_trace/example1/example1.go:8 +0x59
exit status 2
```

The first difference I see is how in 1.17, each individual value is broken into a document like syntax.

Listing 13.11

```
Go 1.16
main.example(0xc000054738, 0x2, 0x4, 0x1073c53, 0x5, 0xa, 0x0, 0xc000054778)

Slice:  0xc000054738, 0x2, 0x4
String: 0x1073c53, 0x5
Int:    0xa
--------------------------------------------------------------------------

Go 1.17
main.example({0x60, 0x10bb6c0, 0xc0000002e8}, {0xc000024060, 0x0},
0xc0000001a0)

Slice:  {0x60, 0x10bb6c0, 0xc0000002e8}
String: {0xc000024060, 0x0}
Int:    {0xc0000001a0}
```

However if I look closer, I see the values are not accurate in Go 1.17. Since these input values are now being passed using registers, when the stack trace occurs, the values are not available for proper display. This is a bummer, but I expect this to improve over time.

13.5 Generating Core Dumps

I can generate a core dump from a running Go program, which is useful if I feel the program is hung or not responding.

Listing 13.12

```
01 package main
02
03 import (
04     "encoding/json"
05     "log"
06     "net/http"
07 )
08
09 func main() {
10     http.HandleFunc("/sendjson", sendJSON)
11
12     log.Println("listener : Started : Listening on:
http://localhost:8080")
13     http.ListenAndServe(":8080", nil)
14 }
15
16 // sendJSON returns a simple JSON document.
17 func sendJSON(rw http.ResponseWriter, r *http.Request) {
18     u := struct {
19         Name  string
20         Email string
21     }{
22         Name:  "bill",
23         Email: "bill@ardanlabs.com",
24     }
25
26     rw.Header().Set("Content-Type", "application/json")
27     rw.WriteHeader(200)
28     json.NewEncoder(rw).Encode(u)
29 }
```

Now I can build and run the program.

Listing 13.13

```
$ go build
$ ./example3
2021/05/17 14:09:05 listener : Started : Listening on: http://localhost:4000
```

Next, I can send a signal to quit the process.

Listing 13.14

```
$ ps
 6575 ttys002     0:00.01 ./example3
$ kill -3 6575
```

This will result in the Go program producing a core dump.

Listing 13.15

```
SIGQUIT: quit
PC=0x7fff20533c62 m=0 sigcode=0

goroutine 0 [idle]:
runtime.kevent(0x4, 0x0, 0x0, 0x7ffeefbfee78, 0x40, 0x0, 0x0)
        /usr/local/go/src/runtime/sys_darwin.go:349 +0x39
runtime.netpoll(0xffffffffffffffff, 0x0)
        /usr/local/go/src/runtime/netpoll_kqueue.go:127 +0xae
runtime.findrunnable(0xc000028000, 0x0)
        /usr/local/go/src/runtime/proc.go:2923 +0x3ee
runtime.schedule()
        /usr/local/go/src/runtime/proc.go:3169 +0x2d7
runtime.park_m(0xc000000180)
        /usr/local/go/src/runtime/proc.go:3318 +0x9d
runtime.mcall(0x106a196)
        /usr/local/go/src/runtime/asm_amd64.s:327 +0x5b

goroutine 1 [IO wait]:
internal/poll.runtime_pollWait(0x2555eb8, 0x72, 0x0)
        /usr/local/go/src/runtime/netpoll.go:222 +0x55
internal/poll.(*pollDesc).wait(0xc000026098, 0x72, 0x0, 0x0, 0x12a6473)
        /usr/local/go/src/internal/poll/fd_poll_runtime.go:87 +0x45
internal/poll.(*pollDesc).waitRead(...)
        /usr/local/go/src/internal/poll/fd_poll_runtime.go:92
internal/poll.(*FD).Accept(0xc000026080, 0x0, 0x0, 0x0, 0x0, 0x0, 0x0, 0x0)
        /usr/local/go/src/internal/poll/fd_unix.go:401 +0x212
net.(*netFD).accept(0xc000026080, 0x30, 0x30, 0x1544108)
        /usr/local/go/src/net/fd_unix.go:172 +0x45
net.(*TCPListener).accept(0xc00000e150, 0xc0000b1d88, 0x100f578, 0x30)
        /usr/local/go/src/net/tcpsock_posix.go:139 +0x32
net.(*TCPListener).Accept(0xc00000e150, 0x12895c0, 0xc000094db0, 0x125d980,
0x144ac50)
        /usr/local/go/src/net/tcpsock.go:261 +0x65
net/http.(*Server).Serve(0xc0000e6000, 0x12fd100, 0xc00000e150, 0x0, 0x0)
        /usr/local/go/src/net/http/server.go:2981 +0x285
net/http.(*Server).ListenAndServe(0xc0000e6000, 0xc0000e6000, 0x1)
        /usr/local/go/src/net/http/server.go:2910 +0xba
net/http.ListenAndServe(...)
        /usr/local/go/src/net/http/server.go:3164
main.main()
        gotraining/topics/go/profiling/stack_trace/example3/example3.go:13
+0xd6

rax    0x4
rbx    0x7ffeefbfee00
rcx    0x7ffeefbfed48
rdx    0x0
rdi    0x4
rsi    0x0
rbp    0x7ffeefbfed50
rsp    0x7ffeefbfed48
r8     0x40
r9     0x0
r10    0x7ffeefbfee78
r11    0x206
r12    0x0
r13    0x14575e0
r14    0x12f243f
r15    0x0
rip    0x7fff20533c62
rflags 0x207, cs 0x7, fs 0x0, gs 0x0
```

Now I have a stack trace of every Goroutine and register information. I can get a larger core dump by using the GOTRACEBACK variable with the crash option when running the program.

Listing 13.16

```
$ GOTRACEBACK=crash ./example3
```

This will provide stack traces for the runtime Goroutines, like the netpoller and scavenger.

Chapter 14: Blog Posts

This chapter contains the material on the blog posts that are listed in the book for convenience.

14.1 Stacks And Pointer Mechanics

Prelude

As of version 1.17, Go changed the ABI (application binary interface) to implement a new way of passing function input and output arguments using registers instead of memory on the stack. This is enabled for Linux, MacOS, and Windows on the 64-bit x86 architectures. This means that some function arguments won't be copied on the stack, but some may depending on the viability of using registers. This doesn't change any of the semantics described in this post.

Introduction

I'm not going to sugar coat it, pointers are difficult to comprehend. When used incorrectly, pointers can produce nasty bugs and even performance issues. This is especially true when writing concurrent or multi-threaded software. It's no wonder so many languages attempt to hide pointers away from programmers. However, if you're writing software in Go, there is no way for you to avoid them. Without a strong understanding of pointers, you will struggle to write clean, simple and efficient code.

Frame Boundaries

Functions execute within the scope of frame boundaries that provide an individual memory space for each respective function. Each frame allows a function to operate within their own context. A function has direct access to the memory inside its frame, through the frame pointer, but access to memory outside its frame requires indirect access. For a function to access memory outside of its frame, that memory must be shared with the function. The mechanics and restrictions established by these frame boundaries need to be understood and learned first.

When a function is called, there is a transition that takes place between two frames. The code transitions out of the calling function's frame and into the called function's frame. If data is required to make the function call, then that data must be transferred from one frame to the other. The passing of data between two frames is done "by value" in Go.

The benefit of passing data "by value" is readability. The value you see in the function call is what is copied and received on the other side. It's why I relate "pass by value" with WYSIWYG, because what you see is what you get. All of this allows you to write code that does not hide the cost of the transition between the two functions. This helps to maintain a good mental model of how each function call is going to impact the program when the transition takes place.

Look at this small program that performs a function call passing integer data "by value".

Listing 1

```
01 package main
02
03 func main() {
04
05     // Declare variable of type int with a value of 10.
06     count := 10
07
08     // Display the "value of" and "address of" count.
09     println("count:\tValue Of[", count, "]\tAddr Of[", &count, "]")
10
11     // Pass the "value of" the count.
12     increment(count)
13
14     println("count:\tValue Of[", count, "]\tAddr Of[", &count, "]")
15 }
16
17 //go:noinline
18 func increment(inc int) {
19
20     // Increment the "value of" inc.
21     inc++
22     println("inc:\tValue Of[", inc, "]\tAddr Of[", &inc, "]")
23 }
```

When your Go program starts up, the runtime creates the main Goroutine to start executing all the initialization code including the code inside the main function. A Goroutine is a path of execution that is placed on an operating system thread that eventually executes on some core. As of version 1.8, every Goroutine is given an initial 2,048 byte block of contiguous memory which forms its stack space. This initial stack size has changed over the years and could change again in the future.

The stack is important because it provides the physical memory space for the frame boundaries that are given to each individual function. By the time the main Goroutine is executing the main function in Listing 1, the Goroutine's stack (at a very high level) would look like this.

Figure 1

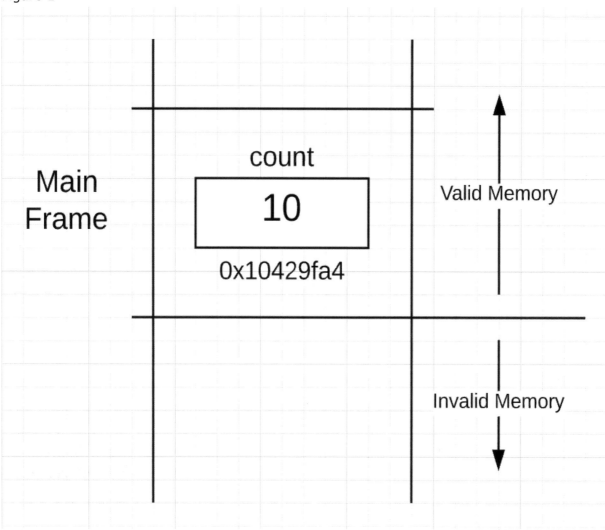

You can see in Figure 1, a section of the stack has been "framed" out for the main function. This section is called a "stack frame" and it's this frame that denotes the main function's boundary on the stack. The frame is established as part of the code that is executed when the function is called. You can also see the memory for the count variable has been placed at address 0x10429fa4 inside the frame for main.

There is another interesting point made clear by Figure 1. All stack memory below the active frame is invalid but memory from the active frame to the top of the stack is valid. I need to be clear about the boundary between the valid and invalid parts of the stack.

Addresses

Variables serve the purpose of assigning a name to a specific memory location for better code readability and to help you reason about the data you are working with. If you have a variable then you have a value in memory, and if you have a value in memory then it must have an address. On line 09, the main function calls the built-in function println to display the "value of" and "address of" the count variable.

Listing 2

```
09      println("count:\tValue Of[", count, "]\tAddr Of[", &count, "]")
```

The use of the ampersand & operator to get the address of a variable's location is not novel, other languages use this operator as well. The output of line 09 should be similar to the output below if you run the code on a 32bit architecture like the playground.

Listing 3

```
count:   Value Of[ 10 ]   Addr Of[ 0x10429fa4 ]
```

Function Calls

Next on line 12, the main function makes a call into the increment function.

Listing 4

```
12      increment(count)
```

Making a function call means the Goroutine needs to frame a new section of memory on the stack. However, things are a bit more complicated. To successfully make this function call, data is expected to be passed across the frame boundary and placed into the new frame during the transition. Specifically, an integer value is expected to be copied and passed during the call. You can see this requirement by looking at the declaration of the increment function on line 18.

Listing 5

```
18 func increment(inc int) {
```

If you look at the function call to increment again on line 12, you can see the code is passing the "value of" the count variable. This value will be copied, passed and placed into the new frame for the increment function. Remember, the increment function can only directly read and write to memory within its own frame, so it needs the inc variable to receive, store and access its own copy of the count value being passed.

Just before the code inside the increment function starts executing, the Goroutine's stack (at a very high level) would look like this:

Figure 2

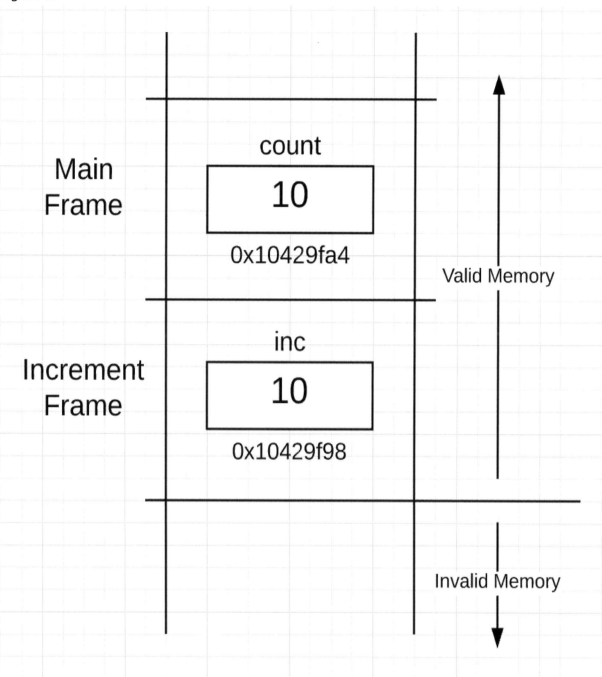

You can see the stack now has two frames, one for main and below that, one for increment. Inside the frame for increment, you see the inc variable and it contains the value of 10 that was copied and passed during the function call. The address of the inc variable is 0x10429f98 and is lower in memory because frames are taken down the stack, which is just an implementation detail that doesn't mean anything.

What's important is that the Goroutines took the value of count from within the frame for main and placed a copy of that value within the frame for increment using the inc variable. The rest of the code inside of increment increments and displays the "value of" and "address of" the inc variable.

Listing 6

```
21      inc++
22      println("inc:\tValue Of[", inc, "]\tAddr Of[", &inc, "]")
```

The output of line 22 on the playground should look something like this:

Listing 7

```
inc:    Value Of[ 11 ]   Addr Of[ 0x10429f98 ]
```

This is what the stack looks like after the execution of those same lines of code:

Figure 3

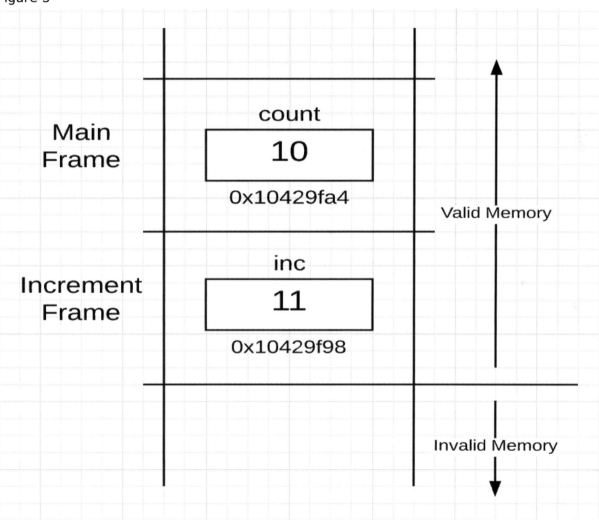

After lines 21 and 22 are executed, the increment function returns and control goes back to the main function. Then the main function displays the "value of" and "address of" the local count variable again on line 14.

Listing 8

```
14      println("count:\tValue Of[",count, "]\tAddr Of[", &count, "]")
```

The full output of the program on the playground should look something like this.

Listing 9

```
count:  Value Of[ 10 ]  Addr Of[ 0x10429fa4 ]
inc:    Value Of[ 11 ]  Addr Of[ 0x10429f98 ]
count:  Value Of[ 10 ]  Addr Of[ 0x10429fa4 ]
```

The value of count in the frame for main is the same before and after the call to increment.

Function Returns

What actually happens to the memory on the stack when a function returns and control goes back up to the calling function? The short answer is nothing. This is what the stack looks like after the return of the increment function.

Figure 4

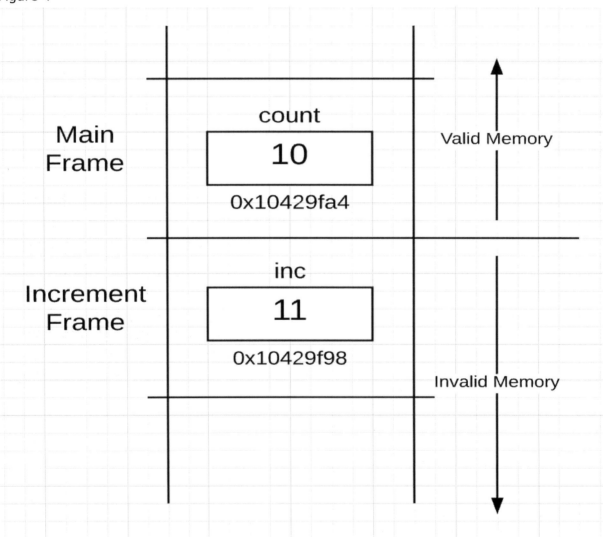

The stack looks exactly the same as Figure 3 except the frame associated with the increment function is now considered to be invalid memory. This is because the frame for main is now the active frame. The memory that was framed for the increment function is left untouched.

It would be a waste of time to clean up the memory of the returning function's frame because you don't know if that memory will ever be needed again. So the memory is left the way it is. It's during each function call, when the frame is taken, that the stack memory for that frame is wiped clean. This is done through the initialization of any values that are placed in the frame. Because all values are initialized to at least their "zero value", stacks clean themselves properly on every function call.

Sharing Values

What if it was important for the increment function to operate directly on the count variable that exists inside the frame for main? This is where pointers come in. Pointers serve one purpose, to share a value with a function so the function can read and write to that value even though the value does not exist directly inside its own frame.

If the word "share" doesn't come out of your mouth, you don't need to use a pointer. When learning about pointers, it's important to think using a clear vocabulary and not operators or syntax. So remember, pointers are for sharing. You should replace the & operator for the word "sharing" as you read code.

Pointer Types

For every type that is declared, either by you or the language itself, you get for free a complement pointer type you can use for sharing. There already exists a built-in type named int so there is a complement pointer type called *int. If you declare a type named User, you get for free a pointer type called *User.

All pointer types have the same two characteristics. First, they start with the character *. Second, they all have the same memory size and representation, which is 4 or 8 bytes that represent an address. On 32bit architectures (like the playground), pointers require 4 bytes of memory and on 64 bit architectures (like your machine), they require 8 bytes of memory.

In the spec, pointer types are considered to be type literals, which means they are unnamed types composed from an existing type.

https://golang.org/ref/spec#PointerType
https://golang.org/ref/spec#Types

Indirect Memory Access

Look at this small program that performs a function call passing an address "by value". This will share the count variable from the main stack frame with the increment function.

Listing 10

```
01 package main
02
03 func main() {
04
05     // Declare variable of type int with a value of 10.
06     count := 10
07
08     // Display the "value of" and "address of" count.
09     println("count:\tValue Of[", count, "]\t\tAddr Of[", &count, "]")
10
11     // Pass the "address of" count.
12     increment(&count)                         <-- CHANGED
13
14     println("count:\tValue Of[", count, "]\t\tAddr Of[", &count, "]")
15 }
16
17 //go:noinline
18 func increment(inc *int) {                    <-- CHANGED
19
20     // Increment the "value of" count that the "pointer points to".
21     *inc++                                    <-- CHANGED
22     println("inc:\tValue Of[", inc, "]\tAddr Of[", &inc, "]\tValue Points
To[", *inc, "]")
23 }
```

There are three interesting changes that were made to this program from the original. Here is the first change on line 12.

Listing 11

```
12     increment(&count)
```

This time on line 12, the code is not copying and passing the "value of" count but instead the "address of" count. You can now say, I am "sharing" the count variable with the increment function. This is what the & operator says, "sharing".

Understand this is still a "pass by value", the only difference is the value you are passing is an address instead of an integer. Addresses are values too; this is what is being copied and passed across the frame boundary for the function call.

Since the value of an address is being copied and passed, you need a variable inside the frame of increment to receive and store this integer based address. This is where the declaration of the integer pointer variable comes in on line 18.

Listing 12

```
18 func increment(inc *int) {
```

If you were passing the address of a User value, then the variable would have needed to be declared as a *User. Even though all pointer variables store address values, they can't be passed any address, only addresses associated with the pointer type. This is the key, the reason to share a value is because the receiving function needs to perform a read or write to that value. You need the type information of any value in order to read and write to it. The compiler will make sure that only values associated with the correct pointer type are shared with that function.

This is what the stack looks like after the function call to increment:

Figure 5

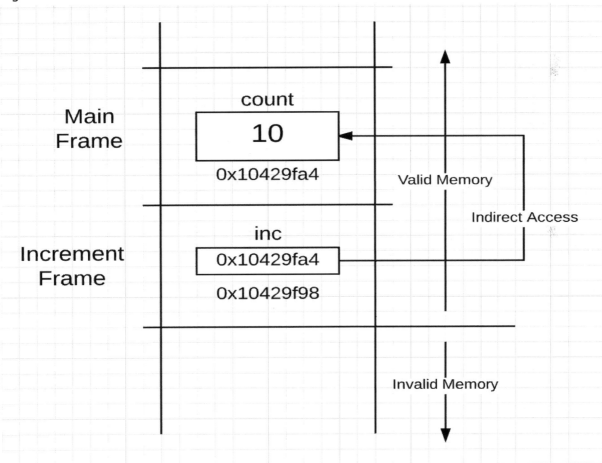

You can see in figure 5 what the stack looks like when a "pass by value" is performed using an address as the value. The pointer variable inside the frame for the increment function is now pointing to the count variable, which is located inside the frame for main.

Now using the pointer variable, the function can perform an indirect read modify write operation to the count variable located inside the frame for main.

Listing 13

```
21   *inc++
```

This time the * character is acting as an operator and being applied against the pointer variable. Using the * as an operator means, "the value that the pointer points to". The pointer variable allows indirect memory access outside of the function's frame that declared it. Sometimes this indirect read or write is called dereferencing the pointer. The increment function still must have a pointer variable within its frame it can directly read to perform the indirect access.

In figure 6 you see what the stack looks like after the execution of line 21.

Figure 6

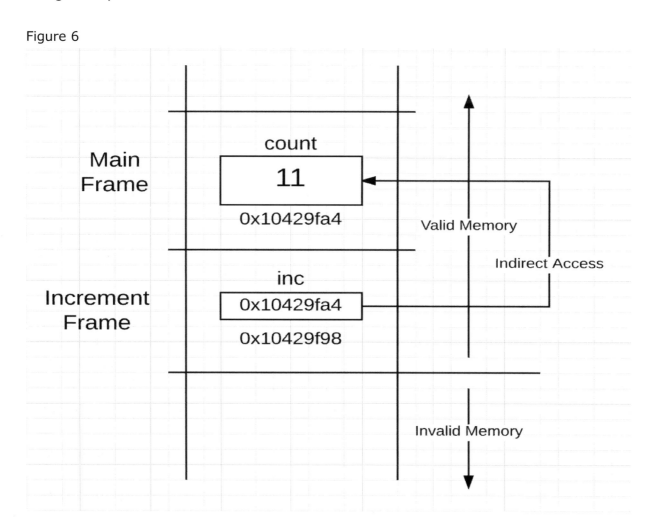

Here is the final output of this program.

Listing 14

```
count:   Value Of[ 10 ]            Addr Of[ 0x10429fa4 ]
inc:     Value Of[ 0x10429fa4 ]   Addr Of[ 0x10429f98 ]   Value Points To[ 11 ]
count:   Value Of[ 11 ]           Addr Of[ 0x10429fa4 ]
```

You can see the "value of" the inc pointer variable is the same as the "address of" the count variable. This sets up the sharing relationship that allowed the indirect access to the memory outside of the frame to take place. Once the write is performed by the increment function through the pointer, the change is seen by the main function when control is returned.

Pointer Variables Are Not Special

Pointer variables are not special because they are variables like any other variable. They have a memory allocation and they hold a value. It just so happens that all pointer variables, regardless of the type of value they can point to, are always the same size and representation. What can be confusing is that the * character is acting as an operator inside the code and is used to declare the pointer type. If you can distinguish the type declaration from the pointer operation, this can help alleviate some confusion.

Conclusion

This post has described the purpose behind pointers and how stack and pointer mechanics work in Go. This is the first step in understanding the mechanics, design philosophies, and guidelines needed for writing consistent and readable code.

In summary this is what you learned:

- Functions execute within the scope of frame boundaries that provide an individual memory space for each respective function.
- When a function is called, there is a transition that takes place between two frames.
- The benefit of passing data "by value" is readability.
- The stack is important because it provides the physical memory space for the frame boundaries that are given to each individual function.
- All stack memory below the active frame is invalid but memory from the active frame and above is valid.
- Making a function call means the Goroutine needs to frame a new section of memory on the stack.
- It's during each function call, when the frame is taken, that the stack memory for that frame is wiped clean.
- Pointers serve one purpose, to share a value with a function so the function can read and write to that value even though the value does not exist directly inside its own frame.
- For every type that is declared, either by you or the language itself, you get for free a compliment pointer type you can use for sharing.
- The pointer variable allows indirect memory access outside of the function's frame that is using it.
- Pointer variables are not special because they are variables like any other variable. They have a memory allocation and they hold a value.

14.2 Escape Analysis Mechanics

Prelude

As of version 1.17, Go changed the ABI (application binary interface) to implement a new way of passing function input and output arguments using registers instead of memory on the stack. This is enabled for Linux, MacOS, and Windows on the 64-bit x86 architectures. This means that some function arguments won't be copied on the stack, but some may depending on the viability of using registers. This doesn't change any of the semantics described in this post.

Introduction

In the first post, I taught the basics of pointer mechanics by using an example in which a value was shared down a Goroutine's stack. What I did not show you is what happens when you share a value up the stack. To understand this, you need to learn about another area of memory where values can live: the "heap". With that knowledge, you can begin to learn about "escape analysis".

Escape analysis is the process that the compiler uses to determine the placement of values that are created by your program. Specifically, the compiler performs static code analysis to determine if a value can be placed on the stack frame for the function constructing it, or if the value must "escape" to the heap. In Go, there is no keyword or function you can use to direct the compiler in this decision. It's only through the convention of how you write your code that you can impact this decision.

Heaps

The heap is a second area of memory, in addition to the stack, used for storing values. The heap is not self-cleaning like stacks, so there is a bigger cost to using this memory. Primarily, the costs are associated with the garbage collector (GC), which must get involved to keep this area clean. When the GC runs, it will use 25% of your available CPU capacity. Plus, it can potentially create microseconds of "stop the world" latency. The benefit of having the GC is that you don't need to worry about managing heap memory, which historically has been complicated and error prone.

Values on the heap constitute memory allocations in Go. These allocations put pressure on the GC because every value on the heap that is no longer referenced by a pointer needs to be removed. The more values that need to be checked and removed, the more work the GC must perform on every run. So, the pacing algorithm is constantly working to balance the size of the heap with the pace it runs at.

Sharing Stacks

In Go, no Goroutine is allowed to have a pointer that points to memory on another Goroutine's stack. This is because the stack memory for a Goroutine can be replaced with a new block of memory when the stack has to grow or shrink. If the runtime had to track pointers to other Goroutine stacks, it would be too much to manage and the "stop the world" latency in updating pointers on those stacks would be overwhelming.

Here is an example of a stack that is replaced several times because of growth. Look at the output for lines 2 and 6. You will see the address of the string value inside the stack frame of main changes twice.

Listing 1

```
package main

const size = 4096

func main() {
        s := "HELLO"
        stackCopy(&s, 0, [size]int{})
}

func stackCopy(s *string, c int, a [size]int) {
        println(c, s, *s)

        c++
        if c == 10 {
                return
        }

        stackCopy(s, c, a)
}

Output:
0 0xc00011ff68 HELLO
1 0xc00011ff68 HELLO

2 0xc00015ff68 HELLO        <-- CHANGED
3 0xc00015ff68 HELLO
4 0xc00015ff68 HELLO
5 0xc00015ff68 HELLO

6 0xc0001dff68 HELLO        <-- CHANGED
7 0xc0001dff68 HELLO
8 0xc0001dff68 HELLO
9 0xc0001dff68 HELLO
```

Escape Mechanics

When a value is shared outside the scope of a function's stack frame, it will be placed (or allocated) on the heap. It's the job of the escape analysis algorithms to find these situations and maintain a level of integrity in the program. The integrity is in making sure that access to any value is always accurate, consistent and efficient.

Look at this example to learn the basic mechanics behind escape analysis.

Listing 2

```
01 package main
02
03 type user struct {
04     name  string
05     email string
06 }
07
08 func main() {
09     u1 := createUserV1()
10     u2 := createUserV2()
11
12     println("u1", &u1, "u2", &u2)
13 }
14
15 //go:noinline
16 func createUserV1() user {
17     u := user{
18         name:  "Bill",
19         email: "bill@ardanlabs.com",
20     }
21
22     println("V1", &u)
23     return u
24 }
25
26 //go:noinline
27 func createUserV2() *user {
28     u := user{
29         name:  "Bill",
30         email: "bill@ardanlabs.com",
31     }
32
33     println("V2", &u)
34     return &u
35 }
```

I am using the go:noinline directive to prevent the compiler from inlining the code for these functions directly in main. Inlining would erase the function calls and

280

complicate this example.

In Listing 2, you see a program with two different functions that create a user value and return the value back to the caller. Version 1 of the function is using value semantics on the return.

Listing 3

```
16 func createUserV1() user {
17      u := user{
18          name:  "Bill",
19          email: "bill@ardanlabs.com",
20      }
21
22      println("V1", &u)
23      return u
24 }
```

I said the function is using value semantics on the return because the user value created by this function is being copied and passed up the call stack. This means the calling function is receiving a copy of the value.

In listing 3, you can see the construction of a user value being performed on lines 17 through 20. Then on line 23, a copy of the user value is passed up the call stack and back to the caller. After the function returns, the stack looks like this.

Figure 1

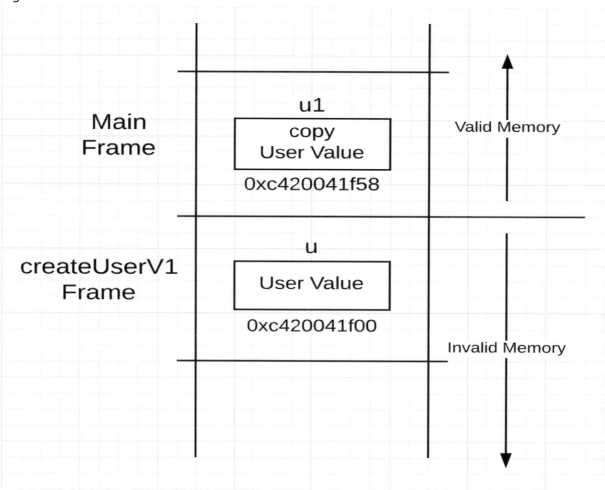

You can see in Figure 1, a user value exists in both frames after the call to createUserV1. In Version 2 of the function, pointer semantics are being used on the return.

Listing 4

```
27 func createUserV2() *user {
28     u := user{
29         name:  "Bill",
30         email: "bill@ardanlabs.com",
31     }
32
33     println("V2", &u)
34     return &u
35 }
```

Note: I said the function is using pointer semantics on the return because the user value created by this function is being shared up the call stack. This means the calling function is receiving a copy of the address for the value.

You can see the same struct literal being used on lines 28 through 31 to construct a user value, but on line 34 the return is different. Instead of passing a copy of the user value back up the call stack, a copy of the address for the user value is passed up. Based on this, you might think that the stack looks like this after the call, but this is NOT what is happening.

Figure 2

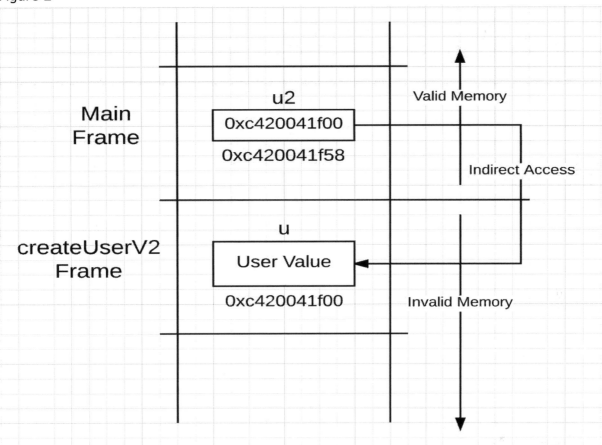

If what you see in Figure 2 was really happening, you would have an integrity issue. The pointer is pointing down the call stack into memory that is no longer valid. On the next function call by main, that memory being pointed to is going to be re-framed and re-initialized.

This is where escape analysis begins to maintain integrity. In this case, the compiler will determine it's not safe to construct the user value inside the stack frame of createUserV2, so instead it will construct the value on the heap. This will happen immediately during construction on line 28.

Readability

As you learned in the last post, a function has direct access to the memory inside its frame, through the frame pointer, but access to memory outside its frame requires indirect access. This means access to values that escape to the heap must be done indirectly through a pointer as well.

Remember what the code looks like for createUserV2.

Listing 5

```
27 func createUserV2() *user {
28     u := user{
29         name:  "Bill",
30         email: "bill@ardanlabs.com",
31     }
32
33     println("V2", &u)
34     return &u
35 }
```

The syntax is hiding what is really happening in this code. The variable u declared on line 28 represents a value of type user. Construction in Go doesn't tell you where a value lives in memory, so it's not until the return statement on line 34, whether you know the value will need to escape. This means, even though u represents a value of type user, access to this user value must be happening through a pointer underneath the covers.

You could visualize the stack looking like this after the function call.

Figure 3

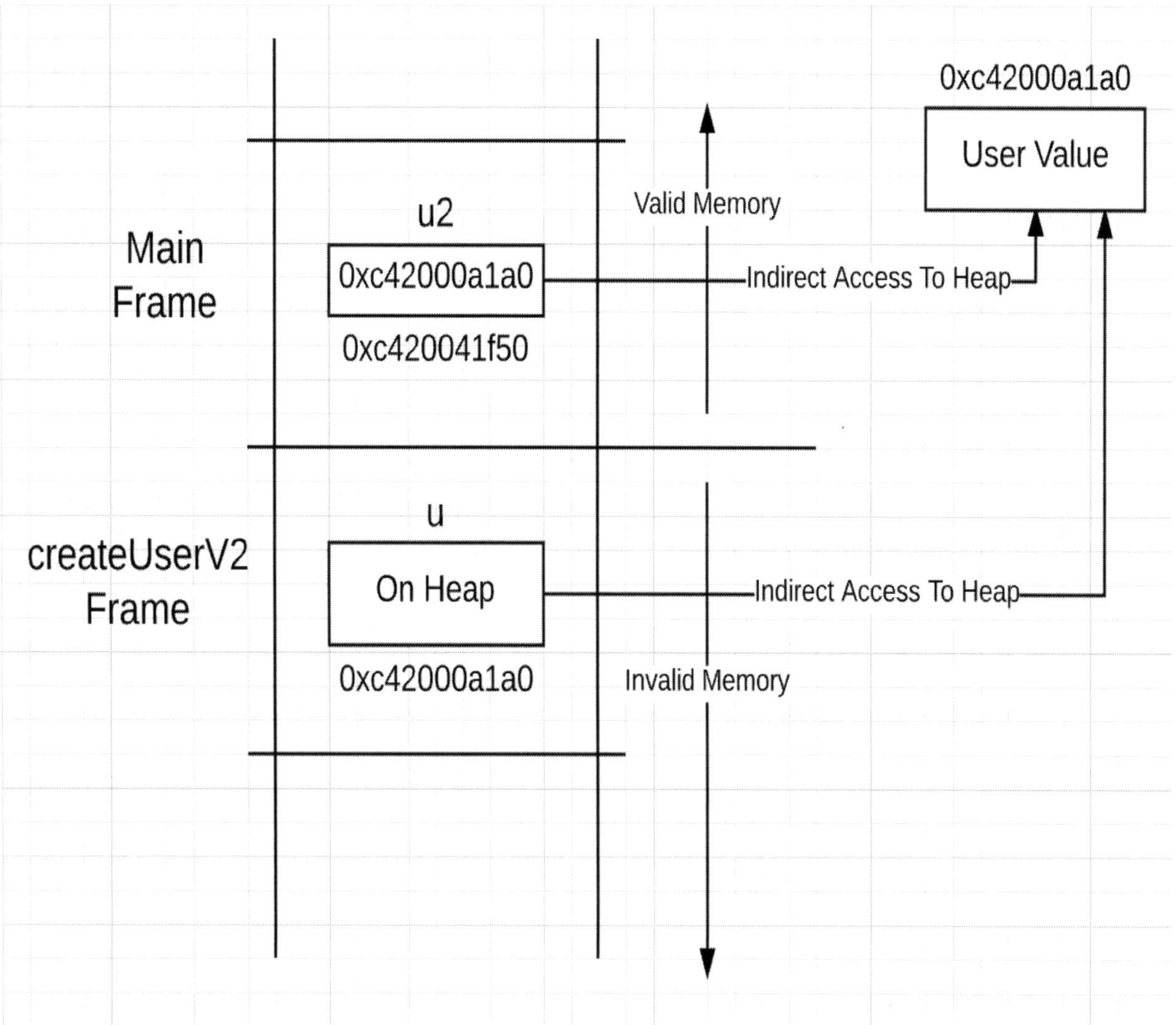

The u variable on the stack frame for createUserV2, represents a value that is on the heap, not the stack. This means using u to access the value requires pointer access and not the direct access the syntax is suggesting. You might think, why not make u a pointer then, since access to the value it represents requires the use of a pointer anyway?

Listing 6

```
27 func createUserV2() *user {
28     u := &user{
29         name:  "Bill",
30         email: "bill@ardanlabs.com",
31     }
32
33     println("V2", u)
34     return u
35 }
```

If you do this, you are walking away from an important readability gain you can have in your code. Step away from the entire function for a second and just focus on the return.

Listing 7

```
34     return u
35 }
```

What does this return tell you? All that it says is that a copy of u is being passed up the call stack. However, what does the return tell you when you use the & operator?

Listing 8

```
34     return &u
35 }
```

Thanks to the & operator, the return now tells you that u is being shared up the call stack and therefore escaping to the heap. Remember, pointers are for sharing. Replace the & operator for the word "sharing" as you read code. This is very powerful in terms of readability, something you don't want to lose.

Here is another example where constructing values using pointer semantics hurts readability.

Listing 9

```
01 var u *user
02 err := json.Unmarshal([]byte(r), &u)
03 return u, err
```

You must share the pointer variable with the json.Unmarshal call on line 02 for this code to work. The json.Unmarshal call will create the user value and assign its address to the pointer variable. https://play.golang.org/p/koI8EjpeIx

What does this code say:

01 : Create a pointer of type user set to its zero value.
02 : Share u with the json.Unmarshal function.
03 : Return a copy of u to the caller.

It is not obviously clear that a user value, which was created by the json.Unmarshal function, is being shared with the caller.

How does readability change when using value semantics during construction?

Listing 10

```
01 var u user
02 err := json.Unmarshal([]byte(r), &u)
03 return &u, err
```

What does this code say:

01 : Create a value of type user set to its zero value.
02 : Share u with the json.Unmarshal function.
03 : Share u with the caller.

Everything is very clear. Line 02 is sharing the user value down the call stack into json.Unmarshal and line 03 is sharing the user value up the call stack back to the caller. This share will cause the user value to escape.

Use value semantics when constructing a value and leverage the readability of the & operator to make it clear how values are being shared.

Compiler Reporting

To see the decisions the compiler is making, you can ask the compiler to provide a report. All you need to do is use the -gcflags switch with the -m option on the go build call.

There are actually 4 levels of -m you can use, but beyond 2 levels the information is overwhelming. I will be using the 2 levels of -m.

Listing 11

```
$ go build -gcflags -m=2

./example4.go:16:6: cannot inline createUserV1: marked go:noinline
./example4.go:27:6: cannot inline createUserV2: marked go:noinline
./example4.go:8:6: cannot inline main: function too complex: cost 132
exceeds budget 80
./example4.go:28:2: u escapes to heap:
./example4.go:28:2:    flow: ~r0 = &u:
./example4.go:28:2:       from &u (address-of) at ./example4.go:34:9
./example4.go:28:2:       from return &u (return) at ./example4.go:34:2
./example4.go:28:2: moved to heap: u
```

You can see the compiler is reporting the escape decisions. What is the compiler saying? First look at the createUserV1 and createUserV2 functions again for reference.

Listing 12

```
16 func createUserV1() user {
17     u := user{
18         name:  "Bill",
19         email: "bill@ardanlabs.com",
20     }
21
22     println("V1", &u)
23     return u
24 }


27 func createUserV2() *user {
28     u := user{
29         name:  "Bill",
30         email: "bill@ardanlabs.com",
31     }
32
33     println("V2", &u)
34     return &u
35 }
```

Look at these lines in the report.

Listing 13

```
./example4.go:28:2: u escapes to heap:
./example4.go:28:2:    flow: ~r0 = &u:
./example4.go:28:2:       from &u (address-of) at ./example4.go:34:9
./example4.go:28:2:       from return &u (return) at ./example4.go:34:2
./example4.go:28:2: moved to heap: u
```

These lines are saying, the user value associated with the u variable, which is constructed on line 28, is escaping because of the return on line 34.

Reading these reports can be confusing and can slightly change depending on whether the type of variable in question is based on a named or literal type.

Change u to be of the literal type *user instead of the named type user that it was before.

Listing 14

```
27 func createUserV2() *user {
28     u := &user{
29         name:  "Bill",
30         email: "bill@ardanlabs.com",
31     }
32
33     println("V2", &u)
34     return u
35 }
```

Run the report again.

Listing 15

```
$ go build -gcflags -m=2

./example4.go:16:6: cannot inline createUserV1: marked go:noinline
./example4.go:27:6: cannot inline createUserV2: marked go:noinline
./example4.go:8:6: cannot inline main: function too complex: cost 132
exceeds budget 80
./example4.go:28:7: &user{...} escapes to heap:
./example4.go:28:7:   flow: u = &{storage for &user{...}}:
./example4.go:28:7:     from &user{...} (spill) at ./example4.go:28:7
./example4.go:28:7:     from u := &user{...} (assign) at ./example4.go:28:4
./example4.go:28:7:   flow: ~r0 = u:
./example4.go:28:7:     from return u (return) at ./example4.go:34:2
./example4.go:28:7: &user{...} escapes to heap
```

Now the report is saying the address to a user value referenced by the u variable, and constructed on line 28, is escaping because of the return on line 34.

Conclusion

The construction of a value doesn't determine where it lives. Only how a value is shared will determine what the compiler will do with that value. Anytime you share a value up the call stack, it is going to escape. There are other reasons for a value to escape which I will explore in the next post.

What these posts are trying to lead you to is guidelines for choosing value or pointer semantics for any given type. Each semantic comes with a benefit and cost. Value semantics keep values on the stack which reduces pressure on the GC.

However, there are different copies of any given value that must be stored, tracked and maintained. Pointer semantics place values on the heap which can put pressure on the GC. However, they are efficient because there is only one value that needs to be stored, tracked and maintained. The key is using each semantic correctly, consistently and in balance.

14.3 Scheduling In Go: OS Scheduler

Introduction

The design and behavior of the Go scheduler allows your multithreaded Go programs to be more efficient and performant. This is thanks to the mechanical sympathies the Go scheduler has for the operating system (OS) scheduler. However, if the design and behavior of your multithreaded Go software is not mechanically sympathetic with how the schedulers work, none of this will matter. It's important to have a general and representative understanding of how both the OS and Go schedulers work to design your multithreaded software correctly.

This multi-part article will focus on the higher-level mechanics and semantics of the schedulers. I will provide enough details to allow you to visualize how things work so you can make better engineering decisions. Even though there is a lot that goes into the engineering decisions you need to make for multithreaded applications, the mechanics and semantics form a critical part of the foundational knowledge you need.

OS Scheduler

Operating system schedulers are complex pieces of software. They have to take into account the layout and setup of the hardware they run on. This includes but is not limited to the existence of multiple processors and cores, CPU caches and NUMA.

http://frankdenneman.nl/2016/07/06/introduction-2016-numa-deep-dive-series

Without this knowledge, the scheduler can't be as efficient as possible. What's great is you can still develop a good mental model of how the OS scheduler works without going deep into these topics.

Your program is just a series of machine instructions that need to be executed one after the other sequentially. To make that happen, the operating system uses the concept of a Thread. It's the job of the Thread to account for and sequentially execute the set of instructions it's assigned. Execution continues until there are no more instructions for the Thread to execute. This is why I call a Thread a path of execution.

Every program you run creates a Process and each Process is given an initial Thread. Threads have the ability to create more Threads. All these different Threads run independently of each other and scheduling decisions are made at the Thread level, not at the Process level. Threads can run concurrently (each taking a turn on an individual core), or in parallel (each running at the same time on different cores). Threads also maintain their own state to allow for the safe, local, and independent execution of their instructions.

The OS scheduler is responsible for making sure cores are not idle if there are Threads that can be executing. It must also create the illusion that all the Threads that can execute are executing at the same time. In the process of creating this illusion, the scheduler needs to run Threads with a higher priority over lower priority Threads. However, Threads with a lower priority can't be starved of execution time. The scheduler also needs to minimize scheduling latencies as much as possible by making quick and smart decisions.

A lot goes into the algorithms to make this happen, but luckily there are decades of work and experience the industry is able to leverage. To understand all of this better, it's good to describe and define a few concepts that are important.

Executing Instructions

The program counter (PC), which is sometimes called the instruction pointer (IP), is what allows the Thread to keep track of the next instruction to execute. In most processors, the PC points to the next instruction and not the current instruction.

Figure 1
https://www.slideshare.net/JohnCutajar/assembly-language-8086-intermediate

The Instruction Pointer (IP)

20

- The computer keeps track of the next line to be executed by keeping its address in a special register called the Instruction Pointer (IP) or Program Counter.

- This register is relative to CS as segment register and points to the next instruction to be executed.

- The contents of this register is updated with every instruction executed.

- Thus a program is executed sequentially line by line

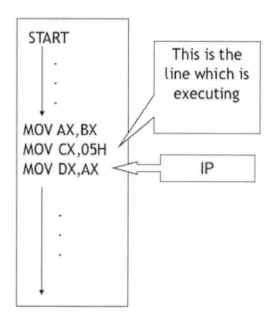

If you have ever seen a stack trace from a Go program, you might have noticed these small hexadecimal numbers at the end of each line. Look for +0x39 and +0x72.

Listing 1

```
goroutine 1 [running]:
    main.example(0xc000042748, 0x2, 0x4, 0x106abae, 0x5, 0xa)
        stack_trace/example1/example1.go:13 +0x39          <- LOOK HERE
    main.main()
        stack_trace/example1/example1.go:8 +0x72           <- LOOK HERE
```

Those numbers represent the PC value offset from the top of the respective function. The +0x39 PC offset value represents the next instruction the Thread would have executed inside the example function if the program hadn't panicked. The 0+x72 PC offset value is the next instruction inside the main function if control happens to go back to that function. More importantly, the instruction prior to that pointer tells you what instruction was executing.

Look at the program below in Listing 2 which caused the stack trace from Listing 1.

292

Listing 2

```
https://github.com/ardanlabs/gotraining/blob/master/topics/go/profiling/
stack_trace/example1/example1.go

07 func main() {
08      example(make([]string, 2, 4), "hello", 10)
09 }

12 func example(slice []string, str string, i int) {
13    panic("Want stack trace")
14 }
```

The hex number +0x39 represents the PC offset for an instruction inside the example function which is 57 (base 10) bytes below the starting instruction for the function. In Listing 3 below, you can see an objdump of the example function from the binary. Find the 12th instruction, which is listed at the bottom. Notice the line of code above that instruction is the call to panic.

Listing 3

```
$ go tool objdump -S -s "main.example" ./example1

func example(slice []string, str string, i int) {
  0x104dfa0        65488b0c2530000000       MOVQ GS:0x30, CX
  0x104dfa9        483b6110                 CMPQ 0x10(CX), SP
  0x104dfad        762c                     JBE 0x104dfdb
  0x104dfaf        4883ec18                 SUBQ $0x18, SP
  0x104dfb3        48896c2410               MOVQ BP, 0x10(SP)
  0x104dfb8        488d6c2410               LEAQ 0x10(SP), BP
       panic("Want stack trace")
  0x104dfbd        488d059ca20000           LEAQ runtime.types+41504(SB), AX
  0x104dfc4        48890424                 MOVQ AX, 0(SP)
  0x104dfc8        488d05a1870200           LEAQ main.statictmp_0(SB), AX
  0x104dfcf        4889442408               MOVQ AX, 0x8(SP)
  0x104dfd4        e8c735fdff               CALL runtime.gopanic(SB)
  0x104dfd9        0f0b                     UD2                  <--- LOOK HERE
PC(+0x39)
```

Remember: the PC is the next instruction, not the current one. Listing 3 is a good example of the amd64 based instructions that the Thread for this Go program is in charge of executing sequentially.

Thread States

Another important concept is Thread state, which dictates the role the scheduler takes with the Thread. A Thread can be in one of three states: Waiting, Runnable or Executing.

Waiting: This means the Thread is stopped and waiting for something in order to continue. This could be for reasons like waiting for the hardware (disk, network), the operating system (system calls) or synchronization calls (atomic, mutexes). These types of latencies are a root cause for bad performance.

Runnable: This means the Thread wants time on a core so it can execute its assigned machine instructions. If you have a lot of Threads that want time, then Threads have to wait longer to get time. Also, the individual amount of time any given Thread gets is shortened, as more Threads compete for time. This type of scheduling latency can also be a cause of bad performance.

Executing: This means the Thread has been placed on a core and is executing its machine instructions. The work related to the application is getting done. This is what everyone wants.

Types Of Work

There are two types of work a Thread can do. The first is called CPU-Bound and the second is called I/O-Bound.

CPU-Bound: This is work that never creates a situation where the Thread may be placed in Waiting states. This is work that is constantly making calculations. A Thread calculating Pi to the Nth digit would be CPU-Bound.

I/O-Bound: This is work that causes Threads to enter into Waiting states. This is work that consists in requesting access to a resource over the network or making system calls into the operating system. A Thread that needs to access a database would be I/O-Bound. I would include synchronization events (mutexes, atomic), that cause the Thread to wait as part of this category.

Context Switching

If you are running on Linux, Mac or Windows, you are running on an OS that has a preemptive scheduler. This means a few important things. First, it means the scheduler is unpredictable when it comes to what Threads will be chosen to run at any given time. Thread priorities together with events, (like receiving data on the network) make it impossible to determine what the scheduler will choose to do and when.

Second, it means you must never write code based on some perceived behavior that you have been lucky to experience but is not guaranteed to take place every time. It is easy to allow yourself to think, because I've seen this happen the same way thousands of times, this is guaranteed behavior. You must control the synchronization and orchestration of Threads if you need determinism in your application.

The physical act of swapping Threads on a core is called context switching. A context switch happens when the scheduler pulls an Executing thread off a core and replaces it with a Runnable Thread. The Thread that was selected from the run queue moves into the Executing state. The Thread that was pulled can move back into the Runnable state (if it still has the ability to run), or into the Waiting state (if was replaced because of an I/O-Bound type of request).

Context switches are considered to be expensive because it takes time to swap Threads on and off a core. The amount of latency incurred during a context switch depends on different factors, but it's not unreasonable for it to take between ~1000 and ~1500 nanoseconds.

https://eli.thegreenplace.net/2018/measuring-context-switching-and-memory-overheads-for-linux-threads

Considering the hardware should be able to reasonably execute (on average) 12 instructions per nanosecond per core, a context switch can cost you ~12k to ~18k instructions of latency.

https://www.youtube.com/watch?v=jEG4Qyo_4Bc&feature=youtu.be&t=266

In essence, your program is losing the ability to execute a large number of instructions during a context switch.

If you have a program that is focused on I/O-Bound work, then context switches are going to be an advantage. Once a Thread moves into a Waiting state, another Thread in a Runnable state is there to take its place. This allows the core to always be doing work. This is one of the most important aspects of scheduling. Don't allow a core to go idle if there is work (Threads in a Runnable state) to be done.

If your program is focused on CPU-Bound work, then context switches are going to be a performance nightmare. Since the Thread always has work to do, the context switch is stopping that work from progressing. This situation is in stark contrast with what happens with an I/O-Bound workload

Less Is More

Improving scheduler latency: https://lwn.net/Articles/404993/

In the early days when processors had only one core, scheduling wasn't overly complicated. Because you had a single processor with a single core, only one Thread could execute at any given time. The idea was to define a scheduler period and attempt to execute all the Runnable Threads within that period of time. No problem: take the scheduling period and divide it by the number of Threads that need to execute.

As an example, if you define your scheduler period to be 1000ms (1 second) and you have 10 Threads, then each thread gets 100ms each. If you have 100 Threads, each Thread gets 10ms each. However, what happens when you have 1000 Threads? Giving each Thread a time slice of 1ms doesn't work because the percentage of time you're spending in context switches will be significantly related to the amount of time you're spending on application work.

What you need is to set a limit on how small a given time slice can be. In the last scenario, if the minimum time slice was 10ms and you have 1000 Threads, the scheduler period needs to increase to 10000ms (10 seconds). What if there were 10,000 Threads, now you are looking at a scheduler period of 100000ms (100 seconds). At 10,000 threads, with a minimal time slice of 10ms, it takes 100 seconds for all the Threads to run once in this simple example if each Thread uses its full time slice.

Be aware this is a very simple view of the world. There are more things that need to be considered and handled by the scheduler when making scheduling decisions as discussed in this post.

https://blog.acolyer.org/2016/04/26/the-linux-scheduler-a-decade-of-wasted-cores/

You control the number of Threads you use in your application. When there are more Threads to consider, and I/O-Bound work happening, there is more chaos and nondeterministic behavior. Things take longer to schedule and execute.

This is why the rule of the game is "Less is More". Less Threads in a Runnable state means less scheduling overhead and more time each Thread gets over time. More Threads in a Runnable state mean less time each Thread gets over time. That means less of your work is getting done over time as well.

Find The Balance

There is a balance you need to find between the number of cores you have and the number of Threads you need to get the best throughput for your application. When it comes to managing this balance, Thread pools are a great answer. I will show you in the next post that this is no longer necessary with Go. I think this is one of the nice things Go did to make multithreaded application development easier.

Prior to coding in Go, I wrote code in C++ and C# on NT. On that operating system, the use of IOCP (IO Completion Ports) thread pools were critical to writing multithreaded software. As an engineer, you needed to figure out how many Thread pools you needed and the max number of Threads for any given pool to maximize throughput for the number of cores that you were given.

When writing web services that talked to a database, the magic number of 3 Threads per core seemed to always give the best throughput on NT. In other words, 3 Threads per core minimized the latency costs of context switching while maximizing execution time on the cores. When creating an IOCP Thread pool, I knew to start with a minimum of 1 Thread and a maximum of 3 Threads for every core I identified on the host machine.

If I used 2 Threads per core, it took longer to get all the work done, because I had idle time when I could have been getting work done. If I used 4 Threads per core, it also took longer, because I had more latency in context switches. The balance of 3 Threads per core, for whatever reason, always seemed to be the magic number on NT.

What if your service is doing a lot of different types of work? That could create different and inconsistent latencies. Maybe it also creates a lot of different system-level events that need to be handled. It might not be possible to find a magic number that works all the time for all the different work loads. When it comes to using Thread pools to tune the performance of a service, it can get very complicated to find the right consistent configuration.

Cache Lines

Accessing data from main memory has such a high latency cost (~100ns or ~1200 instructions) that processors and cores have local caches to keep data close to the hardware threads that need it. Accessing data from caches has a much lower cost (~1.3ns to ~12.3ns or ~16 to ~160 instructions) depending on the cache being accessed. Today, one aspect of performance is about how efficiently you can get data into the processor to reduce these data-access latencies. Writing multithreaded applications that mutate state need to consider the mechanics of the caching system.

Figure 2

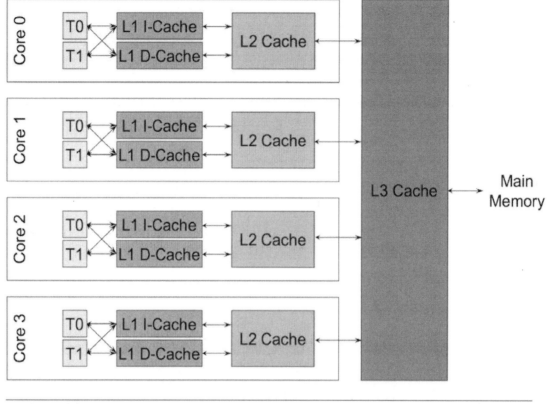

Core i7-9xx Cache Hierarchy

Data is exchanged between the processor and main memory using cache lines.

Note: This talk by Scott Meyers has these details and more:
https://www.youtube.com/watch?v=WDIkqP4JbkE

A cache line is a 64-byte chunk of memory that is exchanged between main memory and the caching system. Each core is given its own copy of any cache line it needs, which means the hardware uses value semantics. This is why mutations to memory in multithreaded applications can create performance nightmares.

When multiple Threads running in parallel are accessing the same data value or even data values near one another, they will be accessing data on the same cache line. Any Thread running on any core will get its own copy of that same cache line.

Figure 3

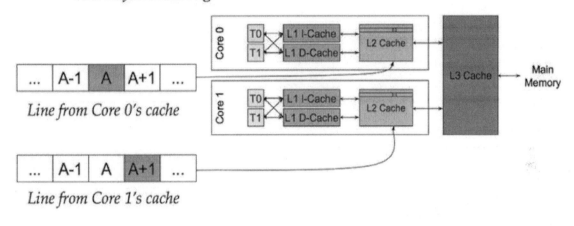

False Sharing

Suppose Core 0 accesses *A* and Core 1 accesses *A+1*.

- *Independent* pieces of memory; concurrent access is safe.

- But *A* and *A+1* probably map to the same cache line.
    - ➡ If so, Core 0's writes to *A* invalidates *A+1*'s cache line in Core 1.
        - ◆ And vice versa.
        - ◆ This is *false sharing*.

If one Thread on a given core makes a change to its copy of the cache line, then through the magic of hardware, all other copies of the same cache line have to be marked dirty. When a Thread attempts to read or write access to a dirty cache line, main memory access (~100 to ~300 clock cycles) is required to get a new copy of the cache line.

Maybe on a 2-core processor this isn't a big deal, but what about a 32-core processor running 32 threads in parallel all accessing and mutating data on the same cache line? What about a system with two physical processors with 16 cores each? This is going to be worse because of the added latency for processor-to-processor communication. The application is going to be thrashing through memory and the performance is going to be horrible and, most likely, you will have no understanding why.

This is called the cache-coherency problem and also introduces problems like false sharing. When writing multithreaded applications that will be mutating shared state, the caching systems have to be taken into account.

Scheduling Decision Scenario

Imagine I've asked you to write the OS scheduler based on the high-level information I've given you. Think about this one scenario that you have to consider. Remember, this is one of many interesting things the scheduler has to consider when making a scheduling decision.

You start your application and the main Thread is created and is executing on core 1. As the Thread starts executing its instructions, cache lines are being retrieved because data is required. The Thread now decides to create a new Thread for some concurrent processing. Here is the question.

Once the Thread is created and ready to go, should the scheduler:

1. Context switch the main Thread off of core 1? Doing this could help performance, as the chances that this new Thread needs the same data that is already cached is pretty good. But the main Thread does not get its full time slice.

2. Have the Thread wait for core 1 to become available pending the completion of the main Thread's time slice? The Thread is not running but latency on fetching data will be eliminated once it starts.

3. Have the Thread wait for the next available core? This would mean cache lines for the selected core would be flushed, retrieved, and duplicated, causing latency. However, the Thread would start more quickly and the main Thread could finish its time slice.

Having fun yet? These are interesting questions that the OS scheduler needs to take into account when making scheduling decisions. Luckily for everyone, I'm not the one making them. All I can tell you is that, if there is an idle core, it's going to be used. You want Threads running when they can be running.

Conclusion

This first part of the post provides insights into what you have to consider regarding Threads and the OS scheduler when writing multithreaded applications. These are the things the Go scheduler takes into consideration as well.

14.4 Scheduling In Go: Go Scheduler

Introduction

When your Go program starts up, it's given a Logical Processor (P) for every virtual core that is identified on the host machine. If you have a processor with multiple hardware threads per physical core Hyper-Threading, each hardware thread will be presented to your Go program as a virtual core. To better understand this, take a look at the system report for my MacBook Pro.

https://en.wikipedia.org/wiki/Hyper-threading

Figure 1

Hardware Overview:

Model Name:	MacBook Pro
Model Identifier:	MacBookPro13,3
Processor Name:	Intel Core i7
Processor Speed:	2.9 GHz
Number of Processors:	1
Total Number of Cores:	4
L2 Cache (per Core):	256 KB
L3 Cache:	8 MB
Memory:	16 GB

You can see I have a single processor with 4 physical cores. What this report is not exposing is the number of hardware threads I have per physical core. The Intel Core i7 processor has Hyper-Threading, which means there are 2 hardware threads per physical core. This will report to the Go program that 8 virtual cores are available for executing OS Threads in parallel.

To test this, consider the following program.

Listing 1

```
package main

import (
    "fmt"
    "runtime"
)

func main() {

    // GOMAXPROCS returns the number of logical
    // CPUs currently being used by the current process.
    fmt.Println(runtime.GOMAXPROCS(0))
}
```

When I run this program on my local machine, the result of the GOMAXPROCS(0) function call will be the value of 8. Any Go program I run on my machine will be given 8 P's.

Every P is assigned an OS Thread ("M"). The M stands for machine. This Thread is still managed by the OS and the OS is still responsible for placing the Thread on a Core for execution. This means when I run a Go program on my machine, I have 8 threads available to execute my work, each individually attached to a P.

Every Go program is also given an initial Goroutine ("G"), which is the path of execution for a Go program. A Goroutine is essentially a Coroutine but this is Go, so we replace the letter C with a G and we get the word Goroutine.

https://en.wikipedia.org/wiki/Coroutine

You can think of Goroutines as application-level threads. They are similar to OS Threads in many ways: eg. just as OS Threads are context-switched on and off a core, Goroutines are context-switched on and off an M.

The last piece of the puzzle is the run queues. There are two different run queues in the Go scheduler: the Global Run Queue (GRQ) and the Local Run Queue (LRQ). Each P is given a LRQ that manages the Goroutines assigned to be executed within the context of a P. These Goroutines take turns being context-switched on and off the M assigned to that P. The GRQ is for Goroutines that have not been assigned to a P yet. There is a process to move Goroutines from the GRQ to a LRQ that we will discuss later.

Figure 2 provides an image of all these components together.

Figure 2

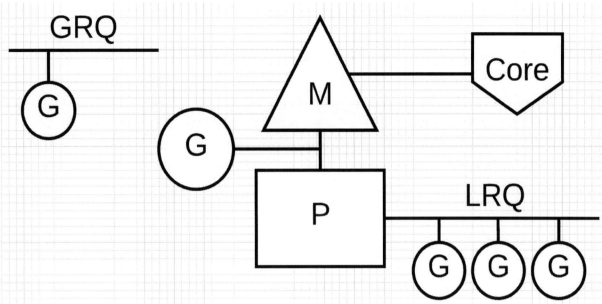

Cooperating Scheduler

As we discussed in the first post, the OS scheduler is a preemptive scheduler. Essentially that means you can't predict what the scheduler is going to do at any given time. The kernel is making decisions and everything is non-deterministic. Applications that run on top of the OS have no control over what is happening inside the kernel with scheduling unless they leverage synchronization primitives like atomic instructions and mutex calls.

https://en.wikipedia.org/wiki/Linearizability
https://en.wikipedia.org/wiki/Lock_(computer_science)

The Go scheduler is part of the Go runtime, and the Go runtime is built into your application. This means the Go scheduler runs in user space, above the kernel.

https://en.wikipedia.org/wiki/User_space

The current implementation of the Go scheduler is a preemptive scheduler.

https://en.wikipedia.org/wiki/Preemption_(computing)

You can't predict what the Go scheduler is going to do. This is because decision making for this scheduler doesn't rest in the hands of developers, but in the Go runtime. It's important to understand the scheduler is non-deterministic.

Goroutine States

Just like Threads, Goroutines have the same three high-level states. These dictate the role the Go scheduler takes with any given Goroutine. A Goroutine can be in one of three states: Waiting, Runnable or Running.

Waiting: This means the Goroutine is stopped and waiting for something in order to continue. This could be for reasons like waiting for the operating system (system calls) or synchronization calls (atomic and mutex operations). These types of latencies are a root cause for bad performance.

Runnable: This means the Goroutine wants time on an M so it can execute its assigned instructions. If you have a lot of Goroutines that want time, then Goroutines have to wait longer to get time. Also, the individual amount of time any given Goroutine gets is shortened as more Goroutines compete for time. This type of scheduling latency can also be a cause of bad performance.

Running: This means the Goroutine has been placed on an M and is executing its instructions. The work related to the application is getting done. This is what everyone wants.

Context Switching

The Go scheduler requires well-defined user-space events that occur at safe points in the code to context switch from. These events and safe points manifest themselves within function calls or in between instructions.

There are several classes of events that occur in your Go programs that allow the scheduler to make scheduling decisions. This doesn't mean it will always happen on one of these events. It means the scheduler gets the opportunity.

These events are:

- The use of the keyword go
- Garbage collection
- System calls
- Synchronization and Orchestration

The use of the keyword go

The keyword go is how you create Goroutines. Once a new Goroutine is created, it gives the scheduler an opportunity to make a scheduling decision.

Garbage collection

Since the GC runs using its own set of Goroutines, those Goroutines need time on an M to run. This causes the GC to create a lot of scheduling chaos. However, the scheduler is very smart about what a Goroutine is doing and it will leverage that intelligence to make smart decisions. One smart decision is context switching a Goroutine that wants to touch the heap with those that don't touch the heap during GC. When GC is running, a lot of scheduling decisions are being made.

System calls

If a Goroutine makes a system call that will cause the Goroutine to block the M, sometimes the scheduler is capable of context switching the Goroutine off the M and context-switch a new Goroutine onto that same M. However, sometimes a new M is required to keep executing Goroutines that are queued up in the P. How this works will be explained in more detail in the next section.

Synchronization and Orchestration

If an atomic, mutex, or channel operation call will cause the Goroutine to block, the scheduler can context-switch a new Goroutine to run. Once the Goroutine can run again, it can be re-queued and eventually context-switched back on an M.

Asynchronous System Calls

When the OS you are running on has the ability to handle a system call asynchronously, something called the network poller can be used to process the system call more efficiently. This is accomplished by using kqueue (MacOS), epoll (Linux) or iocp (Windows) within these respective OS's.

https://golang.org/src/runtime/netpoll.go

Networking-based system calls can be processed asynchronously by many of the OSs we use today. This is where the network poller gets its name, since its primary use is handling networking operations. By using the network poller for networking system calls, the scheduler can prevent Goroutines from blocking the M when those system calls are made. This helps to keep the M available to execute other Goroutines in the P's LRQ without the need to create new Ms. This helps to reduce scheduling load on the OS.

The best way to see how this works is to run through an example.

Figure 3

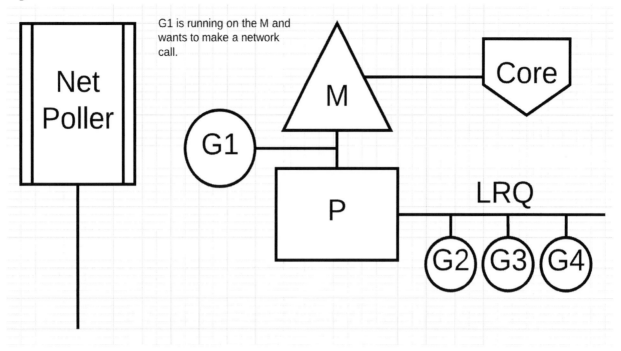

G1 is running on the M and wants to make a network call.

Figure 3 shows our base scheduling diagram. Goroutine-1 is executing on the M and there are 3 more Goroutines waiting in the LRQ to get their time on the M. The network poller is idle with nothing to do.

Figure 4

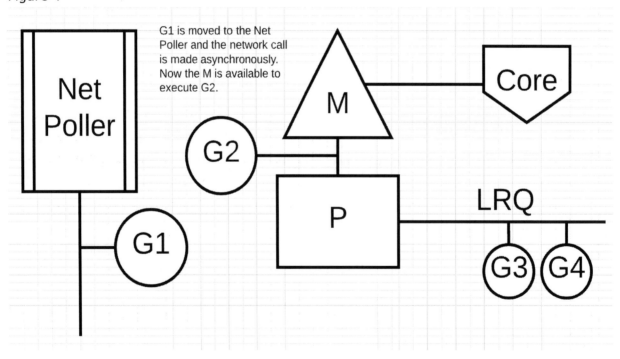

G1 is moved to the Net Poller and the network call is made asynchronously. Now the M is available to execute G2.

In figure 4, Goroutine-1 wants to make a network system call, so Goroutine-1 is moved to the network poller and the asynchronous network system call is processed. Once Goroutine-1 is moved to the network poller, the M is now available to execute a different Goroutine from the LRQ. In this case, Goroutine-2 is context switched on the M.

Figure 5

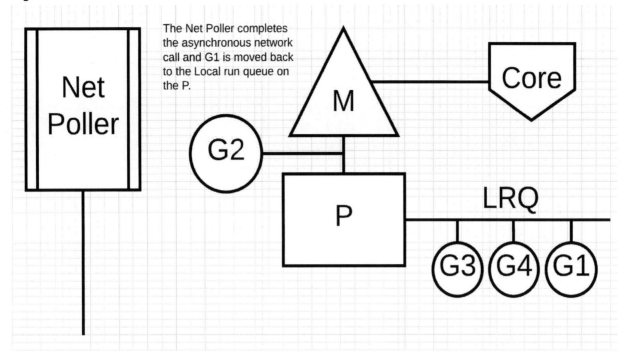

The Net Poller completes the asynchronous network call and G1 is moved back to the Local run queue on the P.

In figure 5, the asynchronous network system call is completed by the network poller and Goroutine-1 is moved back into the LRQ for the P. Once Goroutine-1 can be context switched back on the M, the Go related code it's responsible for can execute again. The big win here is that, to execute network system calls, no extra Ms are needed. The network poller has an OS Thread and it is handling an efficient event loop.

Synchronous System Calls

What happens when the Goroutine wants to make a system call that can't be done asynchronously? In this case, the network poller can't be used and the Goroutine making the system call is going to block the M. This is unfortunate but there's no way to prevent this from happening. One example of a system call that can't be made asynchronously is file-based system calls. If you are using CGO, there may be other situations where calling C functions will block the M as well.

Let's walk through what happens with a synchronous system call (like file I/O) that will cause the M to block.

Figure 6

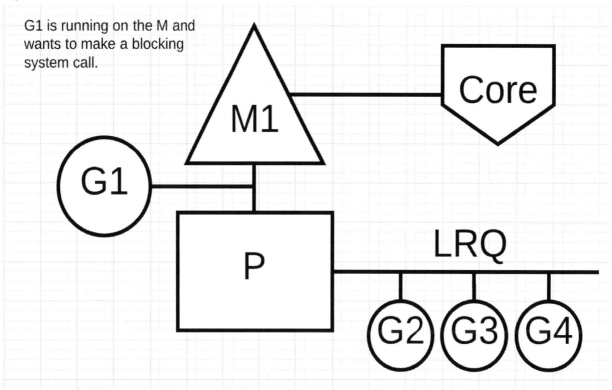

G1 is running on the M and wants to make a blocking system call.

Figure 6 is showing our basic scheduling diagram again but this time Goroutine-1 is going to make a synchronous system call that will block M1.

Figure 7

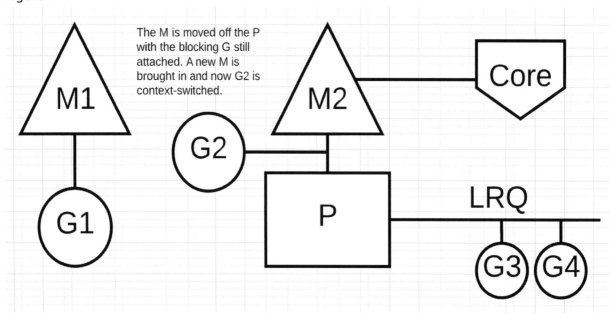

The M is moved off the P with the blocking G still attached. A new M is brought in and now G2 is context-switched.

In figure 7, the scheduler is able to identify that Goroutine-1 has caused the M to block. At this point, the scheduler detaches M1 from the P with the blocking Goroutine-1 still attached. Then the scheduler brings in a new M2 to service the P. At that point, Goroutine-2 can be selected from the LRQ and context switched on M2. If an M already exists because of a previous swap, this transition is quicker than having to create a new M.

Figure 8

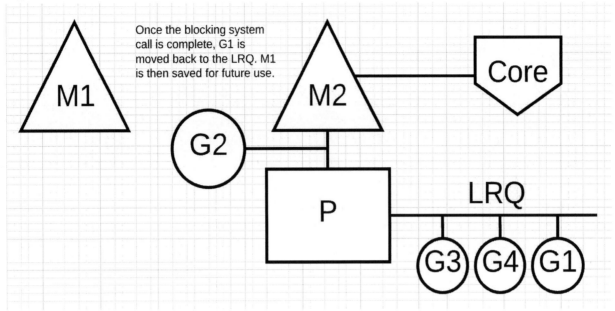

Once the blocking system call is complete, G1 is moved back to the LRQ. M1 is then saved for future use.

In figure 8, the blocking system call that was made by Goroutine-1 finishes. At this point, Goroutine-1 can move back into the LRQ and be serviced by the P again. M1 is then placed on the side for future use if this scenario needs to happen again.

Work Stealing

Another aspect of the scheduler is that it's a work-stealing scheduler. This helps in a few areas to keep scheduling efficient. For one, the last thing you want is an M to move into a waiting state because, once that happens, the OS will context-switch the M off the Core. This means the P can't get any work done, even if there is a Goroutine in a runnable state, until an M is context-switched back on a Core. The work stealing also helps to balance the Goroutines across all the P's so the work is better distributed and getting done more efficiently.

Let's run through an example.

Figure 9

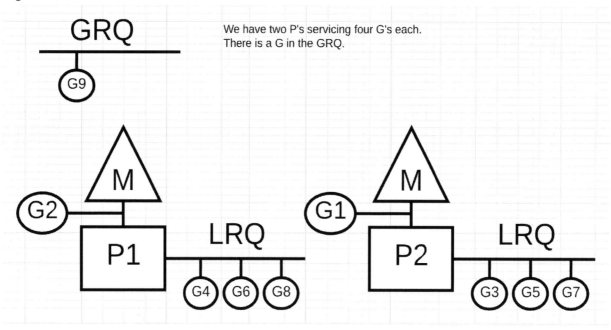

In figure 9, we have a multi-threaded Go program with two P's servicing four Goroutines each and a single Goroutine in the GRQ. What happens if one of the P's services all of its Goroutines quickly?

Figure 10

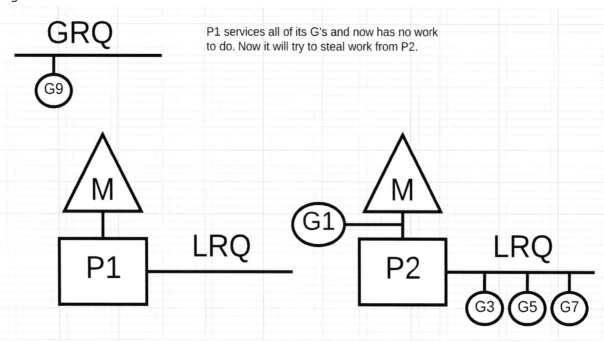

In figure 10, P1 has no more Goroutines to execute. But there are Goroutines in a runnable state, both in the LRQ for P2 and in the GRQ. This is a moment where P1 needs to steal work. The rules for stealing work are as follows.

https://golang.org/src/runtime/proc.go

310

Listing 2

```
runtime.schedule() {
    // only 1/61 of the time, check the global runnable queue for a G.
    // if not found, check the local queue.
    // if not found,
    //      try to steal from other Ps.
    //      if not, check the global runnable queue.
    //      if not found, poll network.
}
```

So based on these rules in Listing 2, P1 needs to check P2 for Goroutines in its LRQ and take half of what it finds.

Figure 11

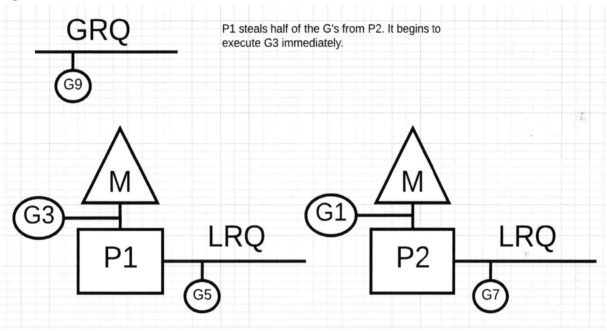

In figure 11, half the Goroutines are taken from P2 and now P1 can execute those Goroutines.

What happens if P2 finishes servicing all of its Goroutines and P1 has nothing left in its LRQ?

Figure 12

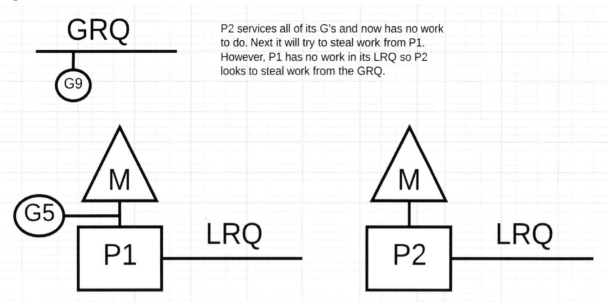

In figure 12, P2 finished all its work and now needs to steal some. First, it will look at the LRQ of P1 but it won't find any Goroutines. Next, it will look at the GRQ. There it will find Goroutine-9.

Figure 13

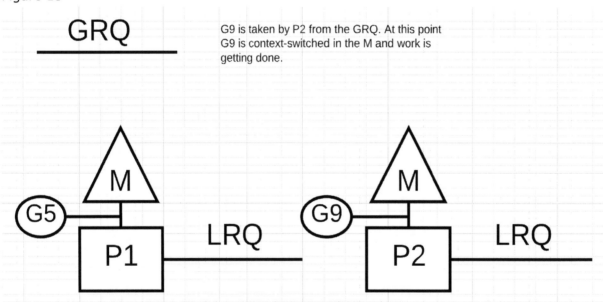

In figure 13, P2 steals Goroutine-9 from the GRQ and begins to execute the work. What is great about all this work stealing is that it allows the Ms to stay busy and not go idle. This work stealing is considered internally as spinning the M. This spinning has other benefits that JBD explains well in her work-stealing blog post.

https://rakyll.org/scheduler

Practical Example

With the mechanics and semantics in place, I want to show you how all of this comes together to allow the Go scheduler to execute more work over time. Imagine a multi-threaded application written in C where the program is managing two OS Threads that are passing messages back and forth to each other.

Figure 14

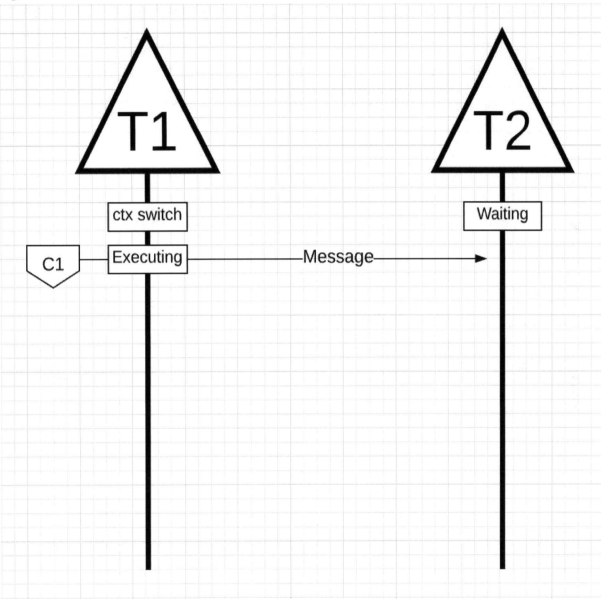

In figure 14, there are 2 Threads that are passing a message back and forth. Thread 1 gets context switched on Core 1 and is now executing, which allows Thread 1 to send its message to Thread 2.

Note: How the message is being passed is unimportant. What's important is the state of the Threads as this orchestration proceeds.

Figure 15

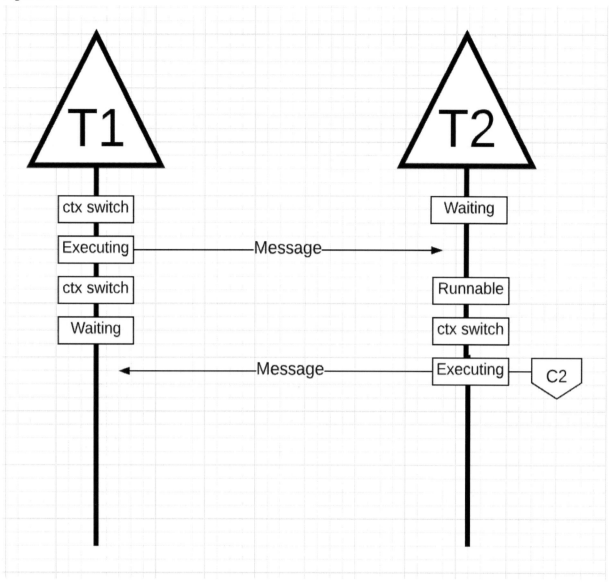

In figure 15, once Thread 1 finishes sending the message, it now needs to wait for the response. This will cause Thread 1 to be context switched off Core 1 and moved into a waiting state. Once Thread 2 is notified about the message, it moves into a runnable state. Now the OS can perform a context switch and get Thread 2 executing on a Core, which happens to be Core 2. Next, Thread 2 processes the message and sends a new message back to Thread 1.

Figure 16

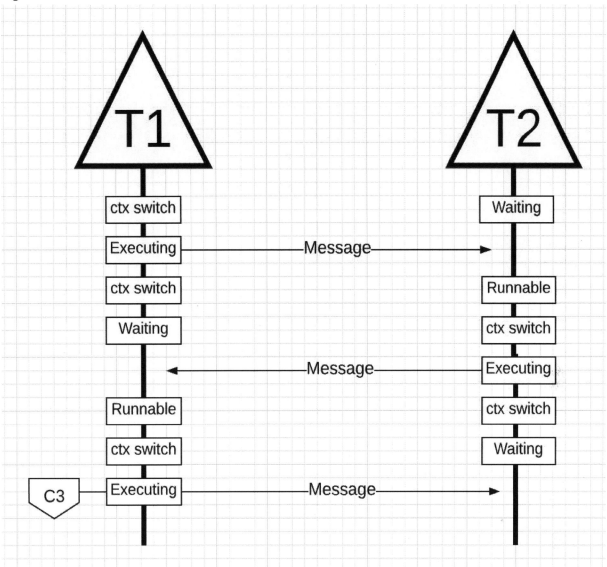

In figure 16, Threads context switch once again as the message by Thread 2 is received by Thread 1. Now Thread 2 context switches from the executing state to the waiting state and Thread 1 context switches from the waiting state to the runnable state and finally back to the executing state, which allows it to process and send a new message back.

All these context switches and state changes require time to be performed which limits how fast the work can get done. With each context switching potential incurring a latency of ~1000ns and hopefully the hardware executing 12 instructions per nanosecond, you are looking at 12k instructions, more or less, not executing during these context switches. Since these Threads are also bouncing between different Cores, the chances of incurring additional latency due to cache-line misses are also high.

Let's take this same example but use Goroutines and the Go scheduler instead.

Figure 17

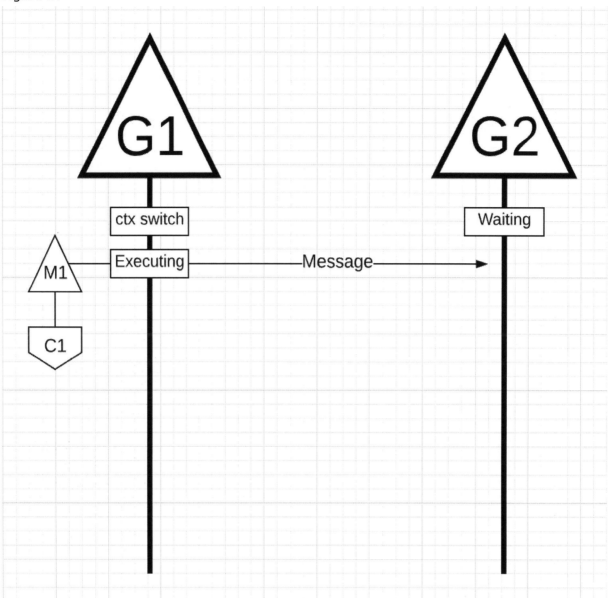

In figure 17, there are two Goroutines that are in orchestration with each other passing a message back and forth. G1 gets context switched on M1, which happens to be running on Core 1, which allows G1 to be executing its work. The work is for G1 to send its message to G2.

Figure 18

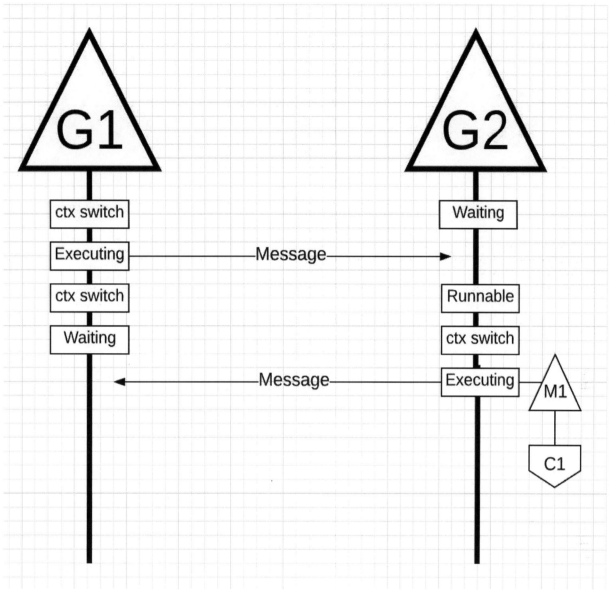

In figure 18, once G1 finishes sending the message, it now needs to wait for the response. This will cause G1 to be context switched off M1 and moved into a waiting state. Once G2 is notified about the message, it moves into a runnable state. Now the Go scheduler can perform a context switch and get G2 executing on M1, which is still running on Core 1. Next, G2 processes the message and sends a new message back to G1.

Figure 19

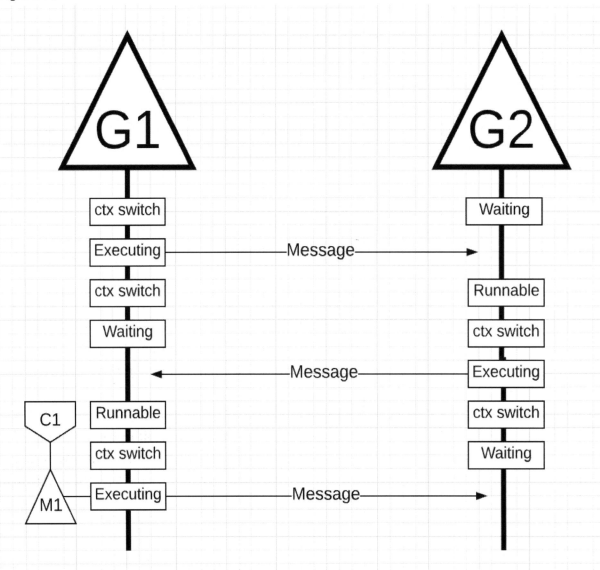

In figure 19, things context switch once again as the message sent by G2 is received by G1. Now G2 context switches from the executing state to the waiting state and G1 context switches from the waiting state to the runnable state and finally back to the executing state, which allows it to process and send a new message back.

Things on the surface don't appear to be any different. All the same context switches and state changes are occurring whether you use Threads or Goroutines. However, there is a major difference between using Threads and Goroutines that might not be obvious at first glance.

In the case of using Goroutines, the same OS Thread and Core is being used for all the processing. This means that, from the OS's perspective, the OS Thread never moves into a waiting state; not once. As a result all those instructions we lost to context switches when using Threads are not lost when using Goroutines.

Essentially, Go has turned I/O-Bound work into CPU-Bound work at the OS level.

Since all the context switching is happening at the application level, we don't lose the same ~12k instructions (on average) per context switch that we were losing when using Threads. In Go, those same context switches are costing you ~200ns or ~2.4k instructions. The scheduler is also helping with gains on cache-line efficiencies and NUMA. This is why we don't need more Threads than we have virtual cores. In Go, it's possible to get more work done, over time, because the Go scheduler attempts to use less Threads and do more on each Thread, which helps to reduce load on the OS and the hardware.

Conclusion

The Go scheduler is really amazing in how the design takes into account the intricacies of how the OS and the hardware work. The ability to turn I/O-Bound work into CPU-Bound work at the OS level is where we get a big win in leveraging more CPU capacity over time. This is why you don't need more OS Threads than you have virtual cores. You can reasonably expect to get all of your work done (CPU and I/O Bound) with just one OS Thread per virtual core. Doing so is possible for networking apps and other apps that don't need system calls that block OS Threads.

As a developer, you still need to understand what your app is doing in terms of the kinds of work you are processing. You can't create an unlimited number of Goroutines and expect amazing performance. Less is always more, but with the understanding of these Go-scheduler semantics, you can make better engineering decisions.

14.5 Scheduling In Go: Concurrency

Introduction

When I'm solving a problem, especially if it's a new problem, I don't initially think about whether concurrency is a good fit or not. I look for a sequential solution first and make sure that it's working. Then, after readability and technical reviews, I will begin to ask the question if concurrency is reasonable and practical. Sometimes it's obvious that concurrency is a good fit and other times it's not so clear.

In this post, I will begin to bring the mechanics and semantics of the OS and Go schedulers together to provide a deeper understanding on what concurrency is and isn't.

The goals of this post are:

- Provide guidance on the semantics you must consider to determine if a workload is suitable for using concurrency.
- Show you how different types of workloads change the semantics and therefore the engineering decisions you will want to make.

What is Concurrency

Concurrency means undefined out of order execution. Taking a set of instructions that would otherwise be executed in sequence and finding a way to execute them out of order and still produce the same result. For the problem in front of you, it has to be obvious that out of order execution would add value. When I say value, I mean add enough of a performance gain for the complexity cost. Depending on your problem, out of order execution may not be possible or even make sense.

It's important to understand that concurrency is not the same as parallelism.

https://blog.golang.org/concurrency-is-not-parallelism

Parallelism means executing two or more instructions at the same time. This is a different concept from concurrency. Parallelism is only possible when you have at least two operating system (OS) and hardware threads available to you, and you have at least two Goroutines, each executing instructions independently on separate OS/hardware threads.

Figure 1

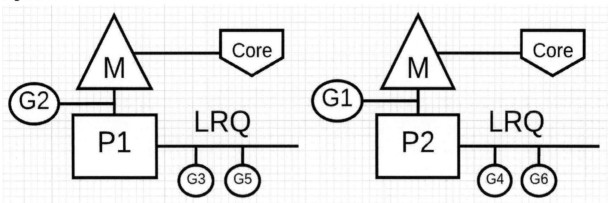

In figure 1, you see a diagram of two logical processors (P) each with their independent OS thread (M) attached to an independent hardware thread (Core) on the machine. You can see two Goroutines (G1 and G2) are executing in parallel, executing their instructions on their respective OS/hardware thread at the same time. Within each logical processor, three Goroutines are taking turns sharing their respective OS thread. All these Goroutines are running concurrently, executing their instructions in no particular order and sharing time on the OS thread.

Here's the rub, sometimes leveraging concurrency without parallelism can actually slow down your throughput. What's also interesting is, sometimes leveraging concurrency with parallelism doesn't give you a bigger performance gain than you might otherwise think you can achieve.

Workloads

How do you know when out of order execution may be possible or make sense? Understanding the type of workload your problem is handling is a great place to start. There are two types of workloads that are important to understand when thinking about concurrency.

CPU-Bound: This is a workload that never creates a situation where Goroutines naturally move in and out of waiting states. This is work that is constantly making calculations. A Thread calculating Pi to the Nth digit would be CPU-Bound.

I/O-Bound: This is a workload that causes Goroutines to naturally enter into waiting states. This is work that consists in requesting access to a resource over the network, or making system calls into the operating system, or waiting for an event to occur. A Goroutine that needs to read a file would be I/O-Bound. I would include synchronization events (mutexes, atomic), that cause the Goroutine to wait as part of this category.

With CPU-Bound workloads you need parallelism to leverage concurrency. A single OS/hardware thread handling multiple Goroutines is not efficient since the

Goroutines are not moving in and out of waiting states as part of their workload. Having more Goroutines than there are OS/hardware threads can slow down workload execution because of the latency cost (the time it takes) of moving Goroutines on and off the OS thread. The context switch is creating a "Stop The World" event for your workload since none of your workload is being executed during the switch when it otherwise could be.

With I/O-Bound workloads you don't need parallelism to use concurrency. A single OS/hardware thread can handle multiple Goroutines with efficiency since the Goroutines are naturally moving in and out of waiting states as part of their workload. Having more Goroutines than there are OS/hardware threads can speed up workload execution because the latency cost of moving Goroutines on and off the OS thread is not creating a "Stop The World" event. Your workload is naturally stopped and this allows a different Goroutine to leverage the same OS/hardware thread efficiently instead of letting the OS/hardware thread sit idle.

How do you know how many Goroutines per hardware thread provides the best throughput? Too few Goroutines and you have more idle time. Too many Goroutines and you have more context switch latency time. This is something for you to think about but beyond the scope of this particular post.

For now it's important to review some code to solidify your ability to identify when a workload can leverage concurrency, when it can't ,and if parallelism is needed or not.

Adding Numbers

We don't need complex code to visualize and understand these semantics. Look at the following function named add that sums a collection of integers.

Listing 1

```
36 func add(numbers []int) int {
37     var v int
38     for _, n := range numbers {
39         v += n
40     }
41     return v
42 }
```

In listing 1 on line 36, a function named add is declared that takes a collection of integers and returns the sum of the collection. It starts on line 37 with the declaration of the v variable to contain the sum. Then on line 38, the function traverses the collection linearly and each number is added to the current sum on line 39. Finally on line 41, the function returns the final sum back to the caller.

Question: is the add function a workload that is suitable for out of order execution? I believe the answer is yes. The collection of integers could be broken up into smaller lists and those lists could be processed concurrently. Once all the smaller lists are summed, the set of sums could be added together to produce the same answer as the sequential version.

However, there is another question that comes to mind. How many smaller lists should be created and processed independently to get the best throughput? To answer this question you must know what kind of workload add is performing. The add function is performing a CPU-Bound workload because the algorithm is performing pure math and nothing it does would cause the goroutine to enter into a natural waiting state. This means using one Goroutine per OS/hardware thread is all that is needed for good throughput.

Listing 2 below is my concurrent version of add.

Listing 2

```
44 func addConcurrent(goroutines int, numbers []int) int {
45      var v int64
46      totalNumbers := len(numbers)
47      lastGoroutine := goroutines - 1
48      stride := totalNumbers / goroutines
49
50      var wg sync.WaitGroup
51      wg.Add(goroutines)
52
53      for g := 0; g < goroutines; g++ {
54          go func(g int) {
55              start := g * stride
56              end := start + stride
57              if g == lastGoroutine {
58                  end = totalNumbers
59              }
60
61              var lv int
62              for _, n := range numbers[start:end] {
63                  lv += n
64              }
65
66              atomic.AddInt64(&v, int64(lv))
67              wg.Done()
68          }(g)
69      }
70
71      wg.Wait()
72
73      return int(v)
74 }
```

Note: There are several ways and options you can take when writing a concurrent version of add. Don't get hung up on my particular implementation at this time. If you have a more readable version that performs the same or better I would love for you to share it.

Listing 2 shows a concurrent version of the add function. This version uses 26 lines of code as opposed to the 5 lines of code for the non-concurrent version. There is a lot of code so I will only highlight the important lines to understand.

Line 48: Each Goroutine will get their own unique but smaller list of numbers to add. The size of the list is calculated by taking the size of the collection and dividing it by the number of Goroutines.

Line 53: The pool of Goroutines is created to perform the adding work.

Line 57-59: The last Goroutine will add the remaining list of numbers which may be greater than the other Goroutines.

Line 66: The sum of the smaller lists are summed together into a final sum.

The concurrent version is definitely more complex than the sequential version, But is the complexity worth it? The best way to answer that question is to create a benchmark. For these benchmarks I have used a collection of 10 million numbers with the garbage collector turned off. Listing 3 shows a sequential version that uses the add function and a concurrent version that uses the addConcurrent function.

Listing 3

```
func BenchmarkSequential(b *testing.B) {
    for i := 0; i < b.N; i++ {
        add(numbers)
    }
}

func BenchmarkConcurrent(b *testing.B) {
    for i := 0; i < b.N; i++ {
        addConcurrent(runtime.NumCPU(), numbers)
    }
}
```

Here are the results when only a single OS/hardware thread is available for all Goroutines. The sequential version is using 1 Goroutine and the concurrent version is using runtime.NumCPU or 8 Goroutines on my machine. In this case, the concurrent version is leveraging concurrency without parallelism.

Listing 4

```
10 Million Numbers using 8 goroutines with 1 core
2.9 GHz Intel 4 Core i7
Concurrency WITHOUT Parallelism
-----------------------------------------------------------------------
$ GOGC=off go test -cpu 1 -run none -bench . -benchtime 3s
goos: darwin
goarch: amd64
pkg: github.com/ardanlabs/gotraining/topics/go/testing/benchmarks/cpu-bound
BenchmarkSequential              1000        5720764 ns/op : ~10% Faster
BenchmarkConcurrent              1000        6387344 ns/op
BenchmarkSequentialAgain         1000        5614666 ns/op : ~13% Faster
BenchmarkConcurrentAgain         1000        6482612 ns/op
```

Note: Running a benchmark on your local machine is complicated. There are so many factors that can cause your benchmarks to be inaccurate. Make sure your machine is as idle as possible and run benchmarks a few times. You want to make sure you see consistency in the results. Having the benchmark run twice by the testing tool is giving this benchmark the most consistent results.

The benchmark in listing 4 shows that the Sequential version is approximately 10 to 13 percent faster than the Concurrent when only a single OS/hardware thread is available for all Goroutines. This is what I would have expected since the concurrent version has the overhead of context switches on that single OS thread and the management of the Goroutines.

Here are the results when an individual OS/hardware thread is available for each Goroutine. The sequential version is using 1 Goroutine and the concurrent version is using runtime.NumCPU or 8 Goroutines on my machine. In this case, the concurrent version is leveraging concurrency with parallelism.

Listing 5

```
10 Million Numbers using 8 goroutines with 8 cores
2.9 GHz Intel 4 Core i7
Concurrency WITH Parallelism
-----------------------------------------------------------------------
$ GOGC=off go test -cpu 8 -run none -bench . -benchtime 3s
goos: darwin
goarch: amd64
pkg: github.com/ardanlabs/gotraining/topics/go/testing/benchmarks/cpu-bound
BenchmarkSequential-8            1000        5910799 ns/op
BenchmarkConcurrent-8            2000        3362643 ns/op : ~43% Faster
BenchmarkSequentialAgain-8       1000        5933444 ns/op
BenchmarkConcurrentAgain-8       2000        3477253 ns/op : ~41% Faster
```

The benchmark in listing 5 shows that the concurrent version is approximately 41 to 43 percent faster than the sequential version when an individual OS/hardware thread is available for each Goroutine. This is what I would have expected since all the Goroutines are now running in parallel, eight Goroutines executing their concurrent work at the same time.

Sorting

It's important to understand that not all CPU-Bound workloads are suitable for concurrency. This is primarily true when it's very expensive to either break work up, and/or combine all the results. An example of this can be seen with the sorting algorithm called Bubble sort. Look at the following code that implements Bubble sort in Go.

Listing 6

```go
01 package main
02
03 import "fmt"
04
05 func bubbleSort(numbers []int) {
06     n := len(numbers)
07     for i := 0; i < n; i++ {
08         if !sweep(numbers, i) {
09             return
10         }
11     }
12 }
13
14 func sweep(numbers []int, currentPass int) bool {
15     var idx int
16     idxNext := idx + 1
17     n := len(numbers)
18     var swap bool
19
20     for idxNext < (n - currentPass) {
21         a := numbers[idx]
22         b := numbers[idxNext]
23         if a > b {
24             numbers[idx] = b
25             numbers[idxNext] = a
26             swap = true
27         }
28         idx++
29         idxNext = idx + 1
30     }
31     return swap
32 }
33
34 func main() {
35     org := []int{1, 3, 2, 4, 8, 6, 7, 2, 3, 0}
36     fmt.Println(org)
```

```
37
38      bubbleSort(org)
39      fmt.Println(org)
40 }
```

In listing 6, there is an example of Bubble sort written in Go. This sorting algorithm sweeps through a collection of integers swapping values on every pass. Depending on the ordering of the list, it may require multiple passes through the collection before everything is sorted.

Question: is the bubbleSort function a workload that is suitable for out of order execution? I believe the answer is no. The collection of integers could be broken up into smaller lists and those lists could be sorted concurrently. However, after all the concurrent work is done there is no efficient way to sort the smaller lists together. Here is an example of a concurrent version of Bubble sort.

Listing 8

```
01 func bubbleSortConcurrent(goroutines int, numbers []int) {
02      totalNumbers := len(numbers)
03      lastGoroutine := goroutines - 1
04      stride := totalNumbers / goroutines
05
06      var wg sync.WaitGroup
07      wg.Add(goroutines)
08
09      for g := 0; g < goroutines; g++ {
10          go func(g int) {
11              start := g * stride
12              end := start + stride
13              if g == lastGoroutine {
14                  end = totalNumbers
15              }
16
17              bubbleSort(numbers[start:end])
18              wg.Done()
19          }(g)
20      }
21
22      wg.Wait()
23
24      // Ugh, we have to sort the entire list again.
25      bubbleSort(numbers)
26 }
```

In Listing 8, the bubbleSortConcurrent function is presented which is a concurrent version of the bubbleSort function. It uses multiple Goroutines to sort portions of the list concurrently. However, what you are left with is a list of sorted values in chunks. Given a list of 36 numbers, split in groups of 12, this would be the resulting list if the entire list is not sorted once more on line 25.

Listing 9

```
Before:
  25 51 15 57 87 10 10 85 90 32 98 53
  91 82 84 97 67 37 71 94 26  2 81 79
  66 70 93 86 19 81 52 75 85 10 87 49

After:
  10 10 15 25 32 51 53 57 85 87 90 98
   2 26 37 67 71 79 81 82 84 91 94 97
  10 19 49 52 66 70 75 81 85 86 87 93
```

Since the nature of Bubble sort is to sweep through the list, the call to bubbleSort on line 25 will negate any potential gains from using concurrency. With Bubble sort, there is no performance gain by using concurrency.

Reading Files

Two CPU-Bound workloads have been presented, but what about an I/O-Bound workload? Are the semantics different when Goroutines are naturally moving in and out of waiting states? Look at an I/O-Bound workload that reads files and performs a text search.

This first version is a sequential version of a function called find.

Listing 10

```
42 func find(topic string, docs []string) int {
43     var found int
44     for _, doc := range docs {
45         items, err := read(doc)
46         if err != nil {
47             continue
48         }
49         for _, item := range items {
50             if strings.Contains(item.Description, topic) {
51                 found++
52             }
53         }
54     }
55     return found
56 }
```

In listing 10, you see the sequential version of the find function. On line 43, a variable named found is declared to maintain a count for the number of times the specified topic is found inside a given document. Then on line 44, the documents are iterated over and each document is read on line 45 using the read function.

Finally on line 49-53, the Contains function from the strings package is used to check if the topic can be found inside the collection of items read from the document. If the topic is found, the found variable is incremented by one.

Here is the implementation of the read function that is being called by find.

Listing 11

```
33 func read(doc string) ([]item, error) {
34     time.Sleep(time.Millisecond) // Simulate blocking disk read.
35     var d document
36     if err := xml.Unmarshal([]byte(file), &d); err != nil {
37         return nil, err
38     }
39     return d.Channel.Items, nil
40 }
```

The read function in listing 11 starts with a time.Sleep call for one millisecond. This call is being used to mock the latency that could be produced if we performed an actual system call to read the document from disk. The consistency of this latency is important for accurately measuring the performance of the sequential version of find against the concurrent version. Then on lines 35-39, the mock xml document stored in the global variable file is unmarshaled into a struct value for processing. Finally, a collection of items is returned back to the caller on line 39.

With the sequential version in place, here is the concurrent version.

Note: There are several ways and options you can take when writing a concurrent version of find. Don't get hung up on my particular implementation at this time. If you have a more readable version that performs the same or better I would love for you to share it.

Listing 12

```
58 func findConcurrent(goroutines int, topic string, docs []string) int {
59     var found int64
60
61     ch := make(chan string, len(docs))
62     for _, doc := range docs {
63         ch <- doc
64     }
65     close(ch)
66
67     var wg sync.WaitGroup
68     wg.Add(goroutines)
69
70     for g := 0; g < goroutines; g++ {
71         go func() {
72             var lFound int64
73             for doc := range ch {
74                 items, err := read(doc)
75                 if err != nil {
76                     continue
77                 }
78                 for _, item := range items {
79                     if strings.Contains(item.Description, topic) {
80                         lFound++
81                     }
82                 }
83             }
84             atomic.AddInt64(&found, lFound)
85             wg.Done()
86         }()
87     }
88
89     wg.Wait()
90
91     return int(found)
92 }
```

Listing 12 shows a concurrent version of the find function. This version uses 30 lines of code as opposed to the 13 lines of code for the non-concurrent version. My goal in implementing the concurrent version was to control the number of Goroutines that are used to process the unknown number of documents. A pooling pattern where a channel is used to feed the pool of Goroutines was my choice.

There is a lot of code so I will only highlight the important lines to understand.

Lines 61-64: A channel is created and populated with all the documents to process.

330

Line 65: The channel is closed so the pool of Goroutines naturally terminates when all the documents are processed.

Line 70: The pool of Goroutines is created.

Line 73-83: Each Goroutine in the pool receives a document from the channel, reads the document into memory and checks the contents for the topic. When there is a match, the local found variable is incremented.

Line 84: The sum of the individual Goroutine counts are summed together into a final count.

The concurrent version is definitely more complex than the sequential version. But is the complexity worth it? The best way to answer this question again is to create a benchmark. For these benchmarks I have used a collection of one thousand documents with the garbage collector turned off. There is a sequential version that uses the find function and a concurrent version that uses the findConcurrent function.

Listing 13

```
func BenchmarkSequential(b *testing.B) {
    for i := 0; i < b.N; i++ {
        find("test", docs)
    }
}


func BenchmarkConcurrent(b *testing.B) {
    for i := 0; i < b.N; i++ {
        findConcurrent(runtime.NumCPU(), "test", docs)
    }
}
```

Listing 13 shows the benchmark functions. Here are the results when only a single OS/hardware thread is available for all Goroutines. The sequential is using 1 Goroutine and the concurrent version is using runtime.NumCPU or 8 Goroutines on my machine.

In this case, the concurrent version is leveraging concurrency without parallelism.

Listing 14

```
10 Thousand Documents using 8 goroutines with 1 core
2.9 GHz Intel 4 Core i7
Concurrency WITHOUT Parallelism
------------------------------------------------------------------
$ GOGC=off go test -cpu 1 -run none -bench . -benchtime 3s
goos: darwin
goarch: amd64
pkg: github.com/ardanlabs/gotraining/topics/go/testing/benchmarks/io-bound
BenchmarkSequential                 3    1483458120 ns/op
BenchmarkConcurrent                20     188941855 ns/op : ~87% Faster
BenchmarkSequentialAgain            2    1502682536 ns/op
BenchmarkConcurrentAgain           20     184037843 ns/op : ~88% Faster
```

The benchmark in listing 14 shows that the concurrent version is approximately 87 to 88 percent faster than the sequential version when only a single OS/hardware thread is available for all Goroutines. This is what I would have expected since all the Goroutines are efficiently sharing the single OS/hardware thread. The natural context switch happening for each Goroutine on the read call is allowing more work to get done over time on the single OS/hardware thread.

Here is the benchmark when using concurrency with parallelism.

Listing 15

```
10 Thousand Documents using 8 goroutines with 1 core
2.9 GHz Intel 4 Core i7
Concurrency WITH Parallelism
------------------------------------------------------------------
$ GOGC=off go test -run none -bench . -benchtime 3s
goos: darwin
goarch: amd64
pkg: github.com/ardanlabs/gotraining/topics/go/testing/benchmarks/io-bound
BenchmarkSequential-8               3    1490947198 ns/op
BenchmarkConcurrent-8              20     187382200 ns/op : ~88% Faster
BenchmarkSequentialAgain-8          3    1416126029 ns/op
BenchmarkConcurrentAgain-8         20     185965460 ns/op : ~87% Faster
```

The benchmark in listing 15 shows that bringing in the extra OS/hardware threads doesn't provide any better performance.

Conclusion

The goal of this post was to provide guidance on the semantics you must consider to determine if a workload is suitable for using concurrency. I tried to provide examples of different types of algorithms and workloads so you could see the differences in semantics and the different engineering decisions that needed to be considered.

You can clearly see that with I/O-Bound workloads parallelism was not needed to get a big bump in performance. This is the opposite of what you saw with the CPU-Bound work. When it comes to an algorithm like Bubble sort, the use of concurrency would add complexity without any real benefit of performance. It's important to determine if your workload is suitable for concurrency and then identify the type of workload you have, to use the right semantics.

14.6 Garbage Collection Semantics

Introduction

Garbage collectors have the responsibility of tracking heap memory allocations, freeing up allocations that are no longer needed, and keeping allocations that are still in-use. How a language decides to implement this behavior is complex but it shouldn't be a requirement for application developers to understand the details in order to build software. Plus, with different releases of a language's VM or runtime, the implementation of these systems is always changing and evolving. What's important for application developers is to maintain a good working model of how the garbage collector for their language behaves and how they can be sympathetic with that behavior without being concerned with the implementation.

As of version 1.16, the Go programming language uses a non-generational, non-compacting, concurrent tri-color mark and sweep collector. If you want to visually see how a mark and sweep collector works, Ken Fox wrote this great article and provides an animation.

https://spin.atomicobject.com/2014/09/03/visualizing-garbage-collection-algorithms

The implementation of Go's collector has changed and evolved with every release of Go. So any post that talks about the implementation details will no longer be accurate once the next version of the language is released.

With all that said, the modeling I will do in this post will not focus on the actual implementation details. The modeling will focus on the behavior you will experience and the behavior you should expect to see for years to come. In this post, I will share with you the behavior of the collector and explain how to be sympathetic with that behavior, regardless of the current implementation or how it changes in the future. This will make you a better Go developer.

Here is more reading you can do about garbage collectors and Go's actual collector as well.

https://github.com/ardanlabs/gotraining/tree/master/reading#garbage-collection)

I will never refer to the heap as a container that you can store or release values from. It's important to understand that there is no linear containment of memory that defines the "Heap". Think that any memory reserved for application use in the process space is available for heap memory allocation. Where any given heap memory allocation is virtually or physically stored is not relevant to our model. This understanding will help you better understand how the garbage collector works.

Collector Behavior

When a collection starts, the collector runs through three phases of work. Two of these phases create Stop The World (STW) latencies and the other phase creates latencies that slow down the throughput of the application. The collector does its best to keep the STW latencies under 100 microseconds for every GC.

I label these three phases as:

- Mark Setup - STW
- Marking - Concurrent
- Mark Termination - STW

Here is a break-down of each phase.

Mark Setup - STW

When a collection starts, the first activity that must be performed is turning on the Write Barrier. The purpose of the Write Barrier is to allow the collector to maintain data integrity on the heap during a collection since both the collector and application Goroutines will be running concurrently.

In order to turn the Write Barrier on, every application Goroutine running must be stopped. That is, as long as the application Goroutines are behaving properly.

Figure 1

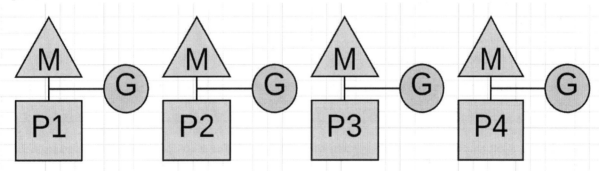

Figure 1 shows 4 application Goroutines running before the start of a collection. Each of those 4 Goroutine must be stopped. The only way to do that is for the collector to watch and wait for each Goroutine to enter into a safe point. A safe point is where the Goroutine is not in the middle of a read or write of memory.

Prior to the Goroutine being a preemptive scheduler, function calls were the only guarantee that a Goroutine was at a safe point to be stopped. Prior to the scheduler change in 1.14, what would happen if one of those four Goroutines didn't make a function call?

Figure 2

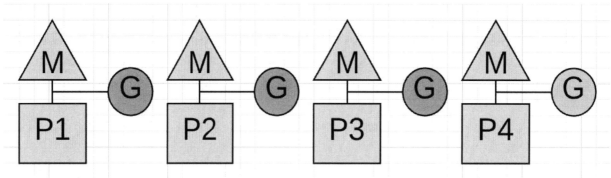

Figure 2 shows a real problem. The collection can't start until the Goroutine running on P4 is stopped and that can't happen because it's in a tight loop performing some math.

Listing 1

```
01 func add(numbers []int) int {
02     var v int
03     for _, n := range numbers {
04         v += n
05     }
06     return v
07 }
```

Listing 1 shows the code that the Goroutine running on P4 is executing. Depending on the size of the slice, the Goroutine could run for an unreasonable amount of time with no opportunity to be stopped. This is the kind of code that could stall a collection from starting. What's worse is the other P's can't service any other Goroutines while the collector waits.

It's critically important if you are using a version of Go prior to 1.14, that Goroutines make function calls in reasonable timeframes.

Marking - Concurrent

Once the Write Barrier is turned on, the collector commences with the Marking phase. The first thing the collector does is take 25% of the available CPU capacity for itself. The collector uses Goroutines to do the collection work and needs the same P's and M's the application Goroutines use. This means for our 4 threaded Go program, one entire P will be dedicated to collection work.

Figure 3

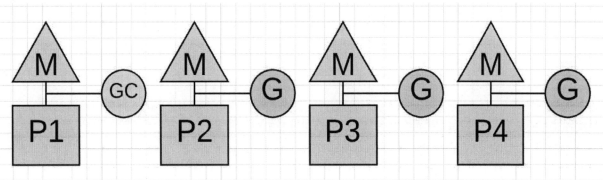

Figure 3 shows how the collector took P1 for itself during the collection. Now the collector can start the Marking phase. The Marking phase consists of marking values in heap memory that are still in-use. This work starts by inspecting the stacks for all existing Goroutines to find root pointers to heap memory. Then the collector must traverse the heap memory graph from those root pointers. While the Marking work is happening on P1, application work can continue concurrently on P2, P3 and P4. This means the impact of the collector has been minimized to 25% of the current CPU capacity.

I wish that was the end of the story, but it isn't. What if it's identified during the collection that the Goroutine dedicated to GC on P1 will not finish the Marking work before the heap memory in-use reaches its goal limit set by the collection before starting? In this case, new allocations have to be slowed down and specifically from those Goroutines.

If the collector determines that it needs to slow down allocations, it will recruit the application Goroutines to assist with the Marking work. This is called a Mark Assist. The amount of time any application Goroutine will be placed in a Mark Assist is proportional to the amount of data it's adding to heap memory. One positive side effect of Mark Assist is that it helps to finish the collection faster.

Figure 4

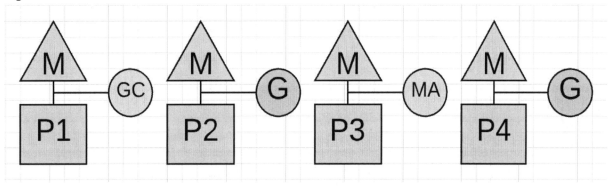

Figure 4 shows how the application Goroutine running on P3 is now performing a Mark Assist and helping with the collection work. Hopefully the other application Goroutines don't need to get involved as well. Applications that allocate heavy could see the majority of the running Goroutines perform small amounts of Mark Assist during collections.

One goal of the collector is to eliminate the need for Mark Assists. If any given collection ends up requiring a lot of Mark Assist, the collector can start the next garbage collection earlier. This is done in an attempt to reduce the amount of Mark Assist that will be necessary on the next collection.

Mark Termination - STW

Once the Marking work is done, the next phase is Mark Termination. This is when the Write Barrier is turned off, various clean up tasks are performed, and the next collection goal is calculated. Goroutines (in versions of Go prior to 1.14) that find themselves in a tight loop during the Marking phase can also cause Mark Termination STW latencies to be extended.

Figure 5

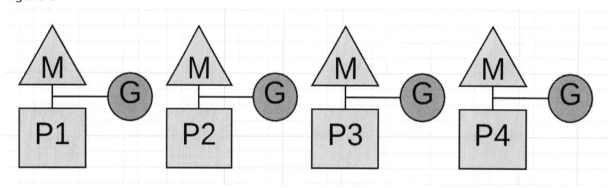

Figure 5 shows how all the Goroutines are stopped while the Mark Termination phase completes. This phase could be done without a STW, but by using a STW, the code is simpler and the added complexity is not worth the small gain.

Once the collection is finished, every P can be used by the application Goroutines again and the application is back to full throttle.

Figure 6

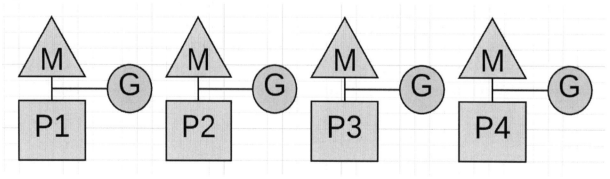

Figure 6 shows how all of the available P's are now processing application work again once the collection is finished. The application is back to full throttle as it was before the collection started.

Sweeping - Concurrent

There is another activity that happens after a collection is finished called Sweeping. Sweeping is when the memory associated with values in heap memory that were not marked as in-use are reclaimed. This activity occurs when application Goroutines attempt to allocate new values in heap memory. The latency of Sweeping is added to the cost of performing an allocation in heap memory and is not tied to any latencies associated with garbage collection.

The following is a sample of a trace on my machine where I have 12 hardware threads available for executing Goroutines.

Figure 7

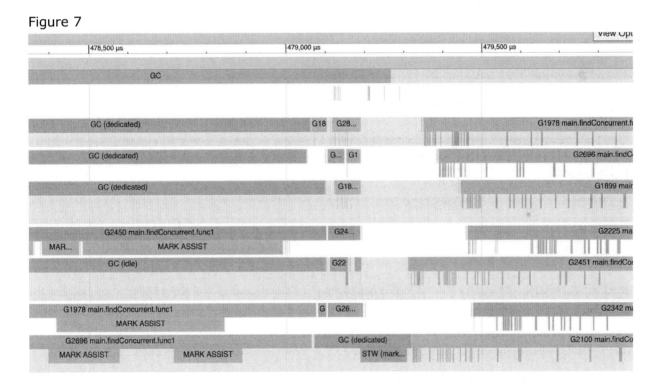

Figure 7 shows a partial snapshot of the trace. You can see how during this collection (keep your view within the blue GC line at the top), three of the twelve P's are dedicated to GC. You can see Goroutine 2450, 1978, and 2696 during this time are performing moments of Mark Assist work and not its application work. At the very end of the collection, only one P is dedicated to GC and eventually performs the STW (Mark Termination) work.

After the collection is finished, the application is back to running at full throttle. Except you see a lot of rose colored lines underneath those Goroutines.

Figure 8

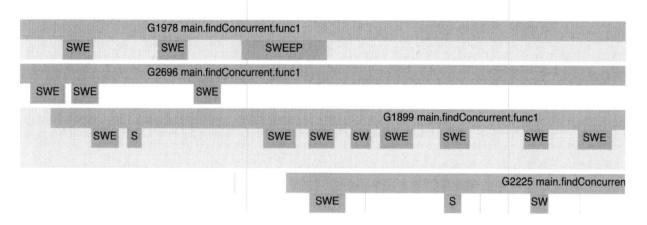

Figure 8 shows how those rose colored lines represent moments when the Goroutine is performing the Sweeping work and not its application work. These are moments when the Goroutine is attempting to allocate new values in heap memory.

Figure 9

1 item selected.	Slice (1)

Title	SWEEP
User Friendly Category	other
Start	479,365,202 ns
Wall Duration	3,636 ns
Start Stack Trace	**Title**

runtime.
(*mcache).nextFree:748
runtime.mallocgc:903

Figure 9 shows the end of the stack trace for one of the Goroutines in the Sweep activity. The call to runtime.mallocgc is the call to allocate a new value in heap memory. The call to runtime.(*mcache).nextFree is causing the Sweep activity. Once there are no more allocations in heap memory to reclaim, the call to nextFree won't be seen any longer.

The collection behavior that was just described only happens when a collection has started and is running. The GC Percentage configuration option plays a big role in determining when a collection starts.

GC Percentage

There is a configuration option in the runtime called GC Percentage, which is set to 100 by default. This value represents a ratio of how much new heap memory can be allocated before the next collection has to start. Setting the GC Percentage to 100 means, based on the amount of heap memory marked as live after a collection finishes, the next collection has to start at or before 100% more new allocations are added to heap memory.

As an example, imagine a collection finishes with 2MB of heap memory in-use.

Note: The diagrams of the heap memory in this post do not represent a true profile when using Go. The heap memory in Go will often be fragmented and messy, and you don't have the clean separation as the images are representing. These diagrams provide a way to visualize heap memory in an easier to understand way that is accurate towards the behavior you will experience.

Figure 10

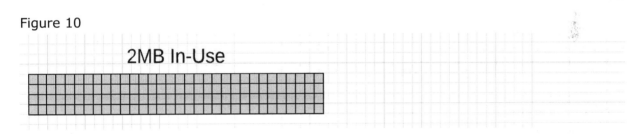

Figure 10 shows the 2MB of heap memory in-use after the last collection finished. Since the GC Percentage is set to 100%, the next collection needs to start at or before 2 more MB of heap memory is added.

Figure 11

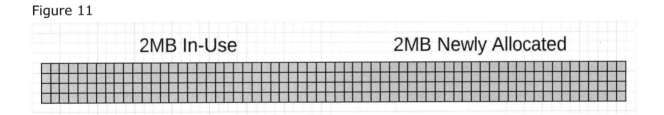

Figure 11 shows that 2 more MB of heap memory is now in-use. This will trigger a collection. A way to view all of this in action, is to generate a GC trace for every collection that takes place.

GC Trace

A GC trace can be generated by including the environment variable GODEBUG with the gctrace=1 option when running any Go application. Every time a collection happens, the runtime will write the GC trace information to stderr.

Listing 2

```
GODEBUG=gctrace=1 ./app

gc 1405 @6.068s 11%: 0.058+1.2+0.083 ms clock, 0.70+2.5/1.5/0+0.99 ms cpu,
7->11->6 MB, 10 MB goal, 12 P

gc 1406 @6.070s 11%: 0.051+1.8+0.076 ms clock, 0.61+2.0/2.5/0+0.91 ms cpu,
8->11->6 MB, 13 MB goal, 12 P

gc 1407 @6.073s 11%: 0.052+1.8+0.20 ms clock, 0.62+1.5/2.2/0+2.4 ms cpu, 8-
>14->8 MB, 13 MB goal, 12 P
```

Listing 2 shows how to use the GODEBUG variable to generate GC traces. The listing also shows 3 traces that were generated by the running Go application.

Here is a break-down of what each value in the GC trace means by reviewing the first GC trace line in the listing.

Listing 3

```
gc 1405 @6.068s 11%: 0.058+1.2+0.083 ms clock, 0.70+2.5/1.5/0+0.99 ms cpu,
7->11->6 MB, 10 MB goal, 12 P

// General
gc 1405      : The 1405 GC run since the program started
@6.068s      : Six seconds since the program started
11%          : Eleven percent of the available CPU has been spent in GC

// Wall-Clock
0.058ms      : STW        : Mark Start      - Write Barrier on
1.2ms        : Concurrent : Marking
0.083ms      : STW        : Mark Termination - Write Barrier off and clean up

// CPU Time
0.70ms       : STW        : Mark Start
2.5ms        : Concurrent : Mark - Assist Time (GC performed in line with
allocation)
1.5ms        : Concurrent : Mark - Background GC time
0ms          : Concurrent : Mark - Idle GC time
0.99ms       : STW        : Mark Term

// Memory
7MB          : Heap memory in-use before the Marking started
11MB         : Heap memory in-use after the Marking finished
6MB          : Heap memory marked as live after the Marking finished
10MB         : Collection goal for heap memory in-use after Marking finished

// Threads
12P          : Number of logical processors or threads used to run Goroutines
```

Listing 3 shows the actual numbers from the first GC trace line broken down by what the values mean. I will eventually talk about most of these values, but for now just focus on the memory section of the GC trace for trace 1405.

Figure 12

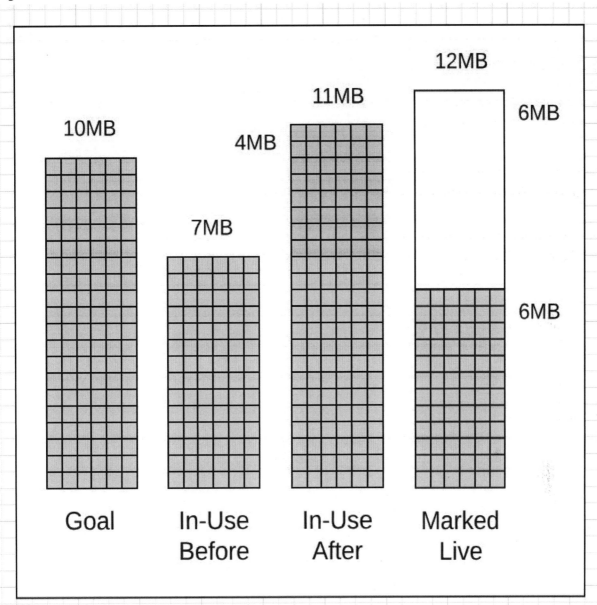

Listing 4

```
// Memory
7MB          : Heap memory in-use before the Marking started
11MB         : Heap memory in-use after the Marking finished
6MB          : Heap memory marked as live after the Marking finished
10MB         : Collection goal for heap memory in-use after Marking finished
```

What this GC trace line is telling you in listing 4, is that the amount of heap memory in-use was 7MB before the Marking work started. When the Marking work finished, the amount of heap memory in-use reached 11MB. Which means there was an additional 4MB of allocations that occurred during the collection. The amount of heap memory that was marked as live after the Marking work finished was 6MB.

This means the application can increase the amount of heap memory in-use to 12MB (100% of the live heap size of 6MB) before the next collection needs to start. You can see that the collector missed its goal by 1MB. The amount of heap memory in-use after the Marking work finished was 11MB not 10MB. That's ok, because the goal is calculated based on the current amount of the heap memory in-use, the amount of heap memory marked as live, and timing calculations about the additional allocations that will occur while the collection is running. In this case, the application did something that required more heap memory to be in-use after Marking than expected.

If you look at the next GC trace line (1406), you will see how things changed within 2ms.

Figure 13

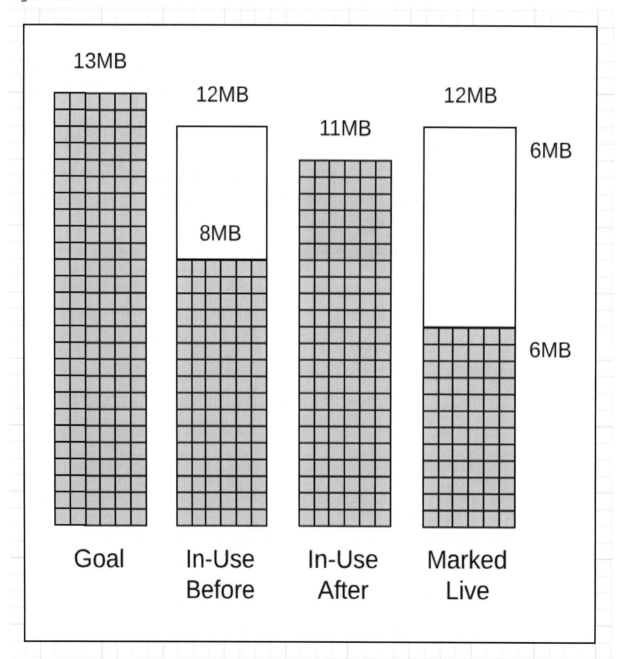

Listing 5

```
gc 1406 @6.070s 11%: 0.051+1.8+0.076 ms clock, 0.61+2.0/2.5/0+0.91 ms cpu,
8->11->6 MB, 13 MB goal, 12 P

// Memory
8MB         : Heap memory in-use before the Marking started
11MB        : Heap memory in-use after the Marking finished
6MB         : Heap memory marked as live after the Marking finished
13MB        : Collection goal for heap memory in-use after Marking finished
```

Listing 5 shows how this collection started 2ms after the start of the previous collection (6.068s vs 6.070s) even though the heap memory in-use had only reached 8MB of the 12MB that was allowed. It's important to note, if the collector decides it's better to start a collection earlier, it will. In this case, it probably started earlier because the application is allocating heavily and the collector wanted to reduce the amount of Mark Assist latency during this collection.

Two more things of note. The collector stayed within its goal this time. The amount of heap memory in-use after Marking finished was 11MB not 13MB, 2 MB less. The amount of heap memory marked as live after Marking finished was the same at 6MB.

As side note, you can get more details from the GC trace by adding the gcpacertrace=1 flag. This causes the collector to print information about the internal state of the concurrent pacer.

Listing 6

```
$ export GODEBUG=gctrace=1,gcpacertrace=1 ./app

Sample output:
gc 5 @0.071s 0%: 0.018+0.46+0.071 ms clock, 0.14+0/0.38/0.14+0.56 ms cpu,
29->29->29 MB, 30 MB goal, 8 P

pacer: sweep done at heap size 29MB; allocated 0MB of spans; swept 3752
pages at +6.183550e-004 pages/byte

pacer: assist ratio=+1.232155e+000 (scan 1 MB in 70->71 MB) workers=2+0

pacer: H_m_prev=30488736 h_t=+2.334071e-001 H_T=37605024 h_a=+1.409842e+000
H_a=73473040 h_g=+1.000000e+000 H_g=60977472 u_a=+2.500000e-001
u_g=+2.500000e-001 W_a=308200 goalΔ=+7.665929e-001 actualΔ=+1.176435e+000
u_a/u_g=+1.000000e+000
```

Running a GC trace can tell you a lot about the health of the application and the pace of the collector. The pace at which the collector is running plays an important role in the collection process.

Pacing

The collector has a pacing algorithm which is used to determine when a collection is to start. The algorithm depends on a feedback loop that the collector uses to gather information about the running application and the stress the application is putting on the heap. Stress can be defined as how fast the application is allocating heap memory within a given amount of time. It's that stress that determines the pace at which the collector needs to run.

Before the collector starts a collection, it calculates the amount of time it believes it will take to finish the collection. Then, once a collection is running, latencies will be inflicted on the running application that will slow down application work. Every collection adds to the overall latency of the application.

One misconception is thinking that slowing down the pace of the collector is a way to improve performance. The idea being, if you can delay the start of the next collection, then you are delaying the latency it will inflict. Being sympathetic with the collector isn't about slowing down the pace.

You could decide to change the GC Percentage value to something larger than 100. This will increase the amount of heap memory that can be allocated before the next collection has to start. This could result in the pace of collection to slow down. Don't consider doing this.

Figure 14

Figure 14 shows how changing the GC Percentage would change the amount of heap memory allowed to be allocated before the next collection has to start. You can visualize how the collector could be slowed down as it waits for more heap memory to become in-use.

Attempting to directly affect the pace of collection has nothing to do with being sympathetic with the collector. It's really about getting more work done between each collection or during the collection. You affect that by reducing the amount or the number of allocations any piece of work is adding to heap memory.

Note: The idea is also to achieve the throughput you need with the smallest heap possible. Remember, minimizing the use of resources like heap memory is important when running in cloud environments.

Figure 15

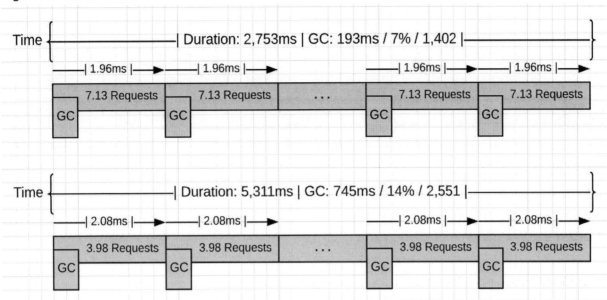

Listing 15 shows some statistics of a running Go application. The version in blue shows stats for the application without any optimizations when 10k requests are processed through the application. The version in green shows stats after 4.48GB of non-productive memory allocations were found and removed from the application for the same 10k requests.

Look at the average pace of collection for both versions (2.08ms vs 1.96ms). They are virtually the same, at around ~2.0ms. What fundamentally changed between these two versions is the amount of work that is getting done between each collection. The application went from processing 3.98 to 7.13 requests per collection. That is a 79.1% increase in the amount of work getting done at the same pace. As you can see, the collection did not slow down with the reduction of those allocations, but remained the same. The win came from getting more work done in-between each collection.

Adjusting the pace of the collection to delay the latency cost is not how you improve the performance of your application. It's about reducing the amount of time the collector needs to run, which in turn will reduce the amount of latency cost being inflicted. The latency costs inflicted by the collector have been explained, but let me summarize it again for clarity.

Collector Latency Costs

There are two types of latencies every collection inflicts on your running application. The first is the stealing of CPU capacity. The effect of this stolen CPU capacity means your application is not running at full throttle during the collection. The application Goroutines are now sharing P's with the collector's Goroutines or helping with the collection (Mark Assist).

Figure 16

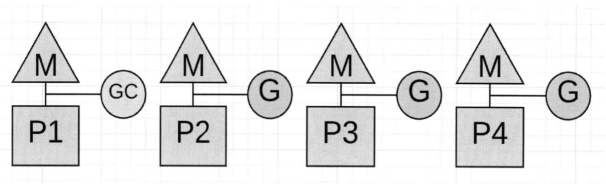

Figure 16 shows how the application is only using 75% of its CPU capacity for application work. This is because the collector has dedicated P1 for itself. This is true for the majority of the collection.

Figure 17

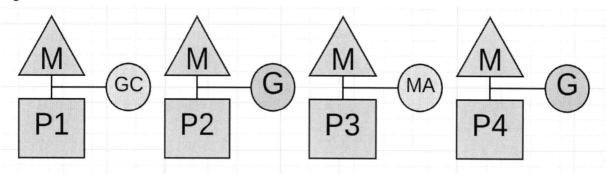

Figure 17 shows how the application in this moment of time (typically for just a few microseconds) is now only using half of its CPU capacity for application work. This is because the Goroutine on P3 is performing a Mark Assist and the collector has dedicated P1 for itself.

*Note: Marking usually takes 4 CPU-milliseconds per MB of live heap (e.g., to estimate how many milliseconds the Marking phase will run for, take the live heap size in MB and divide by 0.25 * the number of CPUs). Marking actually runs at about 1 MB/ms, but only has a quarter of the CPUs.*

The second latency that is inflicted is the amount of STW latency that occurs during the collection. The STW time is when no application Goroutines are performing any of their application work. The application is essentially stopped.

Figure 18

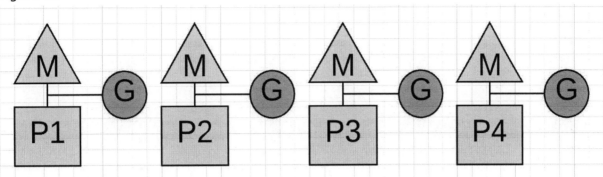

Figure 18 is showing STW latency where all the Goroutines are stopped. This happens twice on every collection. If your application is healthy, the collector should be able to keep the total STW time at or below 100 microsecond for the majority of collections.

You now know the different phases of the collector, how memory is sized, how pacing works, and the different latencies the collector inflicts on your running application. With all that knowledge, the question of how you can be sympathetic with the collector can finally be answered.

Being Sympathetic

Being sympathetic with the collector is about reducing stress on heap memory. Remember, stress can be defined as how fast the application is allocating heap memory within a given amount of time. When stress is reduced, the latencies being inflicted by the collector will be reduced. It's the GC latencies that are slowing down your application.

The way to reduce GC latencies is by identifying and removing unnecessary allocations from your application. Doing this will help the collector to:

* Maintain the smallest heap possible.
* Find an optimal consistent pace.
* Stay within the goal for every collection.
* Minimize the duration of every collection, STW and Mark Assist.

All these things help reduce the amount of latency the collector will inflict on your running application. That will increase the performance and throughput of your application. The pace of the collection has nothing to do with it.

Conclusion

If you take the time to focus on reducing allocations, you are doing what you can as a Go developer to be sympathetic with the garbage collector. You are not going to write zero allocation applications so it's important to recognize the difference between allocations that are productive (those helping the application) and those that are not productive (those hurting the application). Then put your faith and trust in the garbage collector to keep the heap healthy and your application running consistently.

Having a garbage collector is a nice tradeoff. I will take the cost of garbage collection so I don't have the burden of memory management. Go is about allowing you as a developer to be productive while still writing applications that are fast enough. The garbage collector is a big part of making that a reality.

Printed in Poland
by Amazon Fulfillment
Poland Sp. z o.o., Wrocław

80131201R00197